ADDRESSES

UPON

THE AMERICAN ROAD

1941–1945

ADDRESSES

UPON

THE AMERICAN ROAD

BY

Herbert Hoover

World War II

1941-1945

NEW YORK

D. VAN NOSTRAND COMPANY, Inc.

250 FOURTH AVENUE

1946

Contents

v

vii

PART I

MAKING PEACE

Declaration of War

Press Statement, New York City
[December 8, 1941]

AMERICAN soil has been treacherously attacked by Japan. Our decision is clear. It is forced upon us. We must fight with everything we have. I have opposed the foreign policies of our Government. I have believed alternative policies would have been better. But whatever our differences of view may be as to the causes which have led to this situation, those are matters to be threshed out by History. Today there is just one job before the American people. We must defeat this invasion by Japan and we must fight it in any place that will defeat it. Upon this job we must have and will have unity in America. We must have and will have full support for the President of the United States in this war to defend America. We will have victory.

Finland

Press Statement, New York City
[November 4, 1941]

I PROTEST at the United States' using pressure on Democratic Finland on behalf of Communist Russia. The independence of Finland from Russia twenty years ago was largely an American creation. The name of Woodrow Wilson stands on a score of Finnish landmarks. We set Finland on her feet. The Finns were the only people in Europe who repaid the money we loaned them. Only two years ago this peaceful little nation was outrageously attacked by Communist Russia. Our whole country heralded it as the most heroic stand of democracy since Thermopylae. The Finns, to save something, surrendered a third of their country to Russia. Then the Communists drove six hundred thousand Finnish men, women and children from the homes they had held for 500 years without even bedclothes to protect them from the winter. True their armies have gone into Karelia, but that was formerly also mostly Finnish. Can America reproach them for taking the first chance to recover these homes and their former countrymen?

Has America lost all sense of human and moral proportions?

The Approaches to Peace

CHICAGO, ILLINOIS
[*December 16, 1942*]

YOUR committee suggested that you have heard a good deal about war of late, and that it would be a help to you to hear something about peace.

The first of last May Mr. Hugh Gibson and I sent to the publishers a book which among other things proposed tentatively a step in the solution of post-war problems that could be taken before the victory by the United Nations. That idea found favorable support from leaders of thought in several countries. My purpose tonight is to expand this plan into more definite form and indicate its importance.

This idea was that the United Nations should at once agree upon such machinery for peace making as will avoid delay in resumption of economic and political life among the nations when firing ceases and also give time for cooling off and deliberate action and public participation in the major problems of a lasting peace. This idea was propounded before any official declarations upon the subject. It has since found favorable support from leaders of thought and officials in several countries.

The western world has seen these gigantic explosions into revolution, tumult and world war before. When the killing ceased, men met together, resolute upon making lasting peace. But always invisible forces have also sat at the peace table—both for good and evil.

The degenerations and emotions of world wars in many ways reach their most destructive point immediately after firing ceases.

Peacemakers are at the most disadvantageous moment for re-building the world.

THE EXPERIENCE AT VERSAILLES

At the end of the last war we had an Armistice which lasted for nine long months. During that time a thousand diplomats of 40 nations, in daily sessions wrangled and struggled to settle the gigantic problems which had been loosened upon the world. And after that there was a long period of uncertainty in the ratification of the treaty.

My immediate job during that Conference was with the gaunt realities of hunger and pestilence, which threatened to destroy the very foundations upon which peace must be built. But that job brought me hourly into contact with the long struggle to rebuild peace and order—and its defeat. Daily I witnessed the age-old forces of nationalism, imperialism and militarism acting under the direction of subtle diplomacy. I saw the rise of selfish interests, the clash of ideals, of personalities and of ambitions of men. Hate, fear and revenge also sat at those tables.

The very bringing together of all these interests intensified the conflicts and generated new ones. It created a hundred nests of intrigue. The attempt to solve a hundred problems all at once made infinite opportunity for dark corner operations in trades and combinations. The whole world was pressing for haste lest the foundations of order should crumble altogether.

I saw the Conference degenerate into a gigantic struggle for power. Gradually the spiritual forces of idealism and of justice were driven back by the forces of destruction. The peace making was, in the end, swept down the terrible stream of intrigue, power politics and conflict. It was wrecked in the whirlpool of destructive compromise and upon the rocks of selfish interest and emotional action.

It was to be a peace-making open to the world and subject to the check of public opinion. It was to be a "negotiated" peace. All that pretense was soon forgotten. It became an "imposed peace" by the powerful.

The economic clock of the world was slowed down during the long delayed conclusions. Instead of releasing the forces of recovery, the Armistice was a period of social, political and economic degeneration. And that just at the time when the hope of men for the future had risen high.

And all this must not be blamed upon the individuals who led that Peace Conference. There were many able and heroic men there. But they were overwhelmed not only by the forces evolved in the conference but by the emotional tides and demands from home. The peoples of the world had little understanding of the impossibility of solving these problems all at once and in haste. President Wilson and many other leaders deserve credit, not criticism, for the fight they made there.

When victory comes after this war, we must, jointly with our Allies, again try to lead the world to the promised land across this terrible maelstrom of conflicting forces. If we are to have lasting peace, it will be by cooperation with them in finding it and making it secure.

THE SHAPES AT THE NEXT PEACE-MAKING

It does not take a prophet to anticipate that these conflicting forces will again be in motion the instant hostilities cease in this war. And from the outlook of today we are likely to encounter this stream of malevolent conflict in Europe a year before we see the same spectacle in Asia.

The Atlantic Charter promises self-determination and restored sovereignty to all nations. And again there will be a thousand diplomats of 40 or 50 nations involved in peace making. Under these promises the liberated peoples will no doubt again instantly set up their own governments the day after firing ceases. In the enemy countries, the defeated leaders and governments will be overthrown. Revolution will march and new men will come into the ascendency.

Every realist knows that the dynamic forces of nationalism, of economic interest, of ideologies, of militarism, of imperialism, of fear, hate, revenge and personal ambition have not died out in the world. They will clash again. They will haunt the halls of peace making. But I believe the will to peace will be more resolute this time. It must be.

And the world will again clamor for haste. The transportation systems, industries and agriculture of all Europe will be damaged or ruined. There is already a shortage of food, which amounts to famine among 180,000,000 of the people. It will extend to 500,000,000. These nations will be without credit or raw materials. Turning the mass-production swords of total war into mass-production plow-shares is no idle metaphor.

And the Allied world will itself also be disrupted by the shock of reversing gears from war to peace. Our peoples will be war weary and distracted by the new miseries of post-war.

A NEW APPROACH TO PEACE MAKING

If we are not again to see the tragedy of Versailles, we must have a new approach to the whole method and process of peace making. We must avoid the whirlpools and rocks upon which that conference was wrecked. The recovery of the world must not be dangerously delayed again.

There are two separate problems here. The one is the method or machinery by which we make peace and the other is the settlements of the problems of peace themselves. Our first necessity is to provide a stage for peace making that will favor the spiritual forces of good-will and idealism rather than old time diplomacy. We must prevent nests of intrigue that can again do evil. We must take time to solve these problems.

The essence of my proposal is that we have no armistice, no general peace conference, such as Versailles. But that we set the peace making in two stages. The first to be an instant "conditional peace" that will turn the world toward political, economic and spiritual recovery without the delays of last time. And then that the world should take time to cool off and work out one by one and separately the solutions for lasting peace.

To do this the United Nations would need to agree in advance to the terms of a conditional peace and a subsequent program. They will need to impose the conditional peace and enforce it. Enforcement will not be difficult, for immediately at the victory the enemy will obviously be required to surrender his arms. The Allies will possess the only remaining military force. Even a small air force could impose the conditional peace and the subsequent program.

The declaration of conditional peace should embrace the minimum of:

1. Total disarmament of the enemy.

2. The designation of provisional boundaries of nations.

3. Machinery for the repatriation of prisoners and civilians driven from their homes.

4. The removal of the economic blockade the instant the enemy has handed over his arms.

5. The immediate organization to relieve famine, combat pestilence and aid in reconstruction. Otherwise there will be anarchy and no peace.

6. The provisional restoration of all commercial treaties that trade may begin again.

7. Immediate call of freely chosen elective constitutional assemblies or parliamentary leaders in the liberated and enemy countries.

8. Immediate reduction of armaments of the United Nations themselves to the minimum force needed to maintain international order and enforce peace provisions.

With these minimums the world could move forward.

There will be a host of gigantic problems to be solved afterwards. There must be machinery for the preservation of peace. There are the problems of world disarmament and of long-view international economic relations. There are the problems of the disposition of enemy countries, of the government of backward nations, solutions of Europe's irredentas and federations of weaker states. There will be questions of reparations, intergovernmental debts, punishment of criminal actions, and many other measures. And they must be so solved that the dynamic forces in the world which always make for war are extinguished and the forces of peace given strength.

Many of the problems must have time for deliberation. Others must have time for the cooling of war revenge and hatred. Many of them must have time for the development of world opinion and adherence. They should be separated from each other for solution and each saved on its merits.

Some of them might be dealt with before the war ends and included in the conditional peace.

As a practical fact all of these separate questions will need at the start to be dealt with by separate commissions representing the dominant nations. They would be so dealt with if there were a general conference like Versailles.

Therefore the plan proposed is to appoint these Commissions as part of the conditional peace. After each of the problems has been separately examined, reported or negotiated, then the principal governments should act.

Some say this is requiring nations to sign upon the dotted line, that it is an "imposed peace" and is not "negotiation." As a matter of fact the peace terms were imposed upon the enemy last time and much of them was indirectly imposed on the liberated nations. But they were imposed only after the world had been infinitely demoralized and its wounds lacerated. Indeed this plan provides a chance for much more adequate examination of the views and rights of all nations than at Versailles.

And the conclusions of these commissions can be open to expression of public opinion. There can be time for debate.

Even if somebody possessed an absolute and perfect formula for these gigantic problems of disarmament, economic relations and preserving peace, no such settlements could endure unless accepted by at least the democratic peoples themselves. If they are badly formulated they will be upset at the ballot box. And I may add that for America no agreement is binding until it has been ratified by the peoples' representatives. If this is a peoples' war, it must be a peoples' peace.

Again, I may repeat that this plan proposes to leave out an armistice altogether and to substitute a preliminary declared peace to be followed by a cooling-off and deliberating period for the major questions. It proposes to avoid the nests of intrigue and the opportunity for selfish jockeying of a general peace conference. It proposes to separate the problems for settlement and to avoid the trading between them.

Such a conditional peace and the machinery to be set up are not difficult to formulate nor should it be difficult to agree upon among the United Nations, nor difficult to enforce. It would speed recovery of the world. Incidentally it would greatly lessen the amount of financial aid necessary for food and reconstruction, for with the quick resumption of production and trade the world could more quickly help itself.

In suggesting the adoption of such a plan for the machinery of peacemaking, I know it must be hammered out upon the anvil of debate. No man can claim finality in perfection in these problems.

PREPAREDNESS FOR PEACE BY DISCUSSION

It is a favorable and important sign that there is today active debate of the problems of peace throughout the Allied world. It is evidenced by the activity of hundreds of organizations, by thousands of meetings and discussions, by millions of pamphlets and scores of books. I have noticed no such discussions in the Axis world.

And out of these discussions in America there are certain propositions upon which there seem now to be general acceptance. They indicate progress in unity of thought. They indicate a resolution to gain real peace this time. These acceptances are mainly:

1. The major purpose of this unutterable sacrifice, suffering and death is to win a lasting peace for mankind. We are resolute that this time it must be a peace which assures the freedom of men.

2. Lasting peace cannot be attained unless there be cooperation between nations to maintain it.

3. There must be definite machinery for that purpose.

4. We must have just as effective advance preparedness for peace as for war. Part of the failure to win the peace last time

was because we listened to the slogan of "Win the war first and discuss peace afterwards."

5. The foundation of preparedness lies in public discussion. It lies in examination of the causes of failure the last time. It lies in the advancement of new ideas and the hammering of them out on the anvil of debate. Public discussion is not only the basis of preparedness to peace making, but it is vital if there is to be intelligent public support in the settlements that are made.

That even these propositions are so generally accepted is evidence of progress in preparedness for peace.

THE NEED FOR REALISM

Much of the discussion of peace, however, also consists of statements or declarations of ideals and the picture of a better world. They present aspirations, hopes and promises. Such statements are not to be disparaged. But we cannot fly to the realms of peace on the wings of phrases or oratory. The development of one specific intelligent step that leads to peace is more important than a thousand orations on the joys of the world to come. Idealism must have the balance wheel of realism if the day's work is to be done. We cannot ignore the weaknesses of the human animal and the wickedness of some dynamic forces. Our ideals and aspirations are the compass by which we lay out the road to human progress. But that road must be paved with hard realistic thought and realistic action and preparedness if we are to go anywhere.

The Declaration of Independence was an expression of aims, purposes and direction. But the Constitution was the embankment and the pavement of the road to free men. The Declaration came from the yearning of the human heart; the Constitution came from the heads of realistic men cooperating with each other. It was easy to compose the Declaration. It was infinitely more difficult to build unity and find lasting freedom through the Constitution. Settlements that will bring lasting peace and freedom to men can come only the same hard way. We, like the

Fathers, must distill much of these hard practical ideas from human experience.

AMIABILITY IN DEBATE

And I would make an observation upon the general discussion of peace problems now in progress. There are many Americans who believed America could contribute more greatly to lasting peace if she kept out of this war. The die, however, was cast at Pearl Harbor. If we would attain lasting peace now, we must win this war with undoubted victory. And if we win the peace, we must have unity. It does not make for unity to call names. That is not the process of peace making. The Sermon on the Mount says: "Blessed are the Peace Makers, for they are the Children of God." I believe that. But some of those who debate peace act as if they were the children of somebody else.

CONCLUSION

And let me again observe that this is not the first time the western world has experienced long periods of general war and disorder. From them new shapes of civilization and new forms of nations have emerged. Civilization has taken new impulses and new directions. We must expect new forms and new directions from the gigantic explosion that began in 1914. No one can pretend to see these shapes clearly. And even if we are emerging into another era of civilization, then also we will need peace.

In the making of that peace will come a fleeting chance for leaders of mankind to bind the wounds, to restore faith and to bring new hope to the world. And this time the methods and the foundations of peace must be so wrought that the destructive forces shall be controlled, or again the structures which we erect to preserve peace will fail.

Further New Approaches to Lasting Peace

Jointly with Hugh Gibson

Articles Appearing in Collier's Magazine

[May-June, 1943]

ARTICLE I

I T IS imperative that America take its full part in building a lasting peace. Whatever may have been our views before the war as the best course for America to follow in order to maintain our peace, we have now taken up the sword. We shall inevitably suffer dreadful losses in substance and precious lives. Having entered upon this course, there can be only one compensation. That is the chance to produce a situation in the world in which it is possible to live in safety without the burden of arms and the threats of wars.

Peace-making is the second greatest task before our people—the first being absolute victory of arms. For any compromise at once destroys any hope for lasting solutions.

We have a better chance than we have ever had to build for lasting peace. But there is only one way to set about it. We must deliberately seek out the difficulties, identify them and in the light of experience consider what can be done to deal with them. If we go about this intelligently, courageously and realistically, we may hope for lasting peace.

We are presenting this subject in four articles.

In this first article we will discuss the first necessity to successful peace-making, that is, the intellectual and spiritual approach to it.

In Article II, for next week's issue, we will propose for American thinking a new and definite method of transition for the world from war to peace and to an ultimate "world institution" to preserve it.

In Article III we will discuss the settlement of specific problems and issues that must be effected in this transitional period if we are to reduce the causes of war so that a "world institution" to preserve peace can succeed.

In Article IV we will discuss the specific plans for a "world institution" to preserve peace, their limitations and the direction which combined experience, realism and idealism indicate we should travel if we are to secure lasting peace.

THE INTELLECTUAL AND SPIRITUAL APPROACHES

In the intellectual and spiritual approaches to peace, we are dealing with dreams, idealism and realism.

The first necessity of successful peace-making is the intellectual and spiritual approach to it.

There are various sorts of minds engaged in the discussion of peace-making. One group consists of those souls sensitive to the infinite agonies of war who with disregard of human experience are in constant search for some magic, some mystic formula or some patent medicine to cure humanity's greatest scourge. American life is conditioned with headlines, slogans and movie captions which give glamor to panaceas and create belief in shortcuts. To many people global planning is a field where imagination can engage in unrestrained play. It is indeed a playground where they may blow gigantic bubbles by dipping their pipes in suds of human kindness. We can solace ourselves that these iridescent globes are a diversion from the miseries of the times and that the bubbles themselves explode before they reach the heavens.

Much of this sort of discussion starts from the assumption that the instant firing ceases the world will be pervaded with sweetness and light. And that all we have to do is to think up now a great world plan to keep the peace, promote world welfare and all will be well.

If it were that easy, man would long ago have solved his most dreadful and baffling problem.

Another group are the more purposeful idealists whose dreams are by no means to be sniffed at. Without dreams, mankind never would have emerged from savagery. But even their plans must be soaked in a solution of hard realism if they are to be made into lasting parchment.

Nor can peace come to the world by cynical realism devoid of idealism, any more than it can be summoned by incantation of emotional slogans. We cannot dismiss the profound reality that idealism plays in our problem.

It is often said that America is today fighting a war of defense because we were attacked. That is overrealistic. It is not the whole truth. It does not do full justice either to our motives or our past conduct. This is the Second Crusade of America to widen the boundaries of freedom and safety in the world. If we had been prepared to sacrifice China and had not concerned ourselves to save Europe from military aggression we would not have been attacked at Pearl Harbor. With modern weapons, we could no doubt have protected ourselves from any invasion. Sometimes one could wish all this were remembered when we are castigated for not doing enough for this nation or that.

We have a breed of flagellants who simplify world problems by the expedient of blaming everything on our own country. Because American genius has made our country strong and rich out of our own soil and hard work, we seem to have wronged somebody. No matter what goes wrong in the world we are to blame. They hang their heads and beat their breasts and apologize to the rest of the world for our behavior. If the League failed to keep the peace, it was because we did not join, which is untrue. If there is war in the Far East it is because our Government would not co-operate with Britain and France to restrain Japan, which is untrue. Generally, their attitude is that if the present world war has come upon us it is because we have consistently failed to do our duty. If foreigners complain of the insufficiency of our aid, instead of examining the facts to see if they do not show some justification of our country, they promptly espouse the foreign criticism and fill the air with self-denunciation. In general the zeal of these people is equalled only by their disregard of facts.

This sort of mind not only presents America as a sorry spectacle in the eyes of the rest of the world, it weakens American influence in securing the fundamentals of peace.

SOME REALITIES

We are indeed a crusading nation. We won a military victory in the First Crusade. But we lost most of President Wilson's "points" at Versailles.

We will again win military victory. But that is only half way to a lasting peace. And to win peace this time America must start with a much deeper understanding of the hard realities we will encounter. Many of them are more clear today from the experience of last time.

Not only does realistic approach offer the best hope of achievement; it avoids a real danger. If we hold out to our people hopes that cannot be realized, there will be inevitable disillusionment. And disillusionment means isolationism.

One of these realities is that our first purpose must be freedom from wars and threats of wars.

We all know—that is, all of us except those who are incorrigible bubble blowers—that there are many highly desirable things for perfecting the world morally, socially and economically that we cannot hope to achieve now. We should concentrate on the thing we can hope for, which is peace, and not dissipate our energies or start quarreling over the unattainable.

There are certain American ideals in relation to international life which we cannot abandon and still be true to our own spiritual foundations. One of them is the right of every politically capable people to self-government. We were born of that conviction. We have stood for this right ever since. Over the years of our national life we have sympathized with every nation struggling for independence. The Monroe Doctrine was an expression of it. We fought the Spanish War that Cuba and the Philippines might be free. It was one of our first purposes in the last World War; it is one of our proclaimed purposes in this war to restore the sovereignty of those who have been deprived of it. Our national conscience, our national ideals, our national policies, our sons who will have died in hundreds of thousands do not permit the abandonment of this purpose.

We have other national ideals which include representative government, the inalienable rights of the Bill of Rights, the sustained dignity of the individual man. We cannot seek to impose these rights upon other peoples because the very right of peoples to self-government carries also the inherent right to determine their own way of life. In any event, personal liberty cannot be imposed by machine guns. Wrong ideas cannot be even cured by war or by treaty. Personal liberty does not come like manna from heaven. It must grow in the minds and spirits of men. But by aiding them to self-government we open the door for it to their peoples. Although we do not seek to impose the Bill of Rights on other peoples, we must hold to it within our borders with no less tenacity if we are to maintain the light by which mankind is to be redeemed.

We must focus our minds on lasting peace, not on spread of our ideology.

We must make up our minds to deal with governments and their social systems as they are and not as we should like them to be. On the United Nations' side in this war, we have a large variety of these systems. It is a dangerous fallacy to assume that more than a minor portion of the people in the world are democracies in our sense or that they ever will be in our lifetime. While we must hold to ideals of our own, it is entirely possible for us to work with nations which do not share our ideological views. We have to live and get along somehow in the same world. In fact, during the first fifty years of our existence, we were about the sole republic in a sea of kings or dictators. And for the most part we contrived to keep the peace with them.

It is of course easier to collaborate with some countries than with others, and we should make our plans accordingly. Honesty in facing these facts will save us much anguish.

One of the deepest of all spiritual emotions is patriotism. People, proud of their traditions, their countryside, their heroes, their accomplishments, will make any sacrifice in life or death to preserve their altars and their independence. Their symbols, their flags, their songs sustain them in battle; their devotion to their country consoles them in loss and in death. The tensity of Nationalism always rises from the fires of war. Already in this war we have seen the Russians discard a creed of Internationalism and die in millions for the "soil of Holy Russia."

It is our belief from these inherent mores of their peoples that both Russia and Britain will be cold to any commitments which affect their sovereignty or independence of action or control their domestic, economic or political life. We venture the opinion that the American people will not do so either.

We believe that reality calls for emphasis in peace plans on "cooperation" or "joint" or "united" action of independent peoples, not "super-government."

We Americans indulge in too many sonorous phrases to the import that *"America* will make the peace." *"America* will police the world." *"America* must lead." America will do none of these things alone. The other leading nations in the world will take no back seat. America has a great role to play in generous cooperation. Neither victory nor peace can come without our aid. And cooperation is a two-way street.

Realism requires that we accept the fact that most other nations will struggle for the interests of their own peoples in the peace settlements. On this continent we have enjoyed an ease of living rarely found elsewhere; we have never had to fight to get the last farthing. In most of the world outside of the United States, in even peace times living for the masses of people is hard at best. They will be further impoverished by the war, and in consequence their national policies will of necessity drive to secure every economic and other advantage they can obtain for their people. What may appear to us as selfish appears legitimate self-interest to them. We shall also have legitimate self-interests to be defended.

There is another trend in our thinking that calls for correction. It arises from our weakness for simplification. Everybody knows that the world has shrunk in terms of communications. Melbourne and Calcutta are closer to us in flying hours than parts of our own country by train. Radio has made the spread of ideas general and instantaneous. But it is a long flying jump from that to the assumption that we now have one world in terms of political and social or philosophical and religious outlook.

Many naively assume that because Asia is now just over the horizon, Occidental and Oriental thought can be standardized. Or that they are consumed with a desire to adopt our way of life—to have the new world built on American blueprints.

All this is very interesting but it simply isn't true. We can test all this upon ourselves. Are we prepared to adopt Oriental philosophy, religion, economic standards or ways of life because we can more easily know their views and their way of living?

The fact is that the world remains pretty much as it has always been. We are only fooling ourselves by trying to distort a revolution in transport and communications into a world-wide political and social revolution. Though the skies be darkened with planes and the air filled with radio propaganda and messages of good will, life will go on much the same; Chinese and Italians, Americans, Arabs and Swedes will remain pretty much what they were. However beguiling the thought may be the world has not turned into a Great Melting Pot. And we shall not achieve lasting peace by starting with the assumption that we have been transformed into one world by radio and airplanes, for if that were true we should have no problem in making lasting peace.

In this war we Americans have held out great world hopes and promises to suffering humanity that we will perpetually divide our productivity and resources and thus bring to them complete comfort and security in life. Realism with respect to our resources today and our probable situation after the war demands more caution in our oratory. Many of those hopes will appear to peoples as undertakings and obligations on our part.

There is nothing more realistically dangerous than propaganda-stimulated war hates toward whole enemy peoples. Moral indignation at cruelty and wrong is a proper basis of moral action. But artificially created hate is a form of hysteria. It is neither the sign of power nor the badge of courage. It does not make the vital distinction between the peoples and the leaders to whom punishment should be meted out. Such propaganda of general hate prolongs wars by creating desperation in the whole enemy peoples.

Hate adds nothing to the real zeal of our civil population. It beclouds judgment and stimulates rash conduct in nations. The soldiers on the front do not have such hysterias. And like them, the civil population will have a more lasting resolution if it keeps cool. War hate is a venomous infection of men's minds that does not spurt solely toward the enemy. Sooner or later it stirs intolerance and violence in their own countrymen. Its international damage, however, is that a durable peace becomes impossible under its emotional mandates. Such stirrings of hysteria perhaps indicate the war zeal of leaders, but some day it weakens the making of peace. The hate elections in Britain and France after the last armistice crippled their leaders in making a lasting peace. We have grown 300 years away from the fears, dangers and age-old hates which are deeply implanted in the racial mores of Europe and Asia. We have lived a century and a half without fear of our neighbors, without aggression directed against us by them or wrong done to us by them. In the fires of this war these animosities must increase in Europe from a thousand diabolical outrages. We can do a great service to the world if we sustain an objectivity that is so essential in *long-view* statesmanship.

We also need realism as to the causes of war.

The causes of this war, and of war in general, have been obscured by a tendency to over-simplification. That is the assumption that wars are the work of evil men or perverted nations and that they can be ended by a sound spanking. Some years ago the writers set out, as many others have done before, to explore what caused war in the past, why peace has been so precarious and what has given promise of lasting peace. No realistic search for the truth can avoid the conclusion that wars result from no simple causes but are the result of the interplay of long-antecedent dynamic forces, of varying pressures. These destructive forces can be grouped as ideologic and economic pressures, extreme nationalism, imperialism, militarism and the complexes of fear, hate and revenge. And there can be no peace unless these forces are courageously met.

Immense aid in discovering the method of preserving peace can be found in experience as well as in idealistic realism. The explosion of the modern world into total wars and tumult has occurred on three major occasions in a century and a half. Twice the world has tried to build "just" peace and to erect "institutions" to preserve it. The needed solvent of realism can be had from these experiences mixed with realistic extracts from the mores of different branches of the human race with which we have to deal. If this mixture is not compounded and used, we shall have no peace.

If we build the great highway to lasting peace, experience must be our guide. That highway must provide us the way through a wilderness of swamps and precipices where our Crusade can pass. And our way must be lighted by idealism.

Neither goodness nor evil will be abolished by this war. Ideas may shift but human nature will not be greatly changed. We need to be awake and not dreaming.

ARTICLE II

A NEW APPROACH TO THE METHODS AND MACHINERY FOR MAKING PEACE

The world has had some sad failures and disillusionments from its past methods of making peace. The whole question requires a new approach. But before making such suggestions we should examine realistically the immediate situation that will confront us after we have won military victory.

Instantly firing ceases a great load of fear will lift from the minds of men, and a great hope for the future will rise with this relief. But soon the stark scene of devastation will be revealed. Resentment at hideous wrongs will raise the spirits of hate and revenge. They will add fire to the natural demands for punitive action against the enemy.

THE ECONOMIC SITUATION

There will be millions of diseased, maimed and orphaned to be cared for. Every nation outside the Western Hemisphere will be hungry and underclad.

Every nation in the world will be impoverished; millions of homes will be destroyed; millions of tons of ships sunk. Our industrial plants will be greatly deteriorated. We must shift from mass production of swords to mass production of plowshares. In the transition, millions of men will be idle and demanding jobs. Every nation will be loaded with debts; the financial problems of restoring national life will be enormous.

All this will be aggravated by the demand of the people for release from wartime restrictions, discipline and burdens.

THE POLITICAL SITUATION

And what will be the political situation in the world the day after the enemy is disarmed and his forces withdrawn? There are today about 33 nations at war with the Axis or parts of it. The Axis armies have overrun 400,000,000 people belonging to the United Nations. The Axis armies have occupied the capitals in about 12 of these United Nations. These nations have been assured restoration of their sovereignty. When it comes, these nations will instantly set up government. They will organize armies. They will occupy their utmost boundaries. Britain, France and Holland will regain sovereignty over their possessions in the Far East.

And there are the enemy states. They will at once blow up in revolution because their present leaders will be removed to somewhere.

Our boys and the boys in every army will clamor to come home at once the enemy is disarmed. Their wives and parents in every land will demand that they be brought home quickly. When they return they will demand, by right of their service and sacrifice, that their state of life be restored to them. They will rightly make themselves heard. Nor are they coming home to see their countries' substance and rights sacrificed in peace making, whether we like it or not.

In all this welter of hope, suffering, wrong, devastation, hate and idealism, a peace will have to be made. Each and every one of these many nations will appoint representatives to participate in peace-making. The spirit of Nationalism will run high within them. Their delegates must try to secure the utmost in political and economic advantage for their impoverished and suffering people. And greed, arrogance, subtle age-old diplomacy will not be absent.

THE ARMISTICE AND PEACE MAKING

People everywhere will clamor for quick restoration and rebuilding of life. They will demand haste and more haste.

The degenerations and emotions of world wars in many ways reach their climax immediately after firing ceases. It is the most disadvantageous moment for peace makers to set to work rebuilding the world.

That was the situation in 1918. It will confront us again.

When victory comes after this war, we must, jointly with our Allies, again try to lead the world to the Promised Land through all these conflicting forces by virtue of our major sacrifice.

And here we must harken to the voice of experience. We must absolutely avoid the failures of Versailles.

That time some 40 nations, with thousands of skilled diplomats, met in general conference. The authors of this article were there and can well examine what happened.

We had an Armistice which lasted for nine long months. During that time these thousands of diplomats in daily sessions under the leadership of the great nations wrangled and struggled to settle the gigantic problems which had been loosed upon the world. And after that there was a long period of uncertainty in the ratification of the treaty. Daily we witnessed the age-old forces of nationalism, imperialism and militarism acting under the direction of subtle diplomacy. We saw the rise of selfish interests, the clash of ideals, of personalities and of ambitions of men. Hate, fear and revenge were ever in invisible presence.

The very bringing together of all these interests in one place intensified the conflicts and generated new ones. It created a hundred nests of intrigue. The attempt to solve a hundred problems all at once made infinite opportunity for dark corner operations in combinations and logrolling. The whole world was pressing for haste lest the foundations of order should crumble altogether.

The world had been promised open covenants openly arrived at, and it was impossible to make haste under any such plan.

There was no time to enlighten the peoples of the world on each intricate question. Every settlement became a subject first of secret controversy, then of compromise.

We saw the Conference degenerate into a gigantic struggle for power. Gradually the spiritual forces of idealism and of justice were driven back. The peace making was, in the end, swept down the terrible stream of intrigue, power politics and conflict. It was wrecked in the whirlpool of destructive compromise and upon the rocks of selfish interest and emotional action.

The economic clock of the world was slowed down during the long delayed discussions. Instead of releasing the forces of moral and economic recovery, the Armistice was a period of social, political and economic degeneration. Just at the time when the hope of men for the future had risen high it was frustrated by delay.

This must not be blamed on President Wilson. And we should not forget that there were many other able and heroic men there. They deserve credit, not criticism, for the fight they made. But they were overwhelmed not only by the forces evolved in the conference but by the emotional tides and demands from home.

The peoples of the world had little understanding of the impossibility of solving these problems all at once and in haste. The shock to the peoples of the world upon awakening to what had been done in haste and in compromise created antagonism to the settlements made. It bred isolationism in every country in the world.

After the last war, America went to the Versailles Conference unprepared. Through the war we had been told that peace discussions would confuse the war effort, that it behooved us to defeat Germany first, that there would be plenty of time to settle the problems of peace afterward. There was no time. And although we went to Versailles with magnificent aims, we were thoroughly unprepared to formulate the practical terms which would give them life. We secured neither peace, freedom nor safety.

There is nothing more important than getting ready to secure what we are fighting for. Indeed, if we could formulate methods, it would make possible the realization of our aims, and if we could formulate enlightened plans with our associates, it might well be the means of opening a second front within enemy countries and hastening a victorious end of the war.

The first lesson of all this experience is the need for preparation. Peace-making requires just as much preparedness as war. And that preparedness is not alone in the development of realistic plans. Failure to keep public opinion informed involves the risk of musunderstanding and revolt when the people are suddenly awakened from dreaming and in their reaction get nasty.

A FURTHER NEW APPROACH TO PEACE MAKING

The sum of all this experience indicates that we must have a totally new approach to the method and machinery of peace-making. In fact, the making of peace consists of three parts:

1. The machinery for the making of peace.

2. The political, economic, military and other immediate settlements necessary to secure order in the world.

3. The superstructure or "world institution" for the preservation of peace to be built upon these settlements.

We will first extend and elaborate our proposal of a year ago as to the method and machinery of peace-making.

To avoid the quicksands in which Versailles bogged down, we suggested that the world should not undergo either another armistice period or a general peace conference. We proposed that the peace-making should be divided into two stages.

For the first stage we proposed that instead of the usual military "armistice" with its delay in political and economic recovery, there be a quick "conditional" peace which would include not only the usual armistice provisions for ending combat but also the settlement of such *urgent* problems as we mention later and those susceptible of agreement before the end of the war. Thus the armistice period would be eliminated altogether and the "conditional peace" would go into operation instantly, before the forces of degeneration could get in their deadly work.

For the second stage we proposed that there be no general peace conference but a *transitional* period during which there should be negotiation of *long-view* questions by separate regional councils or special commissions, these solutions to be directed towards allaying once and for all the dynamic causes of war. This *transitional* period is needed for the re-growth of political stability, economic recovery, cooling-off of emotions, adequate deliberation and development of public understanding.

TRUSTEES OF PEACE DURING THE TRANSITIONAL PERIOD

At this point we propose a further new approach to thinking on the whole problem of peace-making—not to the machinery alone but a new step in concepts. We suggest that a few of the leading United Nations at some time before the end of the war should by definite agreement of the whole United Nations be constituted "Trustees of Peace," or "Regents of Peace," or "Leaders of Peace" to guide the world through the *transitional* stage from war to peace. They would be "Regents" to bring up the infant peace. It would be their duty to maintain order, to restore international law, to develop the solutions of the *long-view* questions and finally to develop some sort of "world institution" to take their place in the preservation of peace. We suggest later on the nature and limitations of their authority.

Such a trusteeship could well be limited to a term of five to ten years after the conditional peace and subject to renewal. During this transitional period, we could know more of the shape of things to come before entering upon irrevocable commitments.

As a matter of fact the obligation of leadership will rest upon a few leading powers. It will not only be an obligation but a right by virtue of their major sacrifice and their strength to maintain peace.

The leading powers are likely to assume these functions anyway in practice as they have in the past. They assumed these functions at Versailles and for a while afterward. But their assumption of such power without consent led to difficulties. The lack of responsibility definitely imposed by the other nations contributed to the early disintegration of unity.

We are not proposing a military alliance of the leading powers. That would undermine their moral influence and would add nothing to their strength. What we will need is predominantly moral and political development of peace. A policeman is 90% effective from his own and other people's knowledge of his office and his strength and of the authority definitely vested in him.

POLICING THE WORLD DURING THE TRANSITIONAL PERIOD

After fighting ceases there will inevitably be a period during which it will be extremely difficult to maintain order in parts of the world unless there is such a known reserve of strength. In a sense the situation will be worse than during the war itself, for so long as fighting continues there are wartime diciplines that maintain an orderly regime behind the lines. And there is the unity from common peril. With the cessation of hostilities many of these disciplines will break down. Demobilized troops will be freed from military restraints. Wartime disciplines of rationing, distribution and the like will break down overnight, particularly in the vanquished countries.

Under such conditions it is daring to assume that a general "world institution" can be entrusted with the maintenance of world order. However successfully large deliberative bodies may serve the cause of democracy in times of peace, they alone are inadequate for dealing with emergencies. And it may be well for us to face the fact that during a transitional period the maintenance of order and the leadership must be entrusted to a few of the greatest world powers.

Those with a weakness for universal representation of all nations may at once object that this is a proposal aimed at arrogating to a few powers the authority and privileges which should belong to all. This can be disposed of by the statement that the task of maintaining world order after this war will be in no sense a privilege for anybody. It will be a heavy burden and responsibility. In the nature of things the few leading powers will be obliged to furnish the military forces and the financial and other resources to preserve peace.

THE FIRST STAGE

We propose that the prior agreed "conditional peace" should be imposed upon the world by the victorious powers and should, as a minimum, include:

a. The instant surrender of arms and demobilization of all enemy military forces.

b. Return of loot.

c. Repatriation of military prisoners and civil populations driven from their homes.

d. The instant removal of all blockade measures against neutrals and liberated nations—and the removal of blockade against enemy areas the instant they have surrendered their arms.

e. Temporary restoration of pre-war commercial treaties pending general economic solutions. (These treaties regulate communication and enable the movement of commercial ships, planes and goods.)

f. Immediate undertaking of relief for famine and pestilence and aid in reconstruction. Without such organized activity there will be anarchy and no peace. If such a "conditional" peace were established, the more rapid economic recovery would greatly lessen the cost of relief.

g. The designation of provisional boundaries of all liberated and enemy states, with some areas to be occupied and governed by the "Trustees" pending settlement.

h. The immediate call of freely-choosen, elective constitutional assemblies or parliamentary bodies in all liberated and enemy countries in order that there be effective governments with which to deal.

i. Immediate reduction of the armaments of the United Na-

tions themselves to the minimum forces needed to maintain international order and to enforce ultimate peace provisions.

j. The appointment of regional "councils" or special commissions representing all United Nations chiefly concerned to deal with different long-view problems.

These *urgent* questions and such a "conditional peace" are not difficult to formulate nor should they be difficult to agree upon among the United Nations before the war ends, or to impose, nor should they create any disunity among the United Nations. Attempt to settle *long-view* questions, however, might disintegrate our unity of war effort.

These urgent measures are the necessary housekeeping to end a war. As they are not *long-view* commitments, our legislative bodies should have no hesitation in supporting them.

Other proposals might be included in the "conditional" peace if they could be agreed upon. But with these simple minimums the world could move forward toward political order and economic recovery.

The suggestion has been made that instead of a "conditional peace" there should be a much longer armistice—from three to ten years duration—to afford the cooling-off period. In view of the degeneration brought about by the uncertainties of the nine months' armistice and the subsequent delays in ratification of treaties after the first war, we tremble to contemplate what would happen in the economic and political uncertainties under such conditions.

An armistice is not peace. An armistice is merely a cessation of the killing of men, but leaves all the other degenerative forces of war in action. An armistice is worse because it relaxes the war-time disciplines without substituting the disciplines of peace-time. With its uncertainties there can be no restoration of production or stability of political order.

THE SECOND STAGE

The second stage would embrace the *transitional* period for growth of economic and political stability. During the transitional stage the "Trustees" or "Regents of Peace" should have the duty not only to see that the terms of the conditional peace are carried out but they would need to erect machinery for determining the solution of the *long-view* problems. Among these questions are:

a. Disposition of enemy countries.

b. Punishment of Axis leaders and officials for criminal actions.

c. Settlement of private-property questions, reparations and intergovernmental debts.

d. Final determination of boundaries and assignment of disputed areas.

e. Protections of minorities and irridentas.

f. Federations of weaker states.

g. Government and protection of backward peoples.

h. Outlets for emigration.

i. Reestablishment of international law and at least temporary restoration of the World Court pending other arrangements.

j. Permanent reduction of world armaments.

k. And finally, the erection of some sort of "world institution" for the preservation of peace.

Later on we discuss the merits of regional councils separately for Europe, Asia and the Western Hemisphere as the foundations of a "world institution" to preserve peace. In any event such a structure could be invaluable in the *transitional period*. Even if temporary or probationary they could be each of them assigned such of these *long-view* problems as are local to their regions. Moreover, these regional councils could serve to compose many current controversies in their own regions and could refer only insolvable conflicts to the Trustees of Peace.

If such a structure were set up at once, it would relieve the Trustees of Peace of an infinite number of local questions, and if these councils proved a success, it would lay foundations for the "world institution" to preserve peace.

Even if there were a general peace conference with a view to complete peace-making such as Versailles, such *long-view* problems would have to be dealt with by regional or special committees representing the interested victorious nations. Some of these questions involve more than one region, and in any event, are special subjects. Such questions should be in separate commissions each to be solved on its own merits. The work of all these committees should obviously be under the direction and coordination of the "Trustees of Peace."

Some of these problems require time for cooling off of war emotions. Many of them require time for deliberation. Many of them must have time for development of world opinion.

Even if somebody possessed an absolute and perfect formula for solution of these gigantic problems, no such settlements can endure unless accepted at least by the democratic peoples themselves. If they are badly formulated, they will be upset at the ballot box. The people cannot decide intelligently unless they have time to inform themselves.

These regional and special commissions should negotiate and report. The acceptance of their conclusions must be subject to acceptance by the various nations involved.

For America no agreement is binding until it has been ratified by the Senate. There are some people in a hurry who feel we shall get farther, faster, by empowering the Executive to conclude binding agreements without fulfilling our Constitutional requirement of ratification by the representatives of the people. If this is a people's war, it must be a people's peace.

It is difficult to see how we strengthen democratic processes by scrapping constitutional procedure and adopting methods of dictatorship which we are endeavoring to eliminate from the world.

And above all, these *long-view* questions must be so solved and the transitional period so guided that the dynamic forces in the world which make for war are extinguished or allayed and the forces of peace given strength, otherwise any world organization to preserve peace will fail.

We shall in the next article make some suggestions as to the solution of particular problems.

ARTICLE III

THE FOUNDATIONS OF PEACE

The making of lasting peace consists of two clearly defined parts:

1. The political, economic, military and other settlements that secure political order and economic progress in the world.

2. The superstructure or "world institution" for the preservation of peace to be built upon these foundations.

We propose in this article to discuss the first part. We suggest some new approaches to it.

In our last article we indicated a multitude of problems in the political, economic and military fields which must be settled between nations entirely apart from creating the structure of a "world institution" to preserve peace. They are the foundations upon which this superstructure must stand. And in these settlements reside the possibilities of underlying and dynamic causes of future wars.

We must constantly realize that the causes of modern wars arise only secondarily from wicked dictators or perverse peoples. They arise primarily from deep-seated and destructive dynamic forces. And it is in the political, military and economic settlements between nations where their destructive action must first be allayed or stilled. To do that effectively is more important to lasting peace than any superstructure of a "world institution" to preserve peace. For unless the foundations are properly laid the superstructure will fail. It is here that the world has failed before.

These destructive dynamic forces may be grouped as ideologies, economic pressures, imperialism, extreme nationalism, militarism and the complexes of fear, hate and revenge.

It has been maintained that we should not try to grapple with these forces, but should immediately create a "world institution" and leave to it all the solutions. We will, in our next article, set out the reasons why such a program cannot succeed.

We may say here that it was precisely the failure at Versailles to cope with these forces which undermined the foundations of the League of Nations. To repeat the same course will destroy any "world institution."

We may well examine in some detail the world's experience from Versailles in dealing with these destructive forces. And we can formulate some definite recommendations.

IDEOLOGICAL FORCES

It was recognized at Versailles that representative government afforded the best hope of preserving peace. It is the only form of government that is not at war with the rights of man. Governments controlled by the people have not always been free from aggressive action, but there are greater brakes upon war in that form of government than in oligarchies or dictatorships. Out of that war and the settlements, representative governments sprang up in all Europe outside of Russia.

So long as these representative forms of government lasted in Germany, Austria, Italy and the smaller Eastern states, the face of Europe was turned toward peace. The European revolt from liberalism, which laid the trail for this present war, was in part due to the attitude of the Allies and in part to the dynamic forces which had not been curbed. Hitler was a product, not a cause.

It should not be the policy of nations to interfere in the domestic life of other nations. But the transition stage from war to peace in the enemy states offers a very practical problem.

We have suggested under the "conditional" peace—"the immediate call of freely chosen representative constitutional assemblies or parliamentary bodies in all liberated and enemy countries." This is absolutely necessary for enemy areas in any event, in order that dictatorship shall be replaced by some sort of authorized and stable government with which to deal.

Representative Government does not necessarily imply our American "unalienable" personal liberties. We do not assume that personal liberty can be imposed by machine guns. But it cannot begin to grow unless the people control the government.

And its growth will depend greatly upon the subsequent encouragement given by the United Nations during the transitional period to the liberty-loving elements in those countries.

Another phase of this same problem of interference of one nation in the domestic life of another arises from the stimulation of ideologic penetration. It is a form of aggression as obnoxious as war. There can be no lasting peace if it is to be allowed to continue, for it is a prime stimulant of hate and controversy.

ECONOMIC PRESSURES

The economic consequences of Versailles were disastrous. It not only failed to heal the economic wounds of the world but opened new ones.

The continuation of the blockade during the Armistice caused steady economic degeneration. The creation of a host of new small nations with many new boundaries with no restraints on their barriers to trade contributed to impoverishment and despair. In fact, there were few steps toward elimination of trade barriers; they were increased. The preposterous method of collecting reparations created periodic world jitters over its periodic readjustment. The impossible intergovernmental obligations were a running economic sore for 20 years.

Little was done toward relieving the world of the cost of arms; no effort was made to stabilize currencies. The whole economic field was neglected. The consequent destructive economic pressures had much to do with the violence of the hurricane of economic depression and revolution that came ten to fifteen years later.

The most constructive economic action at Versailles was the relief of several hundred million starving people and action under the relief to restore communications and transportation.

To direct the pressures in the economic field toward lasting peace, we have under the "Conditional Peace" suggested that the blockade should be removed the instant the enemy disarms and that the commercial treaties be provisionally restored. This, with similar action to that taken the last time in relief of the starving and restoration of communications and transportation, will prevent delay in the revival of production, of trade and of employment.

The *long-view* program this time, to turn economic pressures toward peace, involves action in many directions. There must be an assurance that international trade will be conducted by private enterprise. Trading by governments or government subsidies to trade at once concentrate the higgling of the markets with their thousand frictions into direct questions between State Departments and Foreign Offices. Under private enterprise these frictions and competitions are represented by profit or loss, or by irritations, subdivided a thousand times among individuals. In the hands of government they concentrate and raise national emotions and become frictions and quarrels between nations. If nations persist in government trading, they must expect anti-dumping action.

The world will sorely need stability of currencies for the movement of trade. It will need sources of credit with which to restart production. America can participate but America cannot be expected to finance the world. We are bound also to be impoverished by the war.

The trade barriers in the world should be reduced to the utmost minimums practicable. This involves the abolition of special agreements between nations which establish any special privilege in trade; the abolition of quotas which are a form of special privilege; and the prevention of monopolies and cartels in international trade. Most of such actions have been directed against the United States.

Economic progress requires freedom of ships to navigate the seas and freedom of planes to fly over them. Both require open port facilities, equal treatment to all nations and contributed services on weather and by radio to increase their safety.

Tariffs should be reduced to a competitive basis founded upon differences in living standards. And here again enters some realism. We can be sure that our farmers and workmen or the farmers and workmen of all countries of high standards of living are not going to allow free imports or free immigration from Asiatic or other low-standard-of-living countries. They will not see it in terms of theoretical equality in trade but rather as the preservation of their very living.

Difficult as it may be, yet economic pressures can be directed to promote prosperity instead of degenerations which furnish the soil of revolution and war.

EXTREME NATIONALISM

We may well repeat that nationalism, with its spiritual content of patriotism, its stimulants to culture and personal dignity of a nation's citizens, is one of the greatest forces in human progress. Its extremes can be dangerous causes of war. The nationalistic spirit inevitably grows with war because the whole process of war is to stir the devotion of men to their flag and country.

Extreme nationalism was little curbed at Versailles. It was even stimulated. It has other phases besides those in the economic field.

One of the theories destructive to international life represented in the Versailles settlements was that both nationalism and government must be based alone upon race. It found extreme expression in the small states of eastern Europe by setting them up without regard to their economic life or defense. These peoples had a right to independence. The new states naturally throbbed with restoration of their freedom from old sufferings. They proceeded not only to erect a multitude of new trade barriers but to build large armies and fortifications along their frontiers, to conclude military alliances and to enter into conspiracies against each other. These frictions and the rattle of their arms rose long before the appearance of Hitler.

All these countries weakened their own prosperity as well as that of the world and by menace kept fear and hate alive among their neighbors. Their boundaries were so set that they included within their borders many minorities from neighboring races. In excessive racialism they sought to curb the cultural expression of these minorities, and each of the mother countries of these minorities clamored for their protection or return. Some part of the present debacle can be attributed to these forces of destruction.

That different races can live amicably together under the same general government is amply demonstrated by the Swiss Confederation and the British Commonwealth. We should not seek the disappearance of the small states. Their cultural development has been, and will be, an immense contribution to civilization.

Experience calls for different action than last time. The major method of curbing the cause of war and economic degeneration from these quarters is to encourage the federation of these states economically and defensively under some cantonal system such as Switzerland or by some other method which will preserve their racial cultures and at the same time promote their economic and political stability. There are 16 states in Europe that would fall naturally into four or five groups.

Many acute "irridentist" sores would be incidentally thus relieved. Where this does not happen, populations should in extreme cases be exchanged—drastic as that may be. The exchange of population between Turkey and Greece carried out after the last war has contributed to the peace and welfare of both peoples.

Another phase of Nationalism will arise in larger states. Proposals forcibly to dismember Germany are a folly that would add only to the economic and political Balkanizing of Europe. The history of Europe is a procession of German separations and explosions into war every time the fragments insisted upon reuniting. If they were separated they would have to be federated again for the same reasons that the small nations should be federated. There can no more be a lasting peace with a dismembered Germany than there could be lasting peace with a dismembered United States.

IMPERIALISM

Imperialism has been the cause of literally hundreds, perhaps thousands, of wars. The subjugation of races capable of self-government is inevitably followed by their striving for independence. The rivalries for areas to exploit create wars between empires.

Imperialism ran rampant out of the treaty of Versailles. While several nations received their independence from old imperial oppressions; yet the British, French and Japanese empires were swelled enormously. The failure of Italy to secure her promised share added fuel to war.

The first cure for Imperialism is to stop the expansion of Empire and the subjugation of peoples.

At once however we wish to point out the exceptional evolution of the British Empire. Whatever its origins may have been, it alone among Empires has been transformed into a commonwealth of nations where self-government has been steadily developed and peace maintained among its components. Such "commonwealths" in other empires would lessen Imperialism and would help insure peace.

A further solution is that the important "mandates," especially those in Africa, should be conducted with full economic and immigration equality for all nations and in such a way that they can be gradually developed toward self-government. Some other areas which contain backward peoples should be placed in a real trust of international government. It is the realistic way to lessen the war-breeding struggles of the have-nots for "colonies" with their exclusive economic privileges.

MILITARISM

Far from Militarism being checked at Versailles, it was stimulated. The cure for militarism is not alone the reduction of armament. Germany, Japan and Italy possess a class—a caste—who live by arms, who are descendants of a caste of arms, who maintain skills and the traditions of war, who believe that war is not only the path to glory but that war rejuvenates races. At Versailles, Germany was reduced to a small army and navy. But it was so organized as to perpetuate the military caste.

The first cure for militarism is to break up the military class or caste in Germany, Italy and Japan. Its descent and traditions must be interrupted and destroyed. And the only way to achieve this is by complete disarmament. The preservation of order in those countries should be delegated to a constabulary where no man having held an officer's commission would be allowed to serve. Thus only can the continuity of these war machines be broken and the menace wiped out.

The Allies in the last peace made binding promises to disarm on land and sea. Under the leadership of the United States we did effect naval reductions which removed billions of taxes from the backs of those who toil. Until the rise of dictators these agreements helped toward peace by lessening naval rivalry. But before the rise of Hitler the land military establishments of the world were still three times the size they had been before the World War. This failure in land arms was due to the division, jealousy and lack of trust among the major powers. The moment for action was immediately after the war when its horrors were still alive in our memories. Then only would it have been possible to obtain a reduction and limitation of land arms among the victorious powers. This moment was allowed to slip away until new formations and new antagonisms had developed.

Again the victorious countries will need drastically to reduce their own armies and navies both to allow economic recovery and to reduce the spirit of militarism in their own countries as well as the fears of their neighbors. The development of the combat airplane makes this easier. A comparatively small air force in the hands of the "Trustees of Peace" with appropriate bases could, in a disarmed world, preserve order and prevent aggression.

But if there is to be important reduction of armament among the United Nations, it must be done quickly after firing ceases. We have suggested that such an agreement should be part of the "conditional peace." Any delay will allow the oppositions of military elements by stimulation of fear to overcome the public desire for relief. Furthermore, as after the last war, continued arms will create fears and disintegration of unity between the United Nations.

FEAR, HATE AND REVENGE

Hot hate and revenge ran through the settlements at Versailles. France had been brutally invaded, her women and children butchered by Germany twice in a single generation. She could not be expected to act with moderation. And the treaties stretched beyond the necessary restraints and reparations into the explosive area of revenge.

Experience has no uncertain lessons in this field. Unless the forces of fear, hate and revenge between peoples and nations can be turned aside, the world will again enter upon the ceaseless treadmill of war. The hideous brutalities of the Axis powers will leave an inerradicable hate in millions of this generation. We cannot expect a growth of brotherhood in those who have suffered. By statesmanship, however, we can so base the settlements at the end of this war that hate, fear and revenge may ultimately decrease and die.

The purpose of peace making must be to establish a regime of law and justice, not regimes of hate.

The concrete problem will arise at once in punishment of the enemy. The first distinction we must make is between peoples and their leaders. The leaders of the nations who brought this situation upon the world must be made an example for all time. There can be no moral distinction and there should be no legal distinction between such men and common criminals conspiring to murder. Too long has it been assumed that there is something sacrosanct about the heads of state who project or provoke war and this wholesale killing of human beings.

The borderlines between proper restraints and reparations from enemy peoples and the explosive area of revenge are difficult to draw. The enemy must be made to realize war does not pay. But if we want lasting peace, we must realize that nations cannot be kept in chains.

Undoubtedly the greatest contribution by the Treaty of Vienna at the end of the Napoleonic Wars was that it imposed no revenge and no chains upon the French, who were the aggressors of that time. At least there was no recurrence of world war for a century.

We cannot have both revenge and peace. We must make such a setting as will give the decent elements in Axis peoples a chance to lead their countries onto the paths of peace.

IN SUMMARY

Out of all these six destructive dynamic forces, uncurbed or even stimulated, at Versailles, grew economic instability, impoverishment, disillusionment, frustration, revolution and dictatorships. Renewed war in Europe became inevitable.

This experience should emphasize the vital distinction between making and preserving the peace. Unless the peace is well made, no organization can preserve it, for it will be dealing with symptoms rather than causes. Unless these six destructive and dynamic forces be ended or allayed, no "world institution" can keep the peace. The League of Nations did not stand a chance.

ARTICLE IV

THE WORLD INSTITUTION TO PRESERVE PEACE

In previous articles we have suggested certain steps in the making of peace. They ultimately lead up to the creation of some sort of "world institution" to preserve peace.

The steps we have suggested are:

(a) That there be an agreement among the United Nations prior to the end of the war constituting a few of the leading nations the "Trustees" of peace.

(b) That, instead of an armistice, we have a "conditional"

peace immediately upon victory which shall embrace certain simple *urgent* measures to start political and economic recovery on its way immediately.

(c) That, instead of a general peace conference, we have a *transitional* period from war to peace, during which the settlement of *long-view* problems should be decentralized into regional councils for Europe, Asia and the Western Hemisphere or into special commissions where matters affect more than one region. We proposed that these settlements should be governed by a determination to eliminate or reduce the causes of war.

(d) That the regional councils should take care of current controversies and, if they fail to settle them, refer them to the "Trustees."

(e) That the "Trustee" nations preserve order in the world during the *transition* period.

(f) That among the *long-view* questions should be placed the creation of a "world institution" to preserve peace which shall succeed the Trusteeship.

We propose in this article to make some suggestions upon the "world institution."

Suggestions of new approach to this problem which we offer are put forward in the hope that they will stimulate thought. There can be no commitment in a world the form of which is not yet clear.

It is easy to dismiss the difficult problems of peace by saying we will first create a "world institution" and it will do the rest.

We are convinced that world experience clearly shows the utter futility of believing we can pass the buck in this way. That is simply dodging responsibilities in difficult problems which we do not have the courage to face. It ignores the whole bitter experience of the world and the task that lies before us.

We believe strongly that no final form or commitment to the overall "world institution" could be competently formulated until after victory is won when the shape of the world will be far more clear. And we believe strongly that even after victory time must be taken for formulation of plans for such an institution. The "world institution" should be the last phase of peace-making, not the first.

Such an institution should be launched under conditions which favor its survival. We shall be throwing it to the wolves if we set it up to grapple with the unallayed forces in operation at the end of the war. There could be no greater disservice to a "world institution" than to entrust it immediately after firing ceases with the task of maintaining order. To hand it such responsibilities in the immediate maelstrom would be to repeat again one of the greatest of handicaps under which the League labored through being thrown into the violent aftermaths of post-war and required to deal with the mess. The experience should have amply proved that any newly created general organization is ill fitted for such emergency service.

Unless the political, economic, military and other settlements are first so formulated as to allay or silence the destructive forces of ideologies and economics, of imperialism, militarism, extreme nationalism, fear, hate and revenge, there can be no lasting peace, no matter what "world institution" we create.

Furthermore, delay is needed until the heat of war and nationalism has cooled—until the enemy states have gained in good will and stability—until the dynamic forces which create war have been allayed and more tranquillity of mind is possible.

It is essential, if such a "world institution" is to have permanence, that it be rooted in acceptance of the United Nations' peoples themselves. If this is a peoples' war, it must be a peoples' peace. And there can be no peoples' peace unless the people have time for public debate and understanding after a concrete proposal is advanced. We must remember that it was six years from the victory of Yorktown to the Constitution of the United States. And the permanence of that instrument is evidence that this six years of discussion and thought was not wasted time.

There is every reason why discussion of all possible plans should take place now. Ideas must be developed and hammered on the anvil of debate. Americans discussed the form of a constitution for the United States long before the victory at Yorktown.

Experience has much to contribute to our thinking upon this question of a "world institution." We should be foolish as a people if we did not take into account the efforts of the past, its strength and its weaknesses.

The world has seen two major attempts to create a "world institution" to preserve peace. The first followed the Congress of Vienna in 1815, which ended the world wars of the Napoleonic period. This effort embraced only Europe but that was most of the international world at that time.

The second, the League of Nations in 1919, a century later, attempted to reach over the whole globe.

THE CONGRESS OF VIENNA

The Congress of Vienna evolved the Holy Alliance. This was a sort of statement of aims and ideals of justice and peace. It was soon transformed into the Quadruple Alliance of the four major powers in Europe. This institution was based on a determination to keep peace by force and to put down evil thoughts of growing Liberalism. It kept the peace for some time and from it emerged the "Concert of Europe." This was a practical, not a formal organization. The "Concert" came into action whenever a crisis arose. Then the major powers communicated or conferred. It tided over many crises and limited the spread of local wars into general conflagrations. But it failed against the dynamic forces making for the explosion of 1914.

The major lesson from the "Concert" was the assembling of nations "in council" to solve crises. It proved it can be done.

THE PAN-AMERICAN UNION

In these efforts to maintain peace we cannot overlook the Pan-American Union which was evolved in 1910 from preceding Pan-American conferences. This has constituted an effective "council" of the Western Hemisphere. It has no "powers" but much influence and such prestige that the Western Hemisphere has been able to maintain general peace throughout its life.

THE LEAGUE OF NATIONS

The League was the greatest experiment in history of definite organization to keep peace in the world. It was a magnificent attempt.

It is important that we examine this experience critically as a guide to the future. In making this analysis of the League's failures and successes, it is not our purpose to indulge in a controversy about the League, but to discover such lessons as are to be found in avoidance of another failure.

The writers of these articles supported America's entry into the League in the hope that the experiment could be worked out, although they did so with many misgivings expressed to leaders during the drafting of the Covenant.

The successes of the League lay in the erection of a most capable Secretariat and the development of a large number of measures of world cooperation. World cooperative action was proved effective in the labor field, child welfare, white and black slavery, double taxation, drug traffic, public health, the settlement of transportation and transit and other questions.

The League, through the organization of arbitration, conciliation and judicial processes, succeeded in the settlement of many controversies by these pacific means and well proved that an organized instrument set up for this purpose can undertake and bring many such controversies to successful conclusions which otherwise might lead to war.

But the League was born of Liberalism and founded upon liberal ideas; it could not survive the revolt from Liberalism in Europe. That revolt found its roots in the failure of the Treaty (as distinguished from the League Covenant) to allay the dynamic causes of war.

Moreover, it was not set up in times of piping peace when hatreds had died down. It was hurriedly created during the aftermaths of war with all its animosities and divisions. No adequate chance was given for public debate and change before commitments were made and it was not, therefore, rooted in the support of the people.

The first lesson from the League is that time must be taken to formulate such an institution and taken in an atmosphere removed from the emotions of war.

The second lesson to be had from the experience of the League is that its structure was too elaborate, too detailed and contradictory as to its duties. By this structure of the Covenant, it generated a whole system of interpretations and confusions. Discussion of cases before the League often became hair-splitting debates over the meaning of the text of the Covenant. Nations even withdrew from the League over such differences and from jealousies in representation upon it.

The foundation for such a body should be a simple statement as to its broad purpose to preserve peace. It should include the terms of the Kellogg Pact by which nations renounced the use of war as an instrument of national policy. It should be authorized to take cognizance of controversies and seek to bring about their pacific settlement.

The third lesson was in the failure to provide for the revision of onerous treaties. The League became an agency for maintaining the *status quo*. In planning for the future, we should be on our guard against too ready assumption that we can build an edifice of nations, each nation as unchanging as the stones of a material building. Throughout all history nations change in their strength, their influence, their sympathies and their interests. There can be no rigid pattern now or later. Peace cannot be preserved by putting nations into straightjackets. And any attempt to maintain the *status quo* in a changing world is a direct invitation to war. Change is the first law of life and the need for change is made clear by growing pressures. If we fail to provide peaceful and orderly methods of change, war becomes the inevitable solvent.

The fourth lesson from League experience was the fact that it was based on two conflicting philosophies. The first was that it was to settle controversies by pacific methods, such as conciliation, arbitration, negotiation and judicial procedure. The second was that in case of failure of pacific methods it was to organize and apply economic and military force to any recalcitrant.

The penalty for failure to agree was to be shot.

The consequence was that often enough the nations avoided or prevented controversies from coming before the League in fear of the force applications. Moreover, the League was not able to secure unanimity of action in the application of force because nations involved in such controversies had friends and affiliates in the League membership. It quickly developed that aggressive powers would be supported by blocs of followers from among the other member-nations on grounds that had nothing to do with the controversy or at least that some nations, while acquiescing in the adoption of the League measures, would nullify them by refraining from action.

While the League had notable success in pacific methods from which the growth and development of precedent and experience gave it strength, yet the minute it failed to apply force, when faced with the necessity for doing so, it lost such prestige and strength as to weaken it in the field of pacific settlement. And when it tried to apply force and failed, it was so stultified in the eyes of its own members that its moral force was almost destroyed.

The whole experience points to the need of thought upon separation of these two functions.

It might well be considered that there should be one agency solely to apply pacific means to controversies and to have no powers of force. Upon the failure of pacific settlement to stop aggression there might be a second agency to step in and apply force.

A fifth lesson from League experience relates to the character of force measures. The League setup provided for two such methods. The first, the "economic sanctions," to be a blockade where other nations broke off trade and financial relations with the aggressor nation. Thereby unemployment and suffering were to be imposed upon the aggressor's people until their government mended its ways. This idea has been revived under the term "quarantine" and seems to haunt many thinkers. The word itself adds stigma to injury.

Practice has proved there are two illusions in these ideas. The first is that "quarantine" or economic sanctions are something "short of war." Their effect on the peoples of the aggressor nation is the same as war, except for the absence of shooting. Small nations might submit but the large nations have hitherto replied to sanctions or threat of sanctions by counter threats to go to war against the imposing nations, or have even actually gone to war. It is not the fear of small nations that leads to world wars; it is the large ones who are able to fight.

Another of the illusions is that all nations can be brought to support economic sanctions, blockade, boycott or quarantine. Every aggressor nation has friends who may deplore its conduct, but they will not take part in such actions against it. The employment and livelihood of some nations are greatly dependent upon the aggressor nation. They also are sufferers and will refuse to go along. This combination of friendship, economic interest, threat and probability of war defeated the application of sanctions to Japan for her aggression on China in 1932, and Italy for her aggression on Ethiopia in 1935.

It can be concluded that "quarantine," "blockade" or "economic sanctions" applied to great nations mean war and that any other belief is fooling. The world should build up no hopes that such action will be "short of war." The only effective "sanction" in case of aggression is military action.

The sixth lesson of League experience was from the participation in all questions of the member nations, and thus the injection of members into the consideration of regional or even local problems which did not directly concern them. For instance, some 25 members were from the Western Hemisphere and Asia who were not concerned in the secondary problems of Europe. This system of world-wide representation resulted in the inability of the League to formulate major policies for peace in any one of the three great regions of the world. Most serious of all, it failed to formulate peace policies for Europe where it was most needed. As a matter of fact, the nations of Europe, to a very large extent, avoided the use of the League. That is evident in the fact that, during the effective life of the League, 19 important diplomatic conferences covering European questions took place in which the League had no part; 36 military alliances and nonaggression pacts were signed by member states which ignored the League; and 20 violent acts took place between nations where the League did not, or was not allowed to, take any action.

It is certain that very much better results can be obtained from a "world institution" under which the primary responsibility is divided regionally than from a world-wide organization which is charged with responsibility for the detailed problems of the whole earth. Experience indicates that the first step in the prevention of war is the development of regional policies and responsibilities.

Such a method would relieve the "world institution" of all except major world crises. It would, in our view, infinitely better serve to keep the peace. The view that there should be three major areas of Europe, Asia and the Western Hemisphere was advanced by the writers of these articles on May 1, 1942. Confirmation of these ideas has recently come from Mr. Churchill, who, on March 21, 1943, said:

"One can imagine that *under* a world institution embodying or representing the United Nations, and some day all nations, there should come into being a *Council of Europe* and a *Council of Asia* . . . it is upon the creation of the Council of Europe and the settlement of Europe that the first practical task will be centered. Now this is a stupendous business. In Europe lie most of the causes which have led to these two world wars. . . .

" . . . We must try . . . to make the Council of Europe, or

whatever it may be called, into a really effective League, with all the strongest forces concerned woven into its texture, with a High Court to adjust disputes, and with forces, armed forces, national or international or both, held ready to enforce these decisions and prevent renewed aggression and the preparation of future wars."

NEW PLANS

There is some comment that can be made upon some of the plans for the overall "world institution" now being currently proposed or revived. There have been a multitude of such plans. They have all been proposed time and again over the centuries. It is an advantage to have them all weighed again in public discussion. And they should be weighed in the light of experience already gained.

There are those who propose a restoration of the League of Nations. Realism compels any student searching for light from experience to the conclusion that, if the League is to be revived, it must be greatly amended before it could hope for any better success and it would need a far better soil if it is to thrive.

In all plans for world action there arise two practical problems of major importance. That is, the method of representation of the nations concerned and the degree of sovereignty which nations are to cede to the "world institution."

There are several plans of representation. They comprise proposals for equal representation for each independent nation, or are based upon strength or population with or without modifications, or some combination of the two. The latter was the case in the League of Nations where the Assembly represented each nation equally and the Council was originally planned as mainly of the large nations, each having a veto power over the whole mechanism. It was an unadmitted acknowledgment of the responsibilities of the great nations.

There are today 57 independent nations, or there would be if their sovereignty were restored. If we include the British Dominions and the Philippines, there would be about 7 more, or 64. They are located, 11 in Asia, 25 in Europe, 4 in Africa,

2 in Australasia, 11 in South America, 11 in North and Central America, or a total of 22 in the Western Hemisphere.

There are about 2,230 million people in the world, of whom about 1,200,000,000 are in Asia and the Indies, 500,000,000 in Europe, 170,000,000 in Africa, about 10,000,000 in Australasia, 90,000,000 in South America, 170,000,000 in North America, or about 260,000,000 in the Western Hemisphere.

The complication of the problem of representation is indicated by the fact that on a straight population basis Asia and the Indies would have a majority of the representatives. Peoples of advanced Western civilization are less than 30% of the human race. The Western Hemisphere would have about 10% of the voice. The United States' voice would be about 6%. On an equal representation 43 nations would have 70% of the members although they have less than 10% of the world population. And 4 nations alone would have a majority.

The proposed methods of selecting representatives in the "world institution" fall into two groups of thought. One, that representatives be appointed by the governments; the other, that they be elected directly by the people. Plans for election at once run upon two rocks. Less than 20% of the world's population have free electoral systems based even theoretically upon an honest secret ballot. And some of these are not so good. As populations are not equal in literacy, culture or power, suggestions are made of basing the electorate on these factors. Aside from the lack of electoral systems, any attempt to differentiate between countries on grounds of superiority or inferiority in literacy, culture and the like would arouse jealousies and disputes at once. A rough guess is that application of such standards would give Europe and North America overwhelming power.

In any event, no general electoral system is likely to be adopted over the world during this century.

Therefore a difficulty in such plans is that representatives from countries without real electoral systems would of necessity be appointed by their governments, while those from electoral countries would come direct from the people and not under direction of their foreign offices. The foreign offices would tend to become somewhat atrophied.

All these ideas were the subject of endless discussion in 1919. Our belief is that when the discussion is finished again the method of representation will approximate that of the League with the possible change that, if founded upon regional organization, the representatives to the over-all "world institution" might be chosen by the regional councils and comprise mostly the larger victorious nations.

The degree of sovereignty to be delegated to this "world institution" is the most difficult of all questions. The various plans run all the way from an organization devoted to development of peace policies, settling controversies and stopping aggression, to those of the super-government type where World Parliaments would have legislative, executive, military and judicial powers.

The super-government ideas are also embraced in proposed World Unions, or Federations, under which some or all the present National Governments become Provinces. All super-government types seem to include control of international trade, transportation and communication. That would enable such a body to control indirectly the internal economic life of every nation.

We are devoting a great deal of our energy these days to discussing the merits of various schemes of world governments, with their parliaments, courts and armies. We can eliminate a large part of this by recognizing the hard fact that no general super-government can be set up unless all the Great Powers are ready to accept such surrender of sovereignty as is required to create the new authority. As we have already said, it seems extremely unlikely that Britain or Russia or France would surrender such degree of sovereignty, even if the American people were willing to do so.

In the light of this it is perhaps premature to assume that we alone are out of step in a world eager for the adoption of a world government. We might do well to turn our thoughts to solutions where we can hope for general agreement.

And as we said in the beginning that when considering the authorities of such a body, emphasis needs to be made in thinking upon the words "cooperation," "joint action," "united action," "partnership" rather than "super-government."

In any event, we should not forget our own struggles toward safety and freedom. It was eleven years from the Declaration of Independence to the Constitution. Many ideas rose and died before we reached that solution.

On Prime Minister Churchill's Address

Jointly with Hugh Gibson

Press Statement, New York City

[March 22, 1943]

PRIME MINISTER CHURCHILL has made a valuable contribution to thinking on post-war planning in the suggestion of Regional Councils in Europe and Asia to preserve peace. We already have the foundation of such a Council in the Western Hemisphere in the Pan-American Union. Obviously, as he implies, there would be some linking of these Regional Councils on worldwide questions through the leadership of the great nations of the United Nations group. It is an effective declaration of the primary regional responsibilities of Europe and other areas.

The idea of a Council of Europe is founded upon Europe's past tradition and practical experience. The longest periods of European peace have come during the 100 years when the nebular "Concert of Europe" had leadership.

The suggestion of rough grouping of smaller European states for representation on the European Council, for economic and other purposes, would strengthen the whole peace foundations of Europe. It should increase the economic prosperity and greatly lessen the war frictions between these states which so often involves their neighbors.

An Approach to a Lasting Peace

Jointly with Hugh Gibson

The New York Times Magazine
New York City
[April 4, 1943]

PRIME MINISTER CHURCHILL in his address of March 21 made the first British pronouncement of world organization to preserve peace. He suggested that as a basis "one can imagine that *under* a world institution embodying or representing the United Nations, and some day all nations, there should come into being a Council of Europe and a Council of Asia." His ideas are obviously tentative, but Mr. Churchill does not put "tentative" ideas without thought and experience behind them. The ideas were so logical a derivation from long British experience and knowledge of European affairs that they have struck a responsive chord in Britain.

It is important to recall what the Prime Minister said. After discussing the probable defeat of Hitler before the defeat of Japan, the necessity to disarm the enemy, punishment of their leaders, the return of loot from subjugated countries, the need to provide relief and the necessity for unity of the great powers, his pertinent statement on world organization was:

One can imagine that *under* a world institution embodying or representing the United Nations, and some day all nations, there should come into being a *Council of Europe* and a *Council of Asia* . . . it is upon the creation of the Council of Europe and the settlement of Europe that the first practical task will be centered. Now this is a stupendous businêss. In Europe lie most of the causes which have led to these two world wars. * * *

Mr. Churchill has outlined a pattern to complete which requires less speculation than logic. It is obvious in these careful expressions Mr. Churchill puts forward four major ideas:

(1) A "world institution embodying or representing the United Nations and some day all nations."

(2) There should come into being under this "world institution" a "Council of Europe" and a "Council of Asia."

Nicely observing the proprieties, Mr. Churchill made no suggestions as to a "Council of the Western Hemisphere." But, of course, his proposal for Europe implies something of the same sort for our hemisphere. Indeed, we have foundations already laid for cooperative action in preserving peace in our own Pan-American Union, which has behind it years of accomplishment and developing strength from decade to decade.

(3) That the primary responsibility for maintaining peace should rest in the regional councils. That they should inaugurate the machinery for settling controversy and even the armed forces to prevent aggression. At least that is his suggestion for the Council of Europe where he is quite specific, as he says:

I hope we shall not lightly cast aside all the immense work which was accomplished by the creation of the League of Nations. Certainly we must take as our foundation the lofty conception of freedom, law and morality which was the spirit of the League. We must try—I am speaking, of course, only for ourselves—we must try to make the Council of Europe, or whatever it may be called, into a really effective league with all the strongest forces concerned woven into its texture with a high court to adjust disputes and with forces, armed forces, national or international, or both, held ready to enforce these decisions and prevent renewed aggression and the preparation of future wars.

Any one can see that this council, when created, must eventually embrace the whole of Europe and that all the main branches of the European family must some day be partners in it. What is to happen to the large number of small nations whose rights and interests must be safeguarded? Here let me ask what would be thought of an army that consisted only of battalions and brigades and which never formed any of the larger and high organizations like army corps. It would soon get mopped up. It would therefore seem to me, at any rate, worthy of patient study that side by side with the great powers there should be a number of groupings of States or confederations which would express themselves through their own chosen representatives, the whole making a council of great States and groups of States. * * *

(4) Mr. Churchill insists upon the necessity for leadership and unity of Britain, Russia and the United States. No doubt China will expect a larger part in the pattern but that is not part of this discussion. Upon this he says:

* * * it would be our hope that the United Nations, headed by the three great victorious powers, the British Commonwealth of Nations, the United States and Soviet Russia, should immediately begin to confer upon the future world organization which is to be our safeguard against further wars. * * * We must hope and pray that the unity of the three leading victorious powers will be worthy of their supreme responsibility. * * *

Mr. Churchill's suggestion of regional responsibility, as is usual with British statesmen, reflects the long lineage of European experience and British instinct to build upon such experience. This experience is further reflected by the fact that his ideas are advanced not as firm proposals but as problems worthy of study and discussion. This is the right approach. We shall never reach sound solutions by emotional methods but only by honest search and scrutiny.

The experience which reflects in his suggestion has a basis in the two major attempts of Europe at organized effort to preserve peace. The first was at the Congress of Vienna in 1814 which ended that world war. The second was at Versailles in 1919 which ended another world war.

From Vienna sprang the Holy Alliance which was quickly transformed into the Quadruple Alliance by which Great Britain, Austria, Prussia and Russia agreed to work together to preserve or enforce peace. It functioned for a few years somewhat effectively but finally split and there gradually emerged the "Concert of Europe." This "Concert of Europe" was not a defined, regularly meeting organization with definite powers, but a practice of the leading powers of getting together in emergencies. It tided over many crises but finally failed against the forces making for the World War of 1914. Whatever may be said of the "Concert," it gave the world one of the longest periods of freedom from world wars—almost exactly a century.

The second attempt was of course the much more precise and definite organization of the League of Nations. The experience of the League showed the handicaps of having some thirty nation-members from outside Europe taking part in the dealing with obvious troublesome European questions or policies. In the Assembly of the League each of these nations, no matter how remote or how unfamiliar with European problems, had an equal vote with the nations of Europe.

Those of us who witnessed the proceedings of the League or participated in them soon had it borne in upon us that the universality of world organization, instead of being an unmixed blessing, was only too often a drag on the settlement of strictly European questions which made up the vast bulk of League activity.

It suffices to run through the published proceedings of the League to see how clear this is. Take a discussion on any purely local European problem, perhaps of direct concern to a few European powers. Those few powers often figure inconspicuously in the debates, while page after page is devoted to the remarks of delegates from South and Central America, from Near East and Far East. It is surprising how often debates revealed that the delegates from other parts of the world were less concerned with settlement than with creating a precedent that might be useful for their countries later on, stressing the importance of their country in world affairs, or even in many cases indulging in oratory to be reproduced in their home papers. They voted such ideas. And these outside powers also often appeared in blocs supporting one side or the other of a controversy on grounds not relative to the dispute.

The inevitable effect was the action of European nations of

that time in ignoring the League in their settlements and controversies—particularly the principal powers. The European powers at that time were usually intent upon finding some solution of their immediate problems. They were driven to outside discussions if they wanted to reach prompt solution rather than spend months listening to fruitless oratory.

An indication of the unwillingness to make use of the League to formulate European peace policies and actions lies in a bare list of incidents outside the League. During eighteen years of active League life, there were nineteen international diplomatic conferences in Europe outside the League, thirty-six military alliances and non-aggression pacts which ignored the League, twenty violent actions between nations where the League did not, or was not allowed to, take action. One of the most striking examples of this was the conclusion of the Locarno agreements outside the framework of the League. It was a regional problem and they dealt with it in a regional way. All this experience makes it natural that for domestic European questions Mr. Churchill should suggest a regional "Council of Europe."

In an analysis ten months ago of the weaknesses of the League in these particulars, the authors of this article remarked (in "The Problems of Lasting Peace," pages 156-57) that the League had wholly failed, or was unable, to formulate broad policies for European peace, and they continue:

The major scene of danger of war in the world has always been the Continent of Europe. Although it was the transcendent need of the times, the League never had a European policy, even at the moment when every European nation was in its membership. * * *

(For instance) There seems to have been no serious discussions or consideration of the crisis generated by the rise of the Axis. That is, the major danger to the world was ignored by the League. * * * One purpose of the victors in the last war and the real foundation of peace was to implant and hold representative government in Europe. That concept the League never seemed to have grasped and certainly did not vigorously assert or guard. * * *

The whole experience would seem to indicate that *one of the first functions in the prevention of war is the development of regional policies in the different major areas of Europe, Asia and the Western Hemisphere.*

Most of the broad policies of long-view peace are regional either to Europe, Asia or the Western Hemisphere. In the Western Hemisphere, the Pan-American conferences had long and successfully performed that function. Certainly the League failed or was unable to formulate a similar broad policy of European cooperation and of constructive peace.

Mr. Churchill does not elaborate upon the powers or functions of the top "world institution." The implication is that the machinery of settling controversies and enforcement is to rest, at least initially, in the regional organizations. The "world institution" is apparently for emergencies of interregional or world-wide character. Such a regional basis or organization would relieve Europe from becoming engaged in the domestic problems of the Western Hemisphere or Asia unless they threatened world war. In other words, that means not isolationism but cooperative regionalism.

The pattern would also logically express itself that the regional councils in the different settings should have such forms of detailed organization as befit their situation. The Western Hemisphere, under this idea, probably would not require as much machinery as the European Council.

In any event, Mr. Churchill's regional plan simplifies the problem of detailed organization of the "world institution" to preserve peace.

The authors of this article, however, wish to give emphasis to the all-time human experience that whatever this regional or world structure to preserve peace may be, it will be futile unless the foundations are properly laid in the other settlements of the peace. It was in these settlements that Versailles, as distinguished from the League of Nations, failed in peace-making.

That treaty failed to allay or still the destructive and dynamic ideological and economic forces: extreme nationalism, imperialism, militarism, fear, hate and revenge. It even stimulated some of these forces. Not only did these foundations of sand render

the League of Nations futile but they will render any superstructure of Leagues, European Councils, World Institutions,
World Congresses, World Parliaments futile again unless far
better settlements are made upon which this superstructure to
preserve peace is erected.

Unless these destructive forces are rigorously dealt with by
the nations, the seeds of war will be again planted which no
organization can for long curb.

History's Greatest Murder Trial

Jointly with Hugh Gibson

This Week Magazine, New York City

[August 29, 1943]

WITH neutral countries warned that the United Nations would look with disfavor upon any attempt to afford asylum to fleeing Axis criminals, it is none too soon to consider the principles upon which we are going to deal with the enemy after victory. There are two problems: how shall we deal with the war criminals themselves? How shall we deal with the enemy peoples so that they may not organize to attack us again?

These criminals are not only the Hitlers, the Mussolinis and the Tojos—big and little—but the long lists of those guilty of acts of assassination, brutality, cruelty and torture.

The fate of Mussolini is still shrouded in secrecy as we write this. But regardless of what may happen to him before this article is printed, his resignation emphasizes the importance of deciding now on the procedure to be followed in bringing the war criminals to justice. If we leave the question of their fate until the end of the war, there is danger that they will escape the consequences of their crimes, as they did the last time.

A year ago the writers said: "There is a large question of the personal responsibility of heads of state and their associates for violation of treaties and agreements (entered into with free will) in pursuit of militaristic and imperialistic designs which result in the killing of millions of human beings.

"The leaders of the nations who brought this situation upon the world must be made to realize the enormity of their acts. There can be no moral distinction between such men and common criminals conspiring to murder. Too long has it been assumed that there is something sacred about the heads of state who project or provoke war and wholesale murder."

In 1918 there was a great deal of talk of hanging the Kaiser and punishing all those guilty of war crimes, but the Kaiser settled down to end his days peaceably in Holland. The Allies agreed to allow the many other Germans accused of crimes to be tried by German courts. The results were hardly surprising. The German courts went through some solemn formalities and were unable to find evidences of guilt. It was a highly dignified farce.

We cannot permit anything of this sort to be repeated. It is just as demoralizing in world affairs to let systematic cruelty and crime go unpunished as it would be in domestic affairs to grant complete immunity to bank robbers and murderers.

A positive distinction must be made between imposing legal punishment for crime and the problem of what to do with enemy peoples. There should be no question of indiscriminate and wholesale punishment of whole nations, for that merely lays the foundation for future conflicts.

Moral indignation at cruelty and wrong is a proper basis of moral action. But war hate is a form of hysteria that makes no distinction between peoples and their leaders who should be punished. Hate propaganda prolongs war by creating desperation in the whole enemy peoples. One of the Nazis' greatest holds on the German people has been their belief that they can expect no mercy from us. They were told that, to avoid extermination, they had only one choice—to fight to the last.

We shall be soft-headed rather than soft-hearted if we fail to accelerate our efforts to establish clearly who the war criminals are and what they have done, with a view to their being given fair and expeditious trial and dealt with in the light of the evidence. The essence of what we are fighting for is to establish justice and we must ourselves abide within these processes.

However quickly we work after military victory, there is likely to be wholesale bloodletting in occupied countries and in Germany itself. The universal experience with military defeat is revolution in which the leaders meet angry and frustrated peoples. Groups will come to the surface with their own sufferings to right and their own vengeances to impose. It would be preferable if all these war criminals could be arrested and tried by proper courts, but such hope may be denied by events.

Despite the warnings to neutral nations by the Allies, many Axis criminals undoubtedly will try to escape to these countries, and in some cases they may succeed in crossing the frontiers. Here rises a definite problem. International law does not recognize the right of asylum for men who commit criminal acts. It does recognize the right of asylum to political refugees. On this ground Holland declined to extradite the German emperor following the last war.

As a result of Mussolini's downfall these questions are now being extensively discussed. As this is written there is still some doubt as to how many neutrals will accept our interpretation of international law. If we allow this question to drag too long, there may be very little that can be done about it. We should devote attention now to reaching international understanding as to the distinction to be made between the old idea of a political refugee whose greatest fault was disagreement with those in power, and the Hitlers and Tojos! A muddled conception of international law and humanity must not be used as a shield to protect people from punishment for their crimes. It is only by a tremendous stretch of the imagination that many of these misdeeds can be described as political. The ruthless seizure of private property, the machine-gunning of refugees, the shooting of hostages, the execution of prisoners of war, the extermination of the Jews, the excesses against the civil population of Hong Kong, Nanking and the like are fiendish crimes. Furthermore, they were deliberately and systematically organized, which aggravates them by premeditation. And the criminals include not only the hired hands who committed such crimes but the men who commanded the crimes to be carried out and those in authority who refused to intervene to stop the acts.

So far we have taken one preliminary step by notifying the neutrals that we expect them to cooperate in making the Axis gangsters available for trial on the same basis as unofficial people committing the same crimes. If neutrals should fail to cooperate, the Axis criminals could then be tried in absentia, and when convicted, the neutral governments should be summoned to hand them over. The neutral governments might well be represented at the trials to satisfy themselves of their fairness.

If such a course were followed, it is difficult to see on what ground any civilized country could protect such criminals simply because they happen to have been vested with some official authority when they committed the crimes.

It has been advocated that each of the United Nations be entrusted with the trial of any individual in whom it has a special, legitimate interest. To us this proposal seems open to grave objections. There will immediately arise a suspicion that the intention is not so much to mete out justice as to obtain revenge.

The United Nations should agree upon a panel of judges of the highest possible type to sit in such cases, the judges to be assigned to individual trials by a steering committee. This would invest the tribunal with the dignity of siting on behalf of the whole civilized world. Prosecutors who are to appear before the courts on behalf of the United Nations should also be designated before the end of the war.

But we emphasize again that in formulating our plans on this subject, one thing should be clear both in our minds and in our propaganda—that we are intent not upon revenge, not upon punishment, but on justice.

An even greater question should also be settled in advance. That is how to deal with enemy peoples at large. We want them to realize that aggression does not pay. Yet we have to live with these nations if we are to have lasting peace.

This first lesson is sound defeat. Defeat itself is the greatest humiliation that can come to a nation. Moreover defeat will bring revolution, with all its internal violences; and revolution also in punishment.

But if we are not to have the periodic rise of aggressive, military action in these nations, impelled by humiliation, hate and pride, we have to do something more than give them a spanking.

Germany, Japan and Italy all have a long-established warrior caste. This caste likes war, it lives by war, it eulogizes war, and it wants to dominate and exploit other nations. Through class traditions, through sons succeeding fathers as officers, through general staffs whose business it is to plan further wars, the military caste in each of these countries is a menace to the world. These warrior castes must be broken up. One of the failures of Versailles was that Germany was allowed to keep an army of 100,000 men and a small navy. Even the privates in these organizations were potential officers. Their generals and their staffs sat plotting war again.

There is only one answer to that: complete disarmament of the defeated nations. The cry that there must be an army to preserve internal order can be answered by a constabulary in which no man who ever held an officer's commission may serve. And if its arms are limited to those necessary to deal with unarmed citizens, they will have little with which to practice.

There are those who think to re-educate the German, Japanese and Italian youth by forcing United Nations teachers into control of their schools. There are obvious difficulties—ideologies cannot be imposed either by foreign teachers or machine guns. Change must come from within the hearts of the peoples themselves.

We can—and must—insist upon the enemy states freely electing a representative government, so as to have a responsible government with which to deal. But we cannot, for instance, impose our concept of a Bill of Rights upon other peoples, because the very right of peoples to self-government carries also the inherent right to determine their own way of life.

We must focus our minds on lasting peace, not on spread of our ideology.

There are those who propose to dismember defeated peoples

into a multitude of states. That simply will not work, for the yearnings of racial solidarity are forces that will ultimately defeat any such idea. The history of periodically dismembered Germany is of intrigue and wars for unification that have disturbed the whole world. If we were defeated and our states separated, would we not conspire until we were united again?

Our experience is that indemnities such as Versailles imposed cannot be collected over a long term of years. There must be a terminal toward which the defeated peoples can look forward or they will constantly conspire.

The defeated countries after this victory can pay some indemnities, but if we are not to create anew the cesspools of world infection we must not attempt to hold them in bondage. That is not only vengeance—it is a delusion.

One of the greatest difficulties the world will have to meet when victory comes is the inevitable and universal emotional state. The hideous brutalities of the Axis powers will leave an ineradicable hate in millions of this generation. We cannot expect a growth of brotherhood in those who have suffered. Famine and poverty will have enveloped the whole world because of the Axis. Hate, revenge will be the natural emotions of all the peoples of the United Nations.

Unless the forces of fear, hate and revenge between peoples and nations can be turned aside, the world will again enter upon the ceaseless treadmill of war. By statesmanship at the end of this war, that hate, fear and revenge may ultimately decrease and die.

The enemy must be made to realize war does not pay. But if we want lasting peace, we must realize that nations cannot be held in chains. In the end there can be no trustworthy security except by giving the decent elements in a people a chance to cooperate in the work of peace.

And let us not cultivate hate by government propaganda or by private cries. There will be enough of this emotion to deal with without stimulation, for such stimulated hate will poison our own souls and make vision, true justice and lasting peace impossible.

These are questions that call for immediate thought and early action. If we act wisely and in unison, we may achieve the just punishment of criminals, teach the lesson that aggression cannot succeed and, finally, demonstrate that we, the victorious nations, stand for justice and are strong enough to enforce it.

New Approaches to Peace

MINNEAPOLIS, MINNESOTA

[*September 3, 1943*]

VICTORY is now inevitable. There will be many more hard months. But every month brings us nearer to the problems of peace.

The American people are alive to the need and determined that we must have a lasting peace this time. From coast to coast you are thinking and discussing the ways to peace. You want to make your lives again free from war hardships. You want your sons, husbands and fathers home.

The method of making peace is being hourly discussed in books, in the press, over the radio. Congressional resolutions and political offensives are in motion all along the front of peace ideas.

We have two schools of discussion. In the first are those people who are striving to distill from the world's experience something definite and positive. Several notable contributions have been put forward which merit great consideration.

In the second school are those who live in the indefinite or the infinite. Their aims are magnificent; their phrases are sonorous; their slogans are impelling. But when we sift them down, they are mostly nebular words to the effect that we must cooperate or collaborate with the world to preserve peace and restore prosperity. They are a long way from how to do it. Often enough these phrases are doors to political escape. Or alternatively, they are the pavement of good intentions. Theirs is an unreal world of perfect words.

I do not underestimate the usefulness of inspiring words. But most of this is exactly the same verbal road which led to Versailles. When we got there we had high ideals, high aims and great eloquence. Unless we arrive at the end of this war far more realistically prepared, we will have little chance of lasting peace. We must have something far more specific and definite than high aims, high ideals, sixty-four dollar words, good intentions, political avoidance or recriminations. Worse than this, we may out of such material have done no more than lay the kindling for World War III.

On this whole problem, I am daily more and more impressed with the fact that nations have often enough been successful in making war. But nations have never yet been successful in making lasting peace. More and more over the centuries the world has developed the art and method of making war. But the world has never developed an art and method of making peace. More and more the methods of peace have resulted in a wider spread of catastrophe.

Surely it is time we have a new approach to peace-making. And that path must leave the century-old bright lights of eloquence and nebular words and explore the hard road of experience.

Hugh Gibson and I, from considerable participation in these problems over the last 25 years, have suggested for public consideration some ideas of a new approach. Several of the ideas which we originally put forward have now been adopted by powerful voices.

I propose to explore these ideas further with you. The principles and the program are at least realistic and positive. And they suggest common ground over which those of even divergent views on particular questions can travel with unity toward our common purpose of a lasting peace.

I had a teacher once who said, in effect, that wisdom does not consist so much of sixty-four dollar words about the ultimates as in knowing what to do next. And the next thing after that.

Therefore, I am going to examine with you what to do next. I may state the principles and program first and the reasons afterwards. The program consists of four steps and there are twelve reasons.

Before we start on this exploration I may assure you that it does not embrace the usual democratic process of name calling. That is not a unifying or peaceful approach. From the Sermon on the Mount we learn that the peace-makers "shall be called the Children of God."

It would appear that unifying name only applies to the actual peace delegates and not to those who engage in advance discussion of what the delegates should do. In any event I will not take your time discussing "isolationists," "nationalists, "internationalists," "Fascists" or "Communists." Our job is to find common ground, not to widen differences.

We propose that this common ground and the road to real peace lies in creating a *Transitional Period* of a few years from war to peace. But before there can be a Transitional Period there must be two advance steps.

FIRST STEP

The first step in our proposal is to reach an agreement, before firing ceases, between all the United Nations that a few leading nations be appointed the joint *Managers or Custodians or Trustees of Peace*, and that there will not be the usual armistice or the usual general peace conference.

SECOND STEP

The second step is an agreement between all the United Nations before victory over Germany, setting up the terms of a simple *Provisional Peace* or a *Provisional Regime* which the Custodians or Trustees shall impose upon belligerent Europe the moment firing ceases, and later on Asia.

THIRD STEP

The third step is the *Transition Period* from war to peace of a few years, in which the world can have time for deliberate solution of the long-view problems of lasting peace.

FOURTH STEP

The fourth and last step, after the foundations of real peace have been laid, is then to create some sort of *world institution* to replace the Managers or Trustees and preserve peace.

THE TRUSTEESHIP

Some immediate questions will arise in your minds as to the Trusteeship. A few great victorious nations are going to dominate the world anyway for a while after this war. They must do it of necessity to themselves. They always have done so after every great war. They did it after the world wars of the Napoleonic period and after the last World War. It would be a great and new step to peace if they did it out in the open, by a definite authority with positive responsibilities and limitations.

I am not proposing an elaborately written piece of paper committing nations to action in unknown circumstances. A mere joint declaration of purpose by all the United Nations would be sufficient. It needs only to be that we continue collaboration in peace making which we have in war and that we do it under the leadership of the principal nations conducting the war; that we do it in consultation with all our allies in the fields in which they are interested; and that we do it for a limited period. If we can do this without elaborate treaties and documents in war, why not in a Transition Period from war to peace?

I am not proposing a military alliance of a few victorious powers, arrogating to themselves domination over other nations such as has in reality followed those other world wars. Such alliances at once raise the antagonism and suspicion of the balance of the world. A military alliance would undermine the moral influence of the Custodians or Trustees and would add nothing to their strength.

THE PROVISIONAL PEACE

Questions will also arise in your minds as to the terms of the Provisional Peace or the Provisional Regime.

These terms can be made specific and comparatively simple. They are the urgent measures necessary to get the world going again.

The first need of the world, more urgent even than bread, will be order. And the second need will be food. Hungry people abandon all restraint and defy all order. The next imperative need will be to restore economic production, for the starving cannot long be supported on charity. These questions admit no delay. Without them Europe and Asia will dissolve in chaos.

There are other urgent matters. There must be total disarmament of the enemy. Their leaders must be punished for crimes against mankind. They must return their loot, prisoners and displaced peoples.

There must be the restoration of sovereignty to those nations deprived of it. The Trustees would need at once to determine temporary boundaries for everybody.

The defeated nations should be required to hold free elections of representative bodies, excluding Fascist candidates, to initiate government and national life so that there will be some responsible body with which to deal.

There should be provisional restoration of the former treaties about posts, telegraphs, ships and planes which are necessary to the reopening of economic life for the whole world.

And the Trustees should at once set up regional councils for Europe, Asia and the Western Hemisphere and such other committees of the United Nations as are needed to work out each of the host of long-view problems without the solution of which there can be no lasting peace.

These provisional questions are not difficult to settle. But they represent the stark necessities required to start the world housekeeping again.

THE TRANSITION PERIOD

It is in a *Transition Period* that the gigantic problems which confront the world must and can be solved.

In the meantime the Trustee nations would need to guide these committees and police the world against any aggressors.

I may enumerate only a few of these problems to indicate their complexity and that time is needed for their solution.

The future of the three great enemy countries and a lot of little ones must be settled.

There are great territories to be justly disposed of.

Militarism must be abolished.

The face of these nations must be turned toward peace.

Gangsterism cannot be abolished overnight.

There is demobilization of the world to be brought about.

There are many boundaries to be settled.

There are peoples to be freed. There are peoples to be placed under guardianship. The Jewish refugee and the problem of Palestine must be settled.

There are gigantic debts and reparations to be considered.

There are a thousand problems of trade, of currency, of credit to be solved.

And all of these problems must be solved in such a fashion and with such justice as to allay or still the dynamic forces which have hitherto always bred war anew. Those forces must not be stimulated as they were at Versailles, where they were made stronger for evil and more explosive.

And now I come to the eleven reasons for this program and the dangers we must avoid.

FIRST REASON

PROMOTING ALLIED UNITY

The first reason is one that has been made more impressive by the events of the last month.

A statement to the enemy people that there will be a Pro-

visional Peace based upon renewed self-government and revived economic life should convey to them our desire to restore
them to the family of nations. Such an assurance to them might
bring the war to a quicker end and save much human life.

THE SECOND REASON

GAINING PREPAREDNESS FOR PEACE MAKING

The second reason for this program is that we must resolve a
double difficulty. That is how to keep unity during the war and
achieve at the same time preparedness for peace in advance of
victory. There is a well-founded and instinctive fear that negotiation by our officials of the gigantic long-view questions during the war would disrupt the unity of the United Nations.
Hence the escapist policy of every modern world war, "Victory
first, discuss peace afterwards."

In consequence, aside from a few very general aims and plati-
tudes, victorious nations have usually come to the peace table
wholly without any real preparedness for the immense problems they must meet. I agree that we cannot negotiate these
long-view questions without dangers. But we could negotiate
the urgent matters which lay the foundation of *provisional
peace*. There is no ground for disunity in them. Their settlement beforehand would promote unity. And incorporated in
them is the machinery for amiable solution of the long-view
questions after victory.

THIRD REASON

AN ARMISTICE IS DESTRUCTIVE

The third reason is that no lasting peace can be made as was
attempted at Versailles in the middle of a military armistice.
An armistice simply suspends the whole world between war and
peace. The machinery and routines of both war and peace are
out of action. It is thus a period of economic and political degeneration with an agonized world crying out for haste. The
end is hasty compromise of principle and justice, not solution.

FOURTH REASON
TO COOL OFF HATE AND GREED

The fourth reason for this proposal is that the world must have time to cool off and recover a balance of judgment if a lasting peace is to be made. Cooling off is less important than the other reasons for Transitional Period. Yet it is important.

When firing ceases the world will be filled with violent emotions. There will be white-hot hate and indignation at the enemy for having brought the world to this state. The air will be filled with fear and vengeance. This is no atmosphere for long-view statesmanship, which must distinguish between guilty leadership and misled peoples. Do not forget we must live with 90 million Germans, 40 million Italians, 70 million Japs and their increment for some hundreds of years yet. We want to get them into the ways of peace if we can.

There will be another emotion present. That is greed or, more politely, self-interest. Each of the victorious nations will face a grim vista of impoverishment. The peoples of each nation will demand those things they believe will restore prosperity and security to them.

And these are not alone the emotions of statesmen. They are the emotions of the people at home. Statesmen are not their own masters. If they ever expect to be re-elected or have monuments to their memory or get their agreements ratified, they are forced to respond to the emotions of their people.

If there be a general peace conference in the midst of all these emotions, as has been the practice hitherto, then 40 nations will send 2000 diplomats to orate, to conspire, quarrel and grab. The world would be crying aloud for haste, that it be allowed to get back to living again. To keep passion, greed, expediency and compromise of principle out of the settlements under these pressures calls for more than human powers. Certainly if we are to have lasting peace, it must be based on more solid foundations than the emotions of war.

Does not all this suggest the necessity of a cooling-off?

THE FIFTH REASON

TO GET BY THE PERIOD OF REACTION

The fifth reason for this suggested approach to peace is that soon after firing ceases an inevitable reaction sets in. Our boys want to come home—and at once. They want to start life again. Their wives, mothers and fathers want them home. They are bound to bring home all their frictions, dislikes and opinions of the strange peoples with whom they have been operating. At home the people will be war-weary. All the suppressed frictions between Allies will come to the surface. The people just don't want anything more to do with "foreigners." A period of reaction toward isolationism is inevitable. And it would be further fanned by the headlines from a general peace conference, such as Versailles, daily arousing a thousand suspicions or misgivings and confirming their suspicions.

In this period of reaction nationalism will rise to such heights as to endanger all constructive plans. It will be a time of demagoguery and prejudice. The world needs time to let this pass.

THE SIXTH REASON

THE UNKNOWN SHAPE OF THINGS TO COME

The sixth reason for these principles of peace making I suggest is that while nations are actually at war, or in the months after firing ceases, we cannot see the shape of things to come. These shapes are made by forces set in motion by the war and even long before the war. No one can for years predict their ultimate effect. The only thing men can be sure of is that after the war there will be profound change. If it were a question only of putting the world back to where it had been, it would be hard enough to do. But the world will never be like that again.

A peace-making that does not take account of these pressures of change will be certain to burst asunder. Surely we need a transition period in which to measure and accommodate these forces.

THE SEVENTH REASON

REAL FOUNDATIONS UNDER A WORLD INSTITUTION

There are those who believe we have only to quickly set up some League or some Council or some World Institution or some Union or World Parliament and then unload all of our problems upon it. It is not that easy.

When issues are vast and intricate it is easy to dodge them that way and then announce that the world will go to the dogs if evil men fail to agree.

Neither anything like the League of Nations nor any kind of world institution to keep the peace could succeed amid the passions, the political and economic chaos that press on the heels of war.

There are a hundred gigantic problems that must be settled between nations before such an agency would have a chance. To force its adoption prematurely is to condemn it to inevitable failure.

The purpose of any world institution must be to preserve peace, not to make it.

They are two entirely different jobs. They must not be confused. Having lived through Versailles and having had to deal with its consequences, I can give you an idea of what I mean. The Treaty of Versailles consisted of 613 paragraphs, of which only 26 dealt with the League Covenant. It was the 587 outside the League that did most to kill the League, and certainly it was the sins of omission and commission in these 587 paragraphs which laid some of the kindling for this war.

To solve these problems, to allay the forces of destruction and to build a new spirit in the world requires time. And a decisive hand which no world-wide institution can exert.

The Temple of Peace cannot be erected until its foundations are well laid. If we make a good peace, it will largely preserve itself. If we make a bad one like Versailles, we shall simply be laying the kindling for World War III. And no machinery for preserving peace will stop it taking fire.

EIGHTH REASON
PRESERVING AMERICAN UNITY

The next reason I will give you for this program bears upon our American national unity.

The formulation of some sort of World Institution to preserve peace is essential. Yet discussion of its details leads quickly to the most emotional and the most dangerous question that can be raised among us. That is how much we surrender of national independence and sovereignty.

I would like to suggest that, if we adopt the *Transition Period*, we can develop the practice of cooperation in stopping aggression during that time and we will learn much as to method. Of equal importance, our people will have opportunity to consider and debate this whole question away from the emotions of war and the reaction toward isolationism which will inevitably follow. It is my belief that with a growth of experience and understanding the whole sovereignty question will become academic. But it takes time. Decision of this matter at the present time is about as important as the ancient worry over how many angels could stand on the point of a needle.

I have no doubt that with time and deliberation our people will no more consent to liquidate the independence of the United States than Mr. Churchill will consent to liquidate the British Empire or Mr. Stalin to liquidate the Soviet Republic. And none of that is necesary to preserve peace. And I may add that the primary safety of America will always rest in our strong right arm.

THE NINTH REASON
DOCUMENTS ARE NOT PEACE

The ninth reason for these principles of peace making is that out of five thousand years of war an illusion has been built up in the human mind that war can be ended and peace made by signing a piece of paper. Especially if it is signed with pomp and circumstance. The world has deluded itself before now that such a signed paper is the dawn of a new day. Hasty documents written at the end of wars have an infernal way of becoming the prospectus of renewed war.

We must learn that it is the conduct of nations over years which counts, not the papers they sign. A little good will goes further than documents.

TENTH REASON

THERE MUST BE RATIFICATION

If we are to have peace, any agreement or any treaty in democracies must be ratified by the people at home. The people must have time to debate, understand and decide.

And we should be careful that our words do not carry more to other nations than we will perform and confirm. Neither by executive action nor Congressional resolution nor public assurance should we give the impression that the United States can be committed to anything without full free action by the Senate of the United States.

Is it not, therefore, better to go one step at a time and deal with different problems separately?

ELEVENTH REASON

Such a plan will not delay peace. It will expedite it. It enables immediate action on urgent questions which involve restoration of order and economic production instead of months or years of delay such as took place after the last war. It enables time for the settlement of long-view questions in such a fashion as to make for lasting peace instead of the hasty compromises which rekindled world war at Versailles.

TWELFTH REASON
THE SUM OF EXPERIENCE

And I might add an overall reason which comes from the stern Voice of Experience. Do not the great peace settlements which followed the two other world wars of the last 150 years —those at Vienna in 1814 and at Versailles in 1919—confirm every one of these reasons for this program? Does anyone believe that either of these treaties would have been signed five years afterwards? That no abiding successful peace can be written in a few weeks or a few months under these pressures has been proven by the greatest tragedy of modern history— Versailles.

TO SUM UP

For these reasons I am suggesting four principles of peace. A temporary Trusteeship or collaboration of the leading nations, a Provisional Peace for each defeated country, a Transition Period of time, and an ultimate World Institution to preserve peace. Is it not the answer that we must first concentrate our immediate thought on definite principles of peace making? And second, does not any program require defined and responsible leadership? And third, must we not have quick and strong action to restore order and the productivity of mankind? And fourth, must we not have time to settle our gigantic long-view questions? Time for emotions to cool off? Time to pass over the reaction which inevitably sets in from war? Time to assess the forces and change set in motion by war? Time to allay the dynamic forces which cause war? Time to deliberate? Time to deal openly with all proposals? Time for the peoples of the world to understand the solutions proposed? Time to rebuild justice, tolerance and good will? Time to build a real World Institution to preserve peace?

It was six years from the victory of Yorktown to the Constitution of the United States—and it was time well spent.

The die of war has been cast. We have taken up the sword

to win lasting peace. For over one hundred and seventy years Americans have fought on a thousand battlefields and always that men might be more free and have peace. Their million graves demand of us that we do not fail them in the halls of peace-making.

The Transition to Lasting Peace

KANSAS CITY, MISSOURI

[October 28, 1943]

OUR first task today is victory in this war. But we must also prepare for peace.

What does America want from this war? We want no domination over other nations. We want no colonies. We want no special economic privileges. We can secure no consequential indemnities. We have just one great interest. We do not want our youth sacrificed again. We do not want our whole economic and social progress set back another quarter of a century by the aftermaths of another total war. What we want is a lasting peace.

This is the first of all our post-war problems. It is the most difficult of all. Given lasting peace, the business world can restore employment. We can lift the standards of living of the American people to heights of comfort and security beyond men's dreams. But if there are to be world wars every 25 years, civilization itself will be destroyed—our own included.

Our people in every village and our men on every front are discussing the problems of peace as never before.

When I listen to the vast ferment of peace discussion in public addresses, when I read the news in the daily press and the constant output of books, when I study resolutions and the debate on them, I am impressed with a certain lack of reality. And our language is gloriously equipped for mass production of nebular words.

The world has for 5,000 years failed to make lasting peace. And with the birth of total war the problems of peace have been infinitely multiplied. I am convinced that we must abandon old formulae of peace making and adopt a new approach to this gigantic problem.

Beginning some 18 months ago I have urged that instead of a long armistice and a general peace conference we should definitely organize a *Transition Period* of a few years under the Leadership or Trusteeship of the leading victorious nations.

I am glad to see that these ideas, under varied terms, are making headway among leaders of thought.

They offer a common ground upon which Americans of divergent views could work more effectively toward real peace.

I propose tonight to explore further with you the makings of lasting peace. And to do this exploring with our feet on the ground.

There are inevitable shapes in the world to come which must be taken into our national thinking. Some of them are already beginning to emerge, even in the darkness of war.

NATIONALISM

Among those shapes is Nationalism. And that is the most powerful of all forces in international relations. Within it lies the freedom of peoples, their independence, their sovereignty and their equal rights.

And Nationalism is a shape which profoundly affects the organization of lasting peace. It is a problem of legal interpretations, of frank realism and of deep human emotions.

In the field of realism it should be obvious to all Americans that many of the United Nations have already proclaimed nationalistic objectives for which they are fighting. Mr. Stalin has not hesitated to indicate with positive frankness territorial expansion for Russia over previously independent peoples. Mr. Churchill has stated categorically that the British Empire will not be liquidated notwithstanding critics in the United States. Mr. Chiang Kai-shek has been unhesitating in stating that

China will restore her ancient boundaries with all foreign squatters evicted. Holland says she will recover her colonies.

Sixteen nations enslaved by our enemies are trusting in the assurance of the Atlantic Charter that "sovereign rights and self-government be restored to those who have been forcibly deprived of them." And other submerged peoples are clamoring for freedom and sovereignty to govern themselves.

Aside from these practical evidences, the emotional basis of Nationalism is no less a potent force in the shape of things to come.

The furnace of war heats and hardens Nationalism. Each nation has again laid its dead upon the altar of its country. These died with their national flag before their eyes and their national hymns upon their lips. The pride of race has swelled from their suffering and sacrifice.

Nationalism rises from the deepest instincts and emotions of mankind. It springs from the yearning of men to be free of foreign domination, to govern themselves. It springs from a thousand rills of race, of history, of sacrifice and of pride in achievement. Nationalism can run to excesses. It can be either a cause of wars or a bulwark of peace and progress. It can run to greed and domination over others or it can bring the thousand blessings of freedom.

Americans can test this upon themselves. Does not the word America stir something deeper within us than mere geography? Does not the suffering and the sacrifice of our forebears who fought for our independence flash in our minds with every mention of that word? Was it not our independence which gave the most expansive release to the creative spirit of mankind in all history? Was it not the release of intellectual and spiritual freedom on this continent that gave the moral strength and the self-reliance which penetrated these plains and forests?

I am not impressed by the idea that America has grown great by the benevolence of any other government. In 300 years our people have forged new concepts of life. We have departed greatly in our thinking from the many nations from which we sprang.

It was the freeing of the minds of men from the restraints of the old world that stirred the initiative which brought into being these inventions, these discoveries of science, these great industrial tools, these farms, these homes, these magnificent cities, these schools, these churches. It was this release of spirit that developed a higher devotion to the welfare of man than the world has ever seen.

Indeed the word "America" has become an expression of the spirit. It does not mean isolationism. For, just as we have valued our own independence, we have fought for the independence of other peoples.

We are told that we have had no foreign policy. Perhaps future historians, studying this last 130 years, will say that America had the most powerful of foreign policies. That is helping other nations to gain freedom and independence and protecting those who have secured it.

Those historians would point to the Monroe Doctrine which protected and preserved the independence of the nations in the Western Hemisphere. They would point to the war with Mexico to free Texas and California securing to them self-government within our Union. Again the historians would point to the war with Spain to free Cuba and the Philippines. They would point to World War I to establish the independence of nine new nations in Europe. They would point to the present World War where our men are fighting to preserve the independence of Britain, France, Russia, China and sixteen little nations.

And has not the United States been the actuating inspiration of freedom for all nations through all these years?

If this is not a foreign policy, it certainly is a century long crusade. Generations of Americans have died for it.

Other nations, also from their traditions, their trials and their triumphs have developed a Nationalism which runs no less deeply than our own. They too feel more than geography in their words—"Britain," "Russia," "France," "Belgium," "Poland." They are equally proud of their countries. They are equally determined to die if need be to maintain their independence.

Whatever may be said of Nationalism, it is real and it is a part of the shapes to come after this war. If we scan either history or the declarations now being made, we must conclude that other nations will be little inclined to surrender their independence or any part of their sovereignty to anybody. That is an inevitable reality from which there is no escape. Lasting peace will not be built upon any surrender of the independence or sovereignty of nations but that it must be built upon the collaboration of free peoples.

Certainly I do not believe that peace can be built upon any sacrifice of the independence or sovereignty of the United States.

Therefore, I suggest that planners of peace incorporate into their thinking the idea that nations will maintain their full independence and their full sovereignty. And it is only upon such a common ground that we must and can build a lasting peace.

TOTAL WAR REVOLUTIONIZES PEACE MAKING

Another unreality in some of our national discussions is a belief that peace has arrived when firing ceases and a treaty is signed. Peace does not even begin for years afterwards.

We must bring into our national thinking the realization that total war has changed the entire basis of making peace.

The whole nature of war and its aftermaths was changed when total and global war first came to the world thirty years ago. Old methods of making peace have been as much outmoded as have the old methods of making war.

For over a century wars had involved only 2 or 3 nations at a time. They included only a small segment of the world. The consequences were not so far-reaching. The healing processes were not so difficult. But in the last total war, and in the present war, 40 nations with 90 per cent of the people in the world are involved with all their multiple conflicting interests and aspirations.

In old wars civilian life was not much disturbed. Total war not only involves total civilian energies during the war, but involves great loss of life and social and economic destruction; new channels of thought and action are driven deep within the minds and souls of men. The aftermaths of total war are upon the scale of the war itself.

If we take an overall view, we know now that the gigantic upheaval of the last total war generated destructive forces which lasted for years in economic dislocations, revolutions, conflict of national interests, threats of war and finally degenerated into renewed world war.

MAKING PEACE AFTER THE LAST TOTAL WAR

After the last war the world rushed to a great peace conference with thousands of delegates from 40 nations, thinking that the signing of a piece of paper could quiet the forces which had been set in motion.

There was idealism at that conference. But idealism died in the inevitable conflicts of purpose among desperate peoples under the war heat of nationalism. The paper they signed stimulated instead of quieting many of the underlying causes of conflict in the world.

But whatever the sins of omission or commission, whatever the mistakes, we now know that mortals at "cease firing" cannot appraise the depths of the wounds of the world from total war, or the violences that have been turned loose, nor the direction these violences will take. They cannot know the changes from ideas and inventions to come out of the war. Mortals cannot devise a paper contract in advance which will stand the shocks and the aftermaths of total war.

Following the last war, unexpected forces arose from the inadequacies of the peace document itself; nations drifted into crisis after crisis and conflict after conflict. The hastily made treaty itself at times handicapped the nations of good-will in dealing with these problems. The age-old sores and the wounds of war were not healed.

MAKING PEACE AFTER THIS TOTAL WAR

Time does not permit me to explore the political, social or economic shapes which are rising out of this war. Nor to examine the dim shapes of revolution that have already begun to emerge; nor the problems of extreme nationalism, of suppressing militarism or the ambitions of imperialism; nor the multitude of problems of disarmament, famine, trade, exchange, boundaries, conflicts of interest, hates and revenge that inevitably will descend upon the world.

I therefore suggest for American thinking that we must accept the fact that a period of disturbing years must inevitably elapse after the next victory over our enemies.

Whether this transition period results in degeneration and a third world war or whether it becomes a *period of transition* from war to lasting peace depends upon what we do during that period.

And peace-making is not merely a negative process of stopping military aggressions. It must be a dynamic elimination of the causes of war, the creation of good-will and cooperation between nations to advance prosperity and the rule of law.

Yet American thinking and American discussion today assumes that another general peace conference—"the peace table" like Versailles in 1919—will be assembled immediately after this war to settle all these gigantic problems. Different pressure groups in the United States are already demanding seats upon the delegation. And there would be 1,000 delegates from pressure groups of other nations.

Do we believe the conflict of interests and the problems are less than before?

Do we believe that men are greater today than in the past or that they can see further into the dark than they have done before?

No matter with what pomp and circumstance such a treaty be constructed, the unknown and the forces of change would put it again in the waste basket.

I therefore suggest that, in view of what we now know of the consequences of global war, no agreement or treaty can be evolved when firing ceases which will hold against its aftermaths.

THE NEW APPROACH

Do not all these shapes of things to come, all this experience of the last total war and all this need for a healing process and dynamic action demand a new approach, a new departure from these paths so strewn with failure in the past?

For these reasons we, 18 months ago, proposed the definitely organized Transition Period from war to peace under definite leadership.

In order to make the plan workable, the Trustees or Leaders, Executive Committee—whatever they are called—should at once, when firing ceases, impose without argument certain urgent necessities of disarming the enemy and certain measures for re-starting the political and economic life in the world.

Then the mind and the determination of the world must be set toward one goal—the making of a lasting peace. And the Trustees in cooperation with the United Nations should guide the world through the deserts and swamps of the Transition Period until we can arrive at the promised land of some world-wide institution to preserve peace.

This plan of a Transition Period has been referred to as a "cooling-off period." That is a misnomer. Its purpose is far greater than this incidental yet great benefit.

MILITARY ALLIANCES

Nor can the transition from war to peace be organized through military alliances. That is another age-old idea from the grooves of past thinking. That is recreating a world psychology of repression and domination, not turning the mind of the world to peaceful method and cooperation.

And by military alliance I do not mean short-term alliances but long-term commitments. Such military alliances always imply that nations agree to go to war at some future time against unknown nations for some purpose, good or bad. Mr. Gibson and I are discussing this subject at length in tomorrow's Collier's Weekly, but I may say here that inevitably such alliances create fear in other nations. Sooner or later they breed counter alliances. Armies and navies at once begin to pyramid in size.

There is a further fatal defect of all military alliances as an instrument to preserve peace. They at once begin to fall apart under the chafing of peoples against the danger of being involved in war. Inevitably world currents change, interests shift, a new generation arises, and some ally concludes not to go to war despite any agreement. Military alliances never endure for long.

Never has a military alliance produced peace, but many of them have produced war. Certainly they are no bases of enduring peace.

One of the suggestions which has been advanced is some sort of legal ties between the United States and Britain. The proposals include common citizenship, common currency, free trade, and military alliance.

Would not such an act at once raise the fears of all other nations that this is a step to world mastery by the English-speaking people and thus promptly generate organized opposition among the other 90% of the human race?

Whatever the merits may be, it is a divergence from our main purpose which must be unity with all United Nations to victory and to build peace.

Moreover, will not such a marriage involve us in all the problems of the British Empire, and conversely, will not the British Empire be plagued with all of the problems of the United States?

Would not the inevitable discussion about these relatives by marriage lead to many frictions and ultimately to bitter divorce?

I am one who believes that collaboration and cooperation between Britain and the United States is the first necessity for peace. But collaboration does not require amalgamation. The practice of cooperation increases friendship.

For common ground in national thinking we should discard all proposals of military alliances as an instrument of peace.

WORLD INSTITUTION TO PRESERVE PEACE

Nor can this Transition Period from war to peace be organized by quickly setting up some world-wide institution, council or world authority to preserve peace. We must make peace before we preserve it. Such a world-wide institution or authority should be the last phase of peace making, not the first.

I believe we must have such an institution. I believe it can be built without destroying the independence or sacrificing the sovereignty of nations. But we should not only have the experience of collaboration in the Transition Period but also the time to lay some foundations before we can effectively design any such world institution.

And if it is to succeed, it must be launched under conditions which favor its survival. We shall be throwing it to the wolves if we set it up to grapple with the violent forces in motion at the end of this war. That would repeat again one of the greatest of handicaps under which the League of Nations labored. It was thrown into the violent aftermaths of post-war and required to deal with the storm. That experience should amply prove that institutions for the long view are wholly ill fitted for the problems, attitudes and emotions of the Transition Period.

It has been said that unless we first and quickly form some sort of world-wide institution the people will have lost their enthusiasms and relapse again into isolationism. This is a notion that we can set up a lasting peace while we are groggy which will bind us when we have sobered up.

On the contrary, it is essential, if such a "world institution" is to have permanence, that it be rooted in acceptance of the United Nations' peoples themselves. If this is a peoples' war, it must be a peoples' peace. And there can be no peoples' peace unless the people have experience and time for understanding and acceptance.

ORGANIZING THE TRANSITION PERIOD

I therefore suggest for American thinking that we discard these ideas of a long armistice, of an initial and general peace conference, ideas of military alliances or ideas of premature formation of a world-wide institution to preserve peace.

The alternative is an organized Transition Period. The campaign for peace during the Transition Period must have as much leadership as a campaign for war. A few principal nations have given leadership in war. Why should they not at once be openly appointed by the United Nations and charged with the responsibility before the world to direct the Transition Period from war to peace?

Out of this war will come a few transcendent centers of power,—America, Britain, Russia and China. By their open responsibility to build peace would this not turn the whole mind of the world towards the goal of a real peace?

Whether we rush in and sign a document after firing ceases or not, the principal victorious powers in the world will continue to dominate the world. They have done it mostly in secrecy after every other world war.

Would not the world be better if its power politics were out in the open where the people of the world could test the every action of these centers of power on whether it contributed to build lasting peace?

Would it not give a sense of unity, solidarity and purpose to the united governments if it were done now?

And as nations will maintain their independence, the Trustees and the United Nations must operate by collaboration as free nations. Today they are successfully carrying forward one of the most difficult of all human tasks—a joint war. A few powerful nations are giving leadership in this gigantic undertaking. They advise and consult with the smaller nations. We are doing this huge job by collaboration in the problems which

arise from day to day. We are doing it without written agreements or treaties. Our bond is our common interest. Our declared purpose is to rid the world of the menaces to civilization,
to free men and to free nations.

*If we can collaborate to make war, can we not collaborate
during a Transition Period while we lay the foundations for
peace? Does this period need more of a contract than a declared joint purpose? Is not that common purpose to make a
lasting peace this time?*

Nations can be more tightly bound by common purpose than
by chains, and in the unknown shapes to come is not the Transition Period necessary for experience and development of foundations?

You can be sure that nations will strive to preserve their independence. If we cannot collaborate among independent free
nations during a few years of the Transition Period to build a
lasting peace, then no signed papers, no agreements, no world
institution is worth anything. What counts in the long run is
not paper documents but the attitudes of nations.

And inherent in all these attitudes will be the need for American patience and more patience lest we lose heart and faith.

CONCLUSION

In conclusion we must now prepare for peace. We must do
better than last time. And our chances for a lasting peace are
better. For out of the furnace of this war there is a yearning
for peace far more potent than ever before. Mothers, fathers
and wives in every nation, as never before, are praying that
such a calamity may not come again to the world.

Despite all that has happened in 1900 years, the Sermon on
the Mount has thundered down the ages. And it now thunders
anew.

The Futility of Military Alliances

Jointly with Hugh Gibson

Collier's Magazine

[November 6, 1943]

V ARIOUS proposals have recently been made that there should be an immediate British-American military alliance or a military alliance including other powers such as Russia and China. Military alliances have produced many wars but never a lasting peace.

The objective of those who have brought forward these suggestions is, no doubt, to assure collaboration among nations in keeping the peace and stopping aggression. Necessarily, any keeping of the peace implies collaboration between the United States and Britain, and with all the others. In that objective, we heartily agree. It is absolutely essential. The question is whether a military alliance is the right way to achieve our common purpose.

The United States has never accepted an agreement of military alliance in its history. We have had associates in war, but no signed commitments to action in unknown circumstances years ahead. With all our background, the suggestion at once raises a thousand prejudices. Attempting to preserve peace by a military alliance with Britain alone raises special anti-British prejudice, and already the debate of this question is creating acrimonious disruption of national unity. But it is not prejudices we must consider. It is whether such a course would produce lasting peace.

Fortunately, for our guidance in this matter, the world has centuries of experience with military alliances. The last 150 years have seen hundreds of them. We shall examine only a few.

They are usually clothed in the garments of peace—"Treaty for the Preservation of Peace," "Amity and Friendship," "Mutual Guarantees," "Mutual Assistance," "Non-aggression." And almost universally they open with some dedication to peace. Many of them have genuinely had that purpose.

We may begin with the Holy Alliance and its off-shoot, the Quadruple Alliance, which sprang from the Congress of Vienna in 1815, ending the world wars of the Napoleonic period. This was not only a treaty to preserve the doctrine of legitimacy, but it also had a genuine purpose of stopping aggression, and in envisaging Napoleon, they could have included Hitler, Tojo and Mussolini. It sounded a note of highest idealism: "Having acquired the intimate conviction that it is necessary to base the course to be followed by the powers in their mutual relations upon the sublime truths taught by the eternal Religion of the Saviour . . .

"All the powers who desire to avow solemnly the sacred principles . . . will be received into this Holy Alliance with equal earnestness and affection."

And in the military treaty between Prussia, Russia, Austria and Britain we find such phrases as: "Being desirous of . . . putting to an end the miseries of Europe and securing its repose . . . of maintaining against every attempt the order of things which have been the happy consequence of their effort."

Here was a sort of Atlantic Charter accompanied by a military treaty to prevent aggression. The parties to the Alliance split on their separate interests within a relatively few years.

Another gigantic military alliance for defense against aggression was the Triple Alliance of Germany, Austria and Italy beginning about 1882 with the solemn assurance of peaceful intent. Counteraction came with the alliance of France and Russia as a protection against aggression, and later Britain joined in it with France under the term of an *Entente Cordiale*.

The inevitable clash of these military alliances came with the first World War. Italy refused to go to war on the side of the Triple Alliance on the ground that she had signed only a defensive alliance.

A MULTIPLICITY OF ALLIANCES

Between World War I and World War II, there were over fifty signed and sealed treaties or pacts having military provisions, all aimed, in reality or ostensibly, at preserving peace and preventing aggression. Over thirty of these military alliances were made prior to the rise of Hitler.

Soon after Versailles, there was created under French tutelage a network of non-aggression and mutual-guarantee military alliances over Europe, despite the fact that Germany, Austria and Hungary were practically disarmed. This ultimately developed into the Little Entente, including Czechoslovakia, Yugoslavia, Rumania and Poland. Ultimately, a counteralliance to the Little Entente was formed, embracing Italy, Austria and Hungary.

In 1922, there was a Baltic military alliance between Poland, Estonia, Latvia and Finland. In 1926, an alliance was made between Iran, Turkey and Afghanistan. In 1930, began the Balkan Entente of Turkey, Greece, Rumania and Yugoslavia, which defined itself in a military treaty later on.

Notable among these military treaties to stop aggression in the pre-Hitler period was that signed at Locarno in October, 1925. The Locarno system of pacts was looked upon as a sure-fire guarantee against war in Europe. These agreements were concluded by Foreign Ministers Austen Chamberlain, Briand and Stresemann, all men of enthusiastic good will. They were treaties embodying mutual guarantees against aggression and agreements of mutual military assistance. There were arbitration treaties among them.

In March, 1936, Hitler charged that the Locarno Agreements had been violated by the Franco-Soviet Military Alliance and sent his troops into the Rhineland. There is no doubt that the Locarno Agreements were violated by Hitler and that, by any reasonable interpretation of the treaty, joint military action was called for. But the spirit of the agreements had fled.

In ten short years, it ignominiously collapsed because in that period there had been such fundamental changes in the interests of the signatories that, with the exception of France and Belgium, not one would raise a finger to defend what had been the agreed common purpose.

One of Russia's most interesting anti-aggression treaties is that signed on July 3, 1933, which included Poland, Rumania, Latvia, Persia, Estonia and Turkey. The treaty recited that "being desirous of strengthening peace" and "in view of the fact that the Briand-Kellogg Pact to which they were signatories forbids aggression," these countries defined the aggressions which they pledged themselves not to commit as "declaration of war," "invasion," "attack by land, sea and air," "blockade," or "support to armed bands." They further agreed that no political, economic, military or other pretext should be an excuse for such aggression. This agreement seems to have weakened in 1939 and 1940 when Russia invaded Poland, Latvia, Estonia and Rumania and annexed the whole or parts of each of them.

With the coming of Hitler in 1933, new shifts in the balance of power spread over Europe, and in 1934 we had four important military agreements. They comprised a non-aggression pact between Poland and Germany, which the French took very badly; a pact mutually guaranteeing their frontiers between Turkey, Greece, Rumania and Yugoslavia; a renewal of mutual guarantee of frontiers by Russia, Rumania, Poland, Estonia and Lithuania; the "Rome Protocols" between Italy, Austria and Hungary.

In 1935, we saw several more military agreements. The most important were a military alliance between France and Russia and a military alliance between Russia and Czechoslovakia.

The beginning of the Axis was made by Germany and Italy in 1936 and later extended to include Japan. In 1937, Italy and Yugoslavia made a solemn non-aggression pact. Turkey, Iraq, Iran and Afghanistan made a non-aggression alliance. China signed one with Russia. Germany guaranteed the inviolability of Belgium. In 1938, Germany and France mutually guaranteed their frontiers.

In 1939, Britain, France and Poland entered into agreements for "mutual assistance"; and there were Franco-British military guarantees to Rumania and Greece. France and Turkey agreed on mutual military aid in case of aggression. In this year, Germany signed the fateful agreement with Russia which ultimately involved understandings on the division of Poland, Rumania and the Baltic States; thus we arrive at the beginning of World War II.

These are but a few specimens of military alliances over a century and a half. Anyone who wishes to follow the history of such alliances will find that they reek with militarism, balance of power, power politics and imperialism—the whole concepts of which must be abandoned if the world is to have lasting peace.

The first reason why a military alliance has always failed to produce peace lies in the very nature of military alliances. A military alliance must have specific objectives and must have provisions as to what, when and where joint military action shall be invoked. Its purpose must be to accomplish a political objective. Therefore, any military alliance is also a political alliance.

UNPREPARED FOR EVENTUALITIES

Such written agreements, whatever their specifications may be, must commit their members to future action, the precise circumstances of which cannot be foreseen. Their concept necessarily leans to the *status quo* and, in the meantime, the unexpected happens.

World currents, the interests of nations and centers of political strength are constantly shifting. Nations with all their changing economic, ideologic and nationalistic pressures cannot be kept in an iron mold. It is folly to assume that nations will not follow their interests, despite treaties. The application of the alliance gets thrown out of gear and gives rise to distrust and resentment among the partners.

Any analysis of the mass of human experience shows that military alliances have no long endurance and therefore are wholly an ineffective machinery for maintaining lasting peace.

The second reason for failure revolves around the potent phenomenon of fear. Study of past alliances indicates that, no matter how high their purpose has been, they provoke counteraction by other nations. This grouping of opposition nations may be years in forming, but it has been proved inevitable. Nations, although disarmed or of inferior armed strength, are not helpless.

It is easy to say that the United Nations will disarm the rest of the world, but no statesman will believe that nations are rendered morally, spiritually, economically or even politically incapable by being disarmed. They can conspire and bring disintegrating pressures to bear. Their policies can nibble away with diplomatic and propaganda action until some partners fall away or join in new combinations or counteralliances.

The third reason that military alliances fail to keep peace is that, out of the fear on both sides, armament grows. Increasing armament, prompted by fear, is the road to war. This multitude of European alliances resulted in steady increase of arms before the first World War and again even after Germany was disarmed and before Hitler appeared.

The fourth reason that alliances fail is that a military alliance is, as we have said, necessarily also a political alliance. Each partner is affected by every political action of the other lest it stir up friction or aggression. Every action of every ally, wise or unwise, at once becomes a family affair. We marry not only a wife but also all her in-laws. The French political policies after Versailles, which kept their partners, the British, in turmoil, fill pages of history.

This family reason is stronger in democracies than in dictator countries. The policies of our partners become at once subjects of discussion in our domestic arena. In democracies, there are always groups or individuals, vocal and potent in opposition to almost anything. Our democracy, more than any other, is subject to these oppositions because of our large groups of different racial origins who carry their racial prejudices over from generation to generation. That the Irish or German groups in America love Britain, or that our Poles love Russia is an illusion.

Questions of relative sacrifice in providing navies, armies and men at once arise for discussion. The nature of our political machinery inevitably brings all these forces into election appeals and prejudices. In other words, any military alliance will stir up constant controversy, disintegration and opposition at home.

These are the major reasons why every military alliance in history has failed. They are the reasons why they have served to make war rather than peace. They apply to any-sized military alliance, whether it be the Big Four in this war or the Big Four in 1815 and 1919, and they all fail sooner or later.

A very particular danger lies in a single alliance between the United States and Britain. The English-speaking peoples comprise only ten per cent of the world. At once the other ninety per cent will fear, and many of them will cry out, that the intention is to dominate the world. It will again be interpreted as building up a "master race," no matter how benevolent our purposes really are. Anyone familiar with the ferments running through the 1,500,000,000 Asiatics—from India to China, to Burma, to Afghanistan—will realize the steady building up, over a hundred years, of resolution to be rid of white domination.

THE WAR POWERS OF CONGRESS

The world would build counteraction and counteralliance eventually. It envisages more wars, not peace. After all, a military alliance raises particular difficulties for the United States. The Constitution reserves the power to declare war to the Congress. The Congress is not likely to delegate unlimited authority to make war.

These problems involve another factor of great importance.

No document or treaty is worth more than the good-will behind it. The whole of history goes to prove that mere signing of treaties alters nothing unless the causes of war have been allayed. If nations cannot collaborate from day to day to meet great world crises in these times of instantaneous communication, they cannot be constrained to do it with signed specifications on paper. They can, if they will, agree upon declarations of purpose, but detailed treaties in the face of a world changing by a great war are a trap, not a protection.

Certainly, with all the ghastly array of scraps of paper behind us, it would seem we might try some other approach than the Treaty of Versailles with its 613 precisely worded paragraphs attempting to anticipate and fix the world to come, together with the conduct of the people in it.

The writers of this article have said repeatedly that, if we are to have lasting peace, we must have a new approach, and a more effective approach, to this whole problem. The world has long since discovered methods of successful war. It has never yet discovered the method of lasting peace.

It was, in part, the hope of avoiding these difficult issues and the dangers inherent in America's joining any military alliance that led the writers to propose a wholly new approach to peace-making which could accommodate itself to change and daily growing experience.

These proposals were outlined in Collier's last June, and we briefly recapitulate them here in order that they may be borne in mind in comparing the advantages and disadvantages of the military-alliance method.

We suggest that the key to making a lasting peace is a Transition Period from war to peace, of a few years, in which the world can have time for deliberate solution of the gigantic problems that are involved. But in order to have a Transition Period, two steps must be taken in advance. The first is an agreement between all the United Nations before victory over Germany, setting up the simple terms upon which a Provisional Regime can be quickly imposed upon belligerent Europe—and, later, on Asia—the moment firing ceases.

There must be leadership. Therefore, the second step proposed is a simple joint declaration by all the united powers constituting a few leading nations as the Trustees or Managers of Peace.

FOUNDATION FOR WORLD PEACE

The last step, after the foundations of real peace have been laid during the Transition Period, is to create some sort of world institution to relieve the Trustees of their burden based upon the representation of all nations.

Thus we propose four sequent steps: First, creation of Trustees of Peace. Second, a Provisional Regime to get the world moving forward. Third, a Transition Period to settle the long-view problems. Fourth, a World Institution to preserve peace.

We have developed, in Collier's and elsewhere, the multitude of reasons for this course. We proposed setting up Trustees or Managers because it seemed to us vital that there should not only be a steering committee but a definite responsibility on the leading nations to guide the world toward peace, working in the open for all the peoples to see.

This is an important departure from previous practice after great wars where the strongest powers had dominated the situation in their own interests and without responsibility to the whole world. By the method we propose, their actions would be placed upon a legal basis. They would act by delegated authority, not by arrogated authority. It should eliminate the misgivings aroused by military alliances and their consequence in counteralliances. It should free the smaller nations from the necessity to arm against their neighbors.

The reasons for the second step—Provisional Regime—embrace the necessity for quick action in disarming the enemy and for restoring political order and economic productivity in the world. Part of the provisional arrangements should be immediate establishment of Regional Committees for Europe, Asia and the Western Hemisphere, who can go to work at once to formulate solutions of long-view questions.

The third step of a Transition Period is proposed because of the imperative need of time, not only for the incidental benefit of cooling of emotions but, of much more importance, to have time for these committees and the peoples of the world to assess the forces and change set in motion by war—time to allay the dynamic forces which cause war, time to deliberate upon the huge problems, such as disposition of enemy peoples, dislocated peoples who want to be free and backward peoples.

TIME AND EXPERIENCED NEEDED

There are problems of minorities. There are problems of starting nations on the road toward the development of the dignity of men and women. In addition, there are the huge economic problems of the world. We need time to deal openly with all proposals; time for the peoples of the world to understand the solutions proposed; time to rebuild justice, tolerance and good will; time and experience on which to build a real World Institution to preserve peace.

This is not a program of delay. On the contrary, it is a program of expedition. At Versailles, the things that should have been done quickly and imposed on the enemy to start the world again to political life and economic productivity were delayed nine months while the economic world degenerated. The long-view problems that should have been given years of development were settled in nine months and settled wrong, and the world was plunged into war again.

The United Nations are now collaborating in the conduct of a successful war—the most gigantic war of history. They are doing it by day-to-day co-operation without a signed agreement, military or otherwise. We are doing our part in the leadership of a few nations who have the major responsibilities and are co-operating with the less powerful of the United Nations through consultation. Our proposal is, therefore, that we continue this same relationship during a provisional regime and a Transition Period from war to peace.

Surely the same collaboration, after the enemy is disarmed, can enable the leading powers to put down any aggressor who might arise during the Transition Period. The experience gained in settlement of the long-view problems of lasting peace can alone clear the way to a sound world institution which will erect the processes of good will, of peaceful settlement of disputes and will repress aggression.

What the world needs is an approach that gets away from the whole reactionary spirit of military alliances, with their connotations of military domination. Imperialism, power politics, balance of power, threats and fears—these are games which our democracy cannot play. Our suggested alternative is one of continuous authorized collaboration in the interest of world peace as a whole, not a program of military alliance and special interests of a few victorious powers. It is a method of which the connotations are the spirit of peace, the building of good will and co-operation. Moral concepts are far more important than police concepts if there is to be peace.

There is no doubt about the willingness of the American people to collaborate in this spirit. But America needs to make sure that Britain, Russia, China and the other governments of the world will collaborate with us in the framework of American ideals. That can be found out and the spirit can be developed by the test and experience of a Transition Period. Collaboration is not a one-way street.

On Finnish Question

Press Statement, New York City
[March 25, 1944]

THE solution of the Finnish question is of profound
importance to the future of freedom. For 300 years
Finland has been the symbol of the struggle for liberty.
Americans, the friends of Finland, profoundly regretted her
entrance into the war on the side of Germany. As ill-advised
as her action was, the purpose of the Finnish people was not to
spread Nazism but to preserve the liberty and democracy of
the Finnish people. Less than three years before, in the view
of the President and most Americans, she had been subject to
an unprovoked attack. We subscribed millions to help her. In
the end she was compelled to surrender a fourth of her land
while four hundred thousand of her people were expelled overnight from their home of three centuries. Her situation in this
war has indeed been difficult. She had the option of joining
Germany or of being raped by the Germans like Belgium. And
in making her decision she was no doubt impelled by the hope
of recovering her homelands again. But despite all that has
happened, we cannot class her with the other allies of Germany.
We cannot forget that her whole aspiration is democracy and
freedom.

Finland wants to cease fighting. She cannot do the impossible of interning the German Army in her borders. Indeed she
may need all her forces to protect her from seizures such as
have come to Hungary. From her experience, she fears to give

invitation to her enemy of centuries to aid her. The Germans in Finland cannot alone seriously attack Russia.

The United States, Russia and Britain have agreed to collaborate in building self-government and freedom in the world. It would seem that we could use our good offices to secure some way out of the impasse for Finland. The way this problem is handled will be a profound indication of the future of collaboration. Is this not the time and place for the application of those ideals, so lately and so well expressed by Mr. Hull? Does not our government have an obligation to the future which must be exerted now?

In the long view there can be no lasting peace in the world unless such peoples as the Finns are to have their independence and lands restored. Nor are the American people likely to accept any peace which does not extend the independence of nations, much less diminish them.

Good Neighbor Policy

Press Statement, New York City
[December 8, 1943]

IN 1928, as President-elect of the United States, I made a
journey through the South American states. On that journey I made a number of public addresses in which I used
the expression "the good neighbor policy." Following that
journey I revised the previous attitude of the United States,
declaring that the United States should never again intervene
in a military fashion in Latin American states, that we should
under no circumstances use force in support of claims of our
citizens over their contracts or any other question. I emphasized this attitude throughout my administration by the with-
drawal of the Marines from Nicaragua and the occupation
troops from Haiti. I had the old Theodore Roosevelt interpretation of the Monroe Doctrine revised from the concept of right
to interference into a declaration of Western Hemisphere solidarity, of freedom from old world encroachment. I am happy
to say that was the last of these interventions and the last of
American interferences in domestic policy of Latin American
states.

These policies were, therefore, firmly established by a Republican administration and there has been no departure in
them since by any Republican leader, and they have been constantly supported in Republican Party platforms. The whole
Republican attitude is one of equality of states and of cooperation in Western Hemisphere progress and ideals. I am absolutely confident that if a Republican administration should come
into power in Washington, these policies will be carried on as
they were established from 1928 to 1932.

Some Additions to the Dumbarton Oaks Proposals

Four Articles Appearing in Press
[March 25-28, 1945]

ARTICLE I

March 25, 1945

THE most fateful conference in all American history is that which meets at San Francisco to formulate the proposals at Dumbarton Oaks into a world charter of organization for maintenance of peace. During those fleeting moments the future of mankind may be moulded for the next hundred years. A third world war would return the world to the barbarism of the stone age. These discoveries of new methods of killing; this shift from wars between men to war against women and children and the gigantic destruction of men's toil of centuries makes certain the extinction of civilization.

If the charter at San Francisco emerges with a reasonable hope of success, the United States must take its full part in carrying it out. When we in America took up the sword to secure peace, we were committed to join in holding the sword if we would preserve peace as against the inevitable hates and violences of a generation to come.

The modern world has seen these gigantic explosions into world war and revolution before. Each time from the bitterness of its travail, it has groped for organization to preserve a lasting peace.

The Dumbarton Oaks proposals are in most ways patterned upon the world's last great experiment—the League of Nations. The League was a partial success and its failures present vivid experience which it would be folly to ignore. In the light of these experiences there are some important additions which should be infused into the Dumbarton Oaks proposals and thereby greatly strengthen this chart of peace.

I state them at once and I shall in later articles amplify the reasons for them. They include:

First: Positive standards of the political rights of men and nations and the establishment of a World Committee to promote these political rights. This Committee to rank with the Economic and Social Committees already proposed in the Dumbarton Oaks plan.

Second: Provision for revision of onerous treaties between nations at, say, ten year intervals, in order to assure that the peace settlements are dynamic and not static.

Third: Regional organization of the organization to preserve peace into three areas, Asia, Europe and the Western Hemisphere; the regional organizations to be subject of course to the Security Council.

Fourth: Absolute disarmament of the enemy powers.

Fifth: Immediate relative disarmament of the United Nations and the establishment of maximum limit of armies, navies and air power among them.

Sixth: While it is probably not a part of the charter itself, when it is adopted by the Congress the authority to use force should not be given the American delegate on the Security Council, but that power should be delegated to the President of the United States with the provision that he be bound by the majority of the joint Foreign Relations Committees of the Senate and the House as to whether a vote to employ American force shall be submitted to the Congress as a whole.

Seventh: Take enough time in formulating the Charter of Peace to do it right.

These proposals are not counsels of perfection. They are lessons of grim experience.

There are three general methods by which peace can be preserved:

First, through measures of force to stop aggression.

Second, through pacific methods, the immediate effect of which is to settle controversies between nations by negotiation, arbitration and judicial decisions.

Third, beyond all this, are the moral, spiritual, political and social forces which either foment conflicts or allay them. If we are to have lasting peace, we cannot rely wholly upon stopping quarrels. We must set in motion these forces which build for peace.

The weakening of the power to stop military aggression in the Dumbarton proposals by the voting formula now agreed renders it even more imperative that the great underlying forces building for peace should be more greatly developed at San Francisco than they appeared at Dumbarton Oaks. The League of Nations proclaimed its base as the maintenance of honor and justice between nations. Even that wholly nebular enunciation of a standard of conduct between nations does not appear in Dumbarton Oaks.

The great principles of political rights of nations and men, the standards of conduct among nations and the curative functions which eliminate the causes of war are wholly absent from Dumbarton Oaks. These forces must underlie not only the whole basis of international law but of moral and spiritual progress of nations toward peace. We are in danger of setting up a purely mechanistic body without spiritual inspiration or soul.

ARTICLE II

March 26, 1945

THE POLITICAL RIGHTS OF NATIONS AND MEN SHOULD BE PROCLAIMED IN THE CHARTER

In the last article I stated that positive standards of political rights of nations and men should be incorporated at San Francisco if we are to mobilize the moral and spiritual forces of the world in the charter of peace.

Some of these principles and ideals are stated in the Declaration of Independence. Mr. Wilson stated part of them in his 14 Points. Part of them appear in the Atlantic Charter. Some of them are referred to in the Moscow Declaration and the Yalta Declaration. Many of them are thus accepted by the United Nations, but they are not expressed in any binding treaty. It would not seem unreasonable that they should be codified and specifically stated in the new Charter of Peace. If so, we may at least have a hope that the day may come when they will prevail.

From these declarations we can condense some of these principles and standards of conduct between nations:

1. No aggrandizement or annexations, territorial or other.

2. No territorial changes that do not accord with the freely expressed wishes of the people concerned.

3. The restoration of sovereign rights and self-government to those who have been deprived of them.

4. The right of all peoples to choose their form of government by free and unfettered elections and secret ballot.

5. Equality in trade.

6. Freedom of the seas in peace time.

7. Disarmament of aggressor nations.

8. Reduction in arms of all nations.

Of equal importance to these standards of conduct between nations, the history of the last 30 years cries out for the establishment of definite rights and protections to individual human beings. These principles have been eloquently proclaimed time and again as elements of peace by the leaders in this war. They include:

9. Protection from execution or imprisonment without fair trial.

10. Prohibitions against compulsory labor or slavery in any disguise.

11. Protections to minorities and backward peoples.

12. The freedom of the press and of religion.

And why not again try those great banners at the masthead of the charter.

13. Renunciation of war as an instrument of national policy.

14. The relations between nations must be founded upon honor and justice.

My proposal is therefore, first, that such fundamental principles and ideals shall be set out in the Charter itself. The Security Council would then have standards of conduct upon which to make decisions. And of equal importance, if they be proclaimed to the world, at least public opinion can define, judge and support. Without them the San Francisco Charter will not be a chart of peace. It will be simply another transitory pact or a declaration.

My second proposal arises from the fact that the Dumbarton Oaks plan includes the creation of one World Committee to promote Economic welfare and another to promote Social welfare. Therefore, I propose the creation of a third World Committee to Promote Political Rights. It is a more important function than the other two world-wide committees, great as they are.

If we are to delegate any part of our national sovereignty, we have a right to know exactly what the standards of conduct of other nations are to be. If the five great nations are to be above the law through this voting formula, it becomes all the more important that we definitely express the standards of conduct to which they are committed in relation to the smaller nations and ourselves.

ARTICLE III

March 27, 1945

REVISION OF TREATIES

The second proposal I have made for the San Francisco Conference is that there be provision for revision of onerous or inapplicable treaties or of the wrongs of imposed settlements. There is no such suggestion in the Dumbarton Oaks plan.

The future of nations cannot be frozen. The forces which will arise out of this war cannot be foreseen.

If we are going to accomplish anything in our time, we must approach our problem in the knowledge that there is nothing rigid or immutable in human affairs. History is a story of growth, decay and change. If no provision, no allowance is made for change by peaceful means, it will come anyway—and with violence.

There was an indefinite provision for change of onerous or inapplicable treaties in the Covenant of the League of Nations, but it was never allowed to function. This failure to recognize inevitability of change became one of the definite causes leading to World War II.

There is one over-all effect of both the Covenant of the League and Dumbarton Oaks proposals which the American people should understand.

Once we settle down to peace again there will be treaties defining boundaries and other relations or imposed relations of nations. The yardstick of who is an aggressor then becomes one of determining who violates the then existing situation or law. Thus the world organization automatically becomes the guarantor of the existing situation—that is the *status quo*.

Experience demonstrates that there are unpredictable areas of most dangerous controversies which rise from the pressure for change in the relations between nations. Among them are provisions imposed during the heat of war emotions, shift in economic pressures and population, the growth of ideas and inventions. There are shifting rights of minorities and the development of backward nations which become conscious and capable of self government.

Oppressed peoples will agitate and even rebel against oppression. They are hardly likely to go on considering themselves bound by a bargain entered into unwillingly by their fathers. As a rule they would be willing to readjust matters without going to war.

Boundary and peace treaties are not inspired documents. Certainly the whole experience after the last war shows that peace can be preserved, not by preventing change and putting the future in a strait-jacket, but by seeking to control change and direct it. Any attempt to maintain the *status quo* indefinitely is a direct cause of war—for peaceful means being denied, the change can come only through force. War becomes the only available solvent.

Each and every plan for preserving peace, whether it be the Pax Romana, the balance of power, the legitimist theory at the Congress of Vienna, or collective security of the League, however divergent they may appear outwardly, have this one thing in common. They set up a new order, and knowing it to be good, they provide that the new boundaries and other conditions shall be kept and anyone who violates it is evil. Never yet, however, have settlements been made after firing ceases that held against growing and changing forces after the war.

After the last war whenever there was an appeal for revision, the world was flooded with speeches on the "sanctity of treaties," and it was represented that any attempt to reconsider a single article of the Versailles Treaty was nothing less than a sinister attempt to undermine the whole fabric of peace which must be resisted as such by all law-loving people. Many people were led to believe that all change was to be resisted on high moral grounds. We can agree as to the sanctity of the pledged word—but most of this talk meant something quite different. What was really meant was not the "sanctity of treaties" but the "sanctity of the *status quo*."

And this question becomes far more important to Americans today than ever before. The peace settlements, the form of governments and the boundaries of many nations have not yet been determined. Unless there be provision for revision of treaties, we will at San Francisco become the blind guarantors of the peace settlements of which we, as yet, know nothing.

To meet this problem Mr. Gibson and I made a suggestion three years ago and I again propose that there be a definite provision in the United Nations Charter that the application of any nation for revision of treaty provisions, not sooner than ten years after its conclusion, should be considered and, if advisable, negotiated by the Committee on Political Rights, which I have suggested.

There will be continuing gigantic wrongs in the world. Americans for all time will sorrow for the fate of Finland, of Estonia, of Latvia, of Lithuania, the partition of Poland, and other states that will be partly or wholly submerged by this war. We cannot even think of another war to secure their freedoms, but we do not need to sacrifice our ideals by acquiescing in their plight. We could at least leave a hope open for their long future.

REGIONAL ORGANIZATION

My third proposal for the San Francisco Conference is that there should be a much more definite regional organization of the whole machinery of the Charter at San Francisco than that suggested at Dumbarton Oaks.

Three years ago Mr. Gibson and I proposed that regional organization should be the foundation of the whole machinery and that the three regional groups should be established—the Western Hemisphere, Europe and Asia. A year later, Mr. Churchill publicly supported this idea.

In the Western Hemisphere the long development of the Pan American Union pointed in that direction and the recent agreement at Mexico City advances it one step further. The success of the nebulous "concert of Europe" in preventing world war for nearly a century pointed in that direction for Europe, and the practical problems which developed in the League of Nations abundantly confirmed the need for that form of organization.

Such regional councils should embrace all United Nations' areas and should deal in the first instance with all controversies that might lead to war. If they fail to secure settlement by pacific methods, then, and only then, should the World Security Council intervene.

If regional organization were established at once, it would bring six powerful benefits:

First, it would give the smaller nations a greater voice, for they should be more largely represented in the regional councils and could well be given equal standing;

Second, policies which would prevent conflict are different in the three great areas and need separate organization;

Third, these regional organizations would relieve the Security Council of many problems and controversies before they reached it;

Fourth, such an organization would relieve the whole mechanism of much of its present color of a military alliance of a few great powers;

Fifth, regional organization at once lessens the pressure for military alliances.

Sixth, such a regional organization would greatly relieve the anxieties of the American people and probably those of most nations lest they be constantly involved in secondary problems all over the earth.

There is no reason why the proposed Economic, Social and Political Rights Councils should not also be regionalized for the better handling of problems peculiar to those regions. Their top World Councils would be the more free for coordination of the three great areas. It might also be worth consideration that the World Court be organized with three regional courts which would act as courts of first instance in questions involving nations in that region alone.

Some objection has been raised that there would be some implied rivalry of interest between regions which would be thus emphasized. The contrary is the truth, for such decentralization would make cooperation the more easy.

ARTICLE IV

March 28, 1945

DISARMAMENT OF THE ENEMY

My fourth proposal for the San Francisco Conference is that agreement upon continued and total disarmament of the enemy nations must be entered into either as part of the United Nations Charter or a separate agreement. In any event it will have to be enforced by the Security Council. And it profoundly affects the whole question of peace.

Three years ago Mr. Gibson and I proposed that the enemy states must be completely disarmed and kept disarmed for an entire generation. We pointed out one of the great errors of the Treaty of Versailles in which Germany was permitted to retain a professional army of 100,000 men, supposedly for purposes of maintaining internal order. She was permitted to have a navy limited only in tonnage and types of ships.

We stated that this leeway perpetuated her professional armies and navies. It perpetuated the warrior caste and all its traditions. It afforded a skeleton army and navy of skilled men ready for quick expansion. It insured the continuity of the General Staff with its military skill, brains and ambitions. It perpetuated their know-how to make war.

Repeated experience with the warrior caste of these nations in their intimidations, aggressions, blitzes, and attacks without even declaration of war should be enough for the world in this particular. We must make a better job of it this time.

We should require total dissolution of the military establishments of all enemy nations and the substitution, for purposes of a civic order, of a constabulary of the police type, excluding the whole officer and military caste from such organization. And we should prohibit the manufacture of arms of any kind. We could thus assure the disappearance of them and their know how from the world.

And if this were done an occupying force of men of the United Nations of a hundred thousand men in Germany and a hundred thousand in Japan would suffice. But it will need be kept there for a generation.

REDUCTION OF ARMAMENT OF THE UNITED NATIONS

My fifth proposal for the San Francisco Conference is that disarmament of the United Nations be more definitely dealt with. The Dumbarton Oaks proposals appear to contemplate a reduction of arms of the United Nations. But having regard to the fate of the same proposals in the League of Nations a more positive program should be introduced. Obviously our present war establishments will need be reduced. But they should be reduced relatively to each other and systematically. And obviously, huge military establishments are themselves a threat of aggression which should be the purpose of any world peace organization to reduce—and quickly.

In 1932 I proposed to the then World Disarmament Conference that these aggressive weapons be suppressed in order to throw the military advantage into the hands of the defense and thus into the peace-loving nations. That proposal was accepted by over forty nations. It was renewed by Mr. Roosevelt in 1933. At least it is worth reconsideration.

But of more importance is agreement now upon the maximum size of armies, navies and air power for the principal United Nations. We should remember that after the disarmament of the enemy the only dangerous armaments are those in the hands of our allies and it is imperative that we arrive at a method by which we do not start competition with our friends with all the dangers to good will which would flow from that.

The Covenant of the League of Nations provided for limitation of armaments at some future time and the time never came so far as the efforts of the League were concerned.

Therefore there should be incorporated in the new Charter of United Nations a much more definite program for limitation of the size of military establishments in the United Nations than that provided in Dumbarton Oaks if we are not to repeat this failure of the League of Nations.

POWERS OF OUR DELEGATE TO THE SECURITY COUNCIL

My sixth proposal refers to that most thorny question for the American people of whether the American delegate on the Security Council will be given the authority to make war. This is no doubt outside the provisions of the charter, but it will face the Senate when that treaty comes up for adoption. I cannot bring myself to the delegation of such power to any one human being. That is what happens if he votes to apply either economic sanctions or military force against an aggressor. The most vital determination that can be made under the democratic process is war. It means thousands of our people are sent to death in foreign lands. To give that power to some one man who represents us is the negation of the democratic process. The other side of the question, however, is that to delay decision against an aggressor presents dangers that the whole world security may break down at some critical moment.

Extremists are perhaps exaggerating both positions. A study of a hundred years of conflicts which have led to world-wide dangers indicates very few instances, if any where there was not time for ample consideration by the Congress.

Upon this I offer the tentative suggestion that this power should not be given to our delegate on the Security Council but to the President. And the President should be required to secure the majority vote of the joint Foreign Relations Committees of the Senate and the House on whether the issues should be submitted to the full Congress. Thus Congress would have a voice in determining both the urgency and the dimensions of responsibility. In minor and urgent undertakings there would need to be no full Congressional action. If action means war with a great power, the approval of the whole Congress is essential.

LESS HASTE AND LESS HATE

My seventh proposal for action at San Francisco does not as much concern that text as the procedure of the governments in this crisis. I have time and again urged that we should not attempt to determine a final organization for lasting peace until we have laid secure its foundations in the post-war settlements between nations.

We should take time to cool off from the hot emotions of war. Our indignation may lead us away from stern justice into vengeance. Victory with vengeance means ultimate disaster to the victor. We cannot have both peace and revenge. The men who led the world into this war should be hanged for murder and those guilty of other crimes must also be punished, but the masses of great races must be given a chance to enter the paths of peace where fear, hate and revenge may be turned aside and die. Our purpose must be to create a regime of law and justice in the world, not regencies of hate.

We do not know the shape of things in the immediate settlements of this war. And we should take time better to understand the now unknown forces that will come out of this gigantic explosion. No human being can foresee them today. No one foresaw them at Versailles. Such forces will be more powerful than any signed documents.

I suggest, therefore, it would be great wisdom if the peoples of the world should have time in which to consider and perhaps perfect any agreement at San Francisco.

Every thinking man and woman prays for a successful issue of the Conference. The destruction of war is now so terrible and the animosities among nations have become so deep that failure to assure a lasting peace now means the end of all hopes of humanity. America has fought this war for the greatest purpose of all time. That is to secure a lasting peace. And this agreement at San Francisco will determine whether our purpose has been won or lost.

The San Francisco Conference
and Peace

PHILADELPHIA, PENNSYLVANIA

[April 17, 1945]

I KNOW I express the sorrow of the American people that Mr. Roosevelt was not spared to guide the San Francisco Conference. The problems remain and we must carry on. In this spirit President Truman has announced that the Conference will proceed as planned. And it becomes our duty to give every support to our new President in his gigantic task.

I was glad to accept your invitation to speak to your Association. Philadelphia has always been devoted to peace. It was founded by a faith of which I am a member; this city is, indeed, the place where my ancestors landed on American soil.

Tonight I propose to explore the Dumbarton Oaks proposals in the light of experience, particularly of the League of Nations. Indeed, the time has come to appraise frankly the forces we must meet; to explore them with the lamp of experience. The time has gone by for emotional generalizations, and this is no time to engage in destructive debate.

Three years ago Hugh Gibson and I published a study of world experience in making peace. We made some suggestions of principles from this experience that should be incorporated in any organization to preserve peace. Some of this experience was adopted, some important lessons were either wholly omitted or only weakly accepted in the Dumbarton Oaks proposals. President Roosevelt and Secretary Stettinius have both stated that plan is open to amendment.

Three weeks ago I published some suggestions directed to strengthening the Dumbarton Oaks proposals.

It was a great satisfaction that ten days later most of these suggestions were also put forward by the representatives of the peace committees of the three great religious groups, the Protestants, the Catholics and the Jews.

On the same day, Moscow took me to task for these proposals. They obviously did not have my full statement. Anyway Moscow's argument reminds me of an old Quaker friend who said, "If thee does not repent in a measure and change thy ways considerably, thee will be damned to a certain extent."

THE PRESENT SITUATION

But before I discuss these suggestions, I should like to make an observation on the present setting of peace.

With the discovery of new methods of killing, with the shift from wars between men to war against women and children and with the gigantic destruction of centuries of men's toil a third world war will mean the extinction of civilization.

When we in America took up the sword, it was inevitable, from the hates, revenge and violence which would follow this war, that we must hold the sword either alone or jointly with others if we would maintain peace.

If the charter at San Francisco emerges with a reasonable hope of success, the United States must take its full part in carrying it out.

As a consequence of this war, Russia has again, and I hope forever, demonstrated by her gallant armies and by her alliance with General Winter and General Space, that she is impregnable. America by her gallant sons and our alliance with General Ocean and General Invention occupies a similar position. Britain's indomitable people allied with General Endurance and General Diplomacy have shown that they can preserve their Empire. But the survival of Western civilization in the United States and in the world depends upon unity in certain principles common to Britain, France and the other democracies.

It is my hope that no cleavage shall develop between Western civilization and the rest of the world which will involve another world war. Truly the world should be too exhausted to suffer a third world war for another twenty years. In the meantime, it is my belief that with collaboration among the great centers of power in Washington, London, Paris, Moscow and Chungking that peace not only can be preserved but the processes of peace can be developed in an atmosphere of good will and understanding.

TO PRESERVE PEACE

There are two obvious methods by which peace can be preserved:

First, through pacific methods, to settle controversies between nations by negotiation, arbitration and judicial decisions. This is the rule of law and justice.

Second, if these measures fail, then the use of force to stop aggression. This is the police power to enforce justice.

But beyond these direct methods there can be no lasting peace unless we summon the moral, spiritual forces which will diminish or stop the underlying dynamic cause of wars.

DUMBARTON OAKS

The League of Nations, as you know, was set up with an Assembly of all nations and a Council partly of permanent members comprising certain great powers and partly of members elected by the Assembly. The League provided for pacific settlement of controversies and for a World Court. It proposed to use economic and military force against an aggressor. The Dumbarton Oaks plan is patterned closely upon the League with somewhat less authority in the Assembly and more in the Council. In the original Dumbarton proposals the machinery of force to stop an aggressor was made much more powerful than in the League. Force was made its major instrument to preserve peace. At the instant summons of the Security Council, economic boycott, the armies, navies and air forces of the world were to stop an aggressor in his tracks. But a compromise as to voting rights of the permanent members of the Dumbarton Oaks Security Council was agreed upon as the result of Russian protest. By that compromise the great nations who are permanent members of the Security Council have a veto power to prevent any designation of their own actions as aggression. Practically, that puts all the great military powers out of reach. And world wars are not started by small nations.

The power of the Security Council was thus devitalized to practically the same level of effectiveness as the Council of the old League of Nations. We saw the practical destruction of the League when it failed to stop aggression of two of its own permanent Council members. That was, Italy's invasion of Ethiopia and Japan's invasion of China. (Please do not confuse these voting powers with those in the Assembly which I am not discussing.)

This retreat in the potency of force seemed to me to make it imperative to develop at San Francisco the pacific methods of maintaining peace, together with a much stronger mobilization of the forces which would allay or control the underlying causes of war.

AMENDMENTS AND ADDITIONS TO THE DUMBARTON OAKS PROPOSALS

The proposals which I made three weeks ago to this end were seven in number to which I will add two more. They are:

First: There are certain fundamental political rights of men and of nations that should be specified in the Charter. There are certain moral and spiritual standards of conduct among nations that should be proclaimed. I proposed we should make them effective by the establishment of a World Committee to promote these political rights. This Committee should rank with the Economic and Social Committees already contained in the Dumbarton Oaks plan.

Second: We should provide for peaceful revision of onerous

treaties between nations, in order that political progress in the world should not be frozen.

Third: We should create regional subdivision of the organization for preservation of peace into three areas, Asia, Europe and the Western Hemisphere; the regional organizations must of course be in harmony with the Security Council.

Fourth: We should insist upon total disarmament of the enemy powers.

Fifth: We should provide prompt proportional postwar reduction in the armies of the United Nations and the establishment of a maximum limit of armies, navies and air power among them.

Sixth: Although it is not a part of the charter itself, I suggested a method by which the war powers of the Congress could be preserved without delay to action in a crisis.

Seventh: Take enough time in formulating the Charter of Peace to do it right.

And tonight I add two more suggestions. There should be a control of military alliances. There should be a definition of aggression. And Senator Vandenberg's proposal that the Assembly be given freedom of initiative should be adopted.

The purpose of these additions is: First, to surround the mechanistic bones of the Charter with moral and spiritual forces. Second, to create those standards of conduct which should be the base of decision by the Security Council. Third, to reach into the causes of war much more deeply than just the settling of quarrels and the curbing of gangsters. And fourth, to simplify the work of the organization.

Mankind has made gigantic progress in methods to destroy civilization by improving upon its previous inventions. Likewise, in our efforts to save civilization from war we must not neglect our previous inventions in the organization of peace. Their successes and the causes of their failure are equally important experience.

The Holy Alliance of 125 years ago and its enforcement agency, the Quadruple Alliance, were set up on the theory that the peace of Vienna should be frozen fast by military power.

The League of Nations was set up on a more enlightened basis —that if controversies arose between nations they should be settled by pacific means before force was used.

The League of Nations was the greatest experiment in the history of peace making. It succeeded in settling many secondary quarrels, but it suffered from several grave weaknesses and many handicaps. My suggestions are directed to remedy or avoid these weaknesses and handicaps.

ALLAYING THE CAUSES OF WAR

The primary weakness of the Holy Alliance, the League of Nations and Dumbarton Oaks proposals is the failure to face the facts as to the real causes of war.

These gigantic explosions of modern civilization into world wars arise from more powerful forces than incidental quarrels. Quarrels are always the symptoms and not the disease. These forces which cause war are too easily obscured by over simplification. They are not wholly the work of evil men or perverted nations to be reformed even by a periodic spanking or even hanging of aggressors. For purposes of discussion we can group these underlying dynamic forces as:

First—Attempts at domination of other races and the counter-strivings of nations for freedom. That is, modern imperialism.

Second—Its handmaiden, militarism with its train of armies and military alliances.

Third—Economic pressures.

Fourth—Crusades for faiths, including economic faiths. That is, militant ideologies.

Fifth—The impulses to change which are inherent in the progress of civilization.

Sixth—The complexes of fear, hate and revenge.

We cannot make a lasting peace unless these forces be so channeled that they cease to drive the world into wars. That was the major cause of failure at Versailles.

The Versailles Treaty consisted of 623 paragraphs, of which 26 were devoted to the creation of the League of Nations. The origins of the present war lay largely in the 597 paragraphs defining the set up of nations, their boundaries, the reparations, the military and economic questions. Imperialism, militarism, economic pressures, hate and vengeance sat at that peace table. Many of the underlying causes of war were perpetuated and some of them were stimulated to more violence.

Because of the weaknesses and handicaps of the League it was not strong enough in after years to cope with the situation created by the war settlements. Some superficial thinkers assert the League failed because the American people refused to join. That would not have saved the world from the consequences of the Treaty of Versailles.

Men at Versailles realized the weakness of the League, but they said we should avoid difficult questions in the Covenant. They said that what we needed to do was to get some sort of League going and it would solve these questions. It never did. The same kind of voices are being raised today decrying any attempt to improve the San Francisco agreement.

Now we are fighting the second world war because of these sins of omission and commission in the Treaty of Versailles and the League's incapacity to preserve peace.

ESTABLISHING THE RIGHTS OF NATIONS AND MEN
AGAINST DOMINATION

Another weakness of the League was its failure to incorporate a bill of rights and standards of conduct of nations and men. Twenty-eight years ago President Wilson among his points sought to infuse a moral and spiritual element in the peace. He sought to establish the political rights of nations and of men. He sought to formulate standards of conduct and law among nations. He sought to curb and allay the causes of war. These ideas received scant support at Versailles.

When this second world war came twenty years later, we were told repeatedly and eloquently that after the defeat of the enemy the great purpose of the war was to establish the political rights of nations and men. Those rights as proclaimed by

Mr. Wilson's points were again reaffirmed in the Atlantic Charter. Twenty-six countries signed it including Russia. These principles and others were affirmed in the Moscow and in the Yalta declarations and in a hundred speeches of our leaders in war.

A BILL OF RIGHTS AND STANDARDS OF CONDUCT FOR NATIONS

These statements specifically include the right of peoples to equal sovereignty, freedom from aggression and domination by others, and the right of nations to determine their own government without interference. They particularize that there shall be no aggrandizement, no annexations, and no territorial changes without the freely expressed wishes of the peoples; that nations have the right to determine their wishes by unfettered elections, by free secret ballot and under international control if necessary. They assert the right of freedom of the seas in peace times and equality of trade. They also proclaimed disarmament; that nations should never use war as an instrument of national policy; and that peace must be based upon justice.

A BILL OF RIGHTS FOR MEN

Beyond these rights and standards of conduct of nations there are the rights and protections of human beings. These have been eloquently and repeatedly stated by our leaders in this war. Their establishment is proclaimed to be also one of the purposes of the war. Their all-inclusive term is freedom of men. They at least include protection of persons from execution or imprisonment without fair trial; prohibitions against compulsory labor or slavery in any disguise; protections to minorities and backward peoples; the freedom of speech, of the press and of religion.

Nor are these rights of men strange ideas. The essence of them appears in American, British, and also the Soviet Russian constitutions.

THESE RIGHTS AND STANDARDS SHOULD BE ADOPTED
AT SAN FRANCISCO

When, after twenty-five years, we come again to San Francisco to write the Charter of Peace, why do we not remedy the failure of a quarter of a century ago? There is nowhere else in this treaty making after this war to record these bills of rights and these standards of conduct.

Nor should this be done by timid references to the Atlantic Charter with all its qualifying words of "hopes" and "desires." If these principles are right, they should be boldly stated.

Vital experience in all this matter is to be derived from our American experiment in government. There was genius in the mechanism of the American Constitution. But its transcendent genius was its great moral and spiritual base in the Bill of Rights. This government would never have endured had it been a mechanism alone.

And if these rights are to be effective, they cannot be left alone to perform themselves. There should be a World Committee in the new organization whose job is to look after them.

By the magnificent valor of the armies and navies we have won the Battle of the Atlantic, the Battle of the Pacific, the Battle of the Philippines. We are near to victory in the Battle of Germany and the Battle of Japan. But are we winning the Battle of Freedom?

Americans must face brutal facts. As the result of this war the area of human freedom will shrink *by* whole nations. It is shrinking *in* many nations. Are we going to dodge these issues at San Francisco?

PEACEFUL CHANGE OF INTERNATIONAL AGREEMENTS

Three years ago I stated that one great weakness of the League was that it made no adequate provision to ease strains by orderly change in agreements between nations when they became onerous or inapplicable. Inasmuch as violation of peace treaties became aggression, the League became the defender and the guarantor of the *status quo*. In fact the intention of some of its founders was just that. Its failure to ease pressures contributed to World War II.

Once we settle down to peace again there will be treaties defining boundaries and other relations or imposed relations of nations. The aggressor will again be anyone who violates the then existing situation. Thus the new world organization to preserve peace and thus the American people automatically become the guarantor of a new *status quo*. And as the war settlements have not yet been made we are in the dark as to what we are about to guarantee.

Abundant experience after the last war demonstrated that dangerous pressures are sure to arise. There will be provisions imposed during the heat of war emotions. There will be the shift in economic pressures and populations. There will be the growth of ideas and inventions. There will be the development of backward nations which become conscious and capable of self-government.

And let no man think that there will not be unpredictable forces and pressures in the world after this war. If we can scan former convulsions of the modern Western world we see that, following these long periods of general war and disorder, new shapes of civilization and new forms of nations have emerged. Civilization has taken new impulses and new directions. We must expect new forms and new directions from this gigantic explosion. No one can pretend to see these shapes clearly. But we must not attempt to freeze the world again, or it will explode again.

If peaceful means are denied, war becomes the only available solvent.

REGIONAL ORGANIZATION TO RELIEVE STRAINS

Another weakness of the League was that its Council was overburdened with all the minor troubles and confused voices of the world at every session.

To relieve these strains there should be a definite regional set-up into the three great separate areas of the world—Europe, Asia and the Americas. The Asian Council could by virtue of its interests include not only the Asiatic nations but also Britain, Russia, France and the United States.

The regional organizations could each settle most of their problems far better than it can be done by more distant nations. This confusion of voices led Secretaries of State to by-pass the League. And Secretaries of State should be the representatives in person on these regional councils within their own areas. It would lend dignity to the organization. It would thus cure another of the League's weaknesses of sending a boy to do a responsible man's job.

Each region should have the first responsibility to keep the peace and devise policies for peace. Any use of force should be reserved to the Security Council. That Council would thus be free to deal only with questions that contain dangers of world war. This method would also give the smaller nations the larger voice they need. It would relieve America and other nations from the strains of many a minor foreign dispute. This would seem to be practical for Mr. Churchill has endorsed it. The Department of State has already taken a long step in this direction at the Mexico City conference.

STOPPING MILITARISM

Another lesson we learned from the weakness of the League was the lame provision for reduction of arms and the lack of control of military alliances. Herein are the sleepless bacilli of militarism.

I proposed that at San Francisco we should stiffen the whole attack upon these causes of war; that we agree to total disarmament of Germany and Japan with no manufacture of weapons for a whole generation or until they have forgotten the know how of war. And equally important, that the United Nations should set up a program to reduce progressively and proportionately their own arms and do it quickly after the war. There should also be some control of military alliances by the Security Council. The multitude of these alliances after the last war inspired fear, counter-alliances, increase of armament. They made for balances of power, and they created voting blocs in the League. They not only weakened the League but they contributed to World War II.

DEFINING AGGRESSION

Aggression in this world is not confined to the old-fashioned threats or to military action or even to economic pressures. Our experience with the Nazis who infiltrated their poisonous propaganda and fifth columns into the lands of peaceful neighbors should indicate that there is a new form of aggression in the world.

Therefore the San Francisco Charter should agree upon a definition of aggression to include direct or indirect subsidized governmental propaganda in other nations. The enforcement of such a provision would help cure that cause of wars which grows out of crusading faith, political or otherwise.

WE SHOULD NOT BE STAMPEDED INTO BLUNDERS

We cannot hope for perfection at San Francisco. In any event the Dumbarton Oaks press release does not purport to be the form of a treaty. It is a statement of methods. It must be drafted into precise terms. It is the height of wisdom that the people of the world should have a chance to see its final wording and to have a period in which to consider and even improve the agreement before it is signed. It will be more certain to last.

We do not have to hurry. If we take six years to make war it might be a good idea to take a few more months to build a sound organization to keep the peace. It was seven years from Yorktown to the Constitution.

THE WAR SETTLEMENTS

Beyond the San Francisco charter one half of the making of peace will lay in the political, economic and territorial settlements of the war. If we do them well, peace will largely preserve itself. If we do them badly, no organization to maintain peace can succeed. I shall discuss these questions on some other occasion, but here I may say that we must not again sow dragons' teeth. And appeasement is a dragon's tooth.

IN CONCLUSION

Truly peace is a matter of spirit; it rests upon moral forces, upon the building of good-will among mankind.

The Sermon on the Mount launched that transcendent concept of good-will among men as the basis of peace. And despite all his violations man has received from that Divine message an undying inspiration to strive for peace. Those spiritual concepts of peace have at least brought it to pass that every war must be professed by its leaders as a war of defense and for the purpose of securing peace. They have brought into the world the concept that aggression is an infamy. And that domination over unwilling people is immoral.

The great purpose of America in this war is lasting peace. That is all that we can possibly get from this dreadful sacrifice of life and the awful burdens upon our children. If the world will cooperate to give our children this boon, their tears will not be less but their labor over years to come will be brightened with confidence and their future lighted with hope.

We must not fail now.

The San Francisco Charter and the
Progress Toward Enduring Peace

SAN FRANCISCO, CALIFORNIA

[*July 18, 1945*]

To my fellow Americans:

I HAVE received a multitude of requests from members of
Congress, the press and individuals for my views upon the
San Francisco Charter and the progress of peace-making.
I am able to do this through the courtesy of the Columbia
Broadcasting System.

CHARTER SHOULD BE RATIFIED

The San Francisco Charter is better than the Dumbarton
Oaks version and is probably as good as could be obtained under the existing emotions, the present governments, the conflicting ideals and ambitions in the world. It should be ratified
by the Senate promptly.

CHARTER WILL NOT ALONE ASSURE LASTING PEACE

The American people should be under no illusions that the
Charter assures lasting peace. The Charter at best consists only
of an expression of desire and machinery to advance peace.
The problem of enduring peace is far wider than the Charter.
The foundations of peace must also be laid in the economic and
political settlements among nations by which this war is to be

liquidated. The nature of these settlements will have more to do with lasting peace than the Charter. The Charter could not preserve a bad peace.

THE STRENGTH OF THE CHARTER

The major strength of the Charter is a noble preamble and that it provides for continuous meetings of the nations where peace problems can be discussed. It stimulates the methods of peaceful settlement of controversies. It re-establishes the World Court and provides trusteeship for dependent countries. It provides for a limited action to prevent military aggression. It sets up machinery for promotion of social and economic welfare.

THE WEAKNESSES OF THE CHARTER

There are many weaknesses in the Charter. There is no positive Bill of Rights for nations and men, but only a mere suggestion that they should be promoted. They are not expressed in the tones of the American Bill of Rights. The Charter does not recover the principles of the Atlantic Charter which were whittled away at Teheran and after Yalta. The political, moral and spiritual standards of conduct of nations and of men are thus insufficiently defined for the tests by which the conduct of nations should be judged by the Security Council. While the Security Council has the power to stop military aggression among small nations, yet this is not assured among the great nations, because of the veto power. The Charter fails to define aggression even in the admirable terms settled by the Soviet Government for inclusion in its treaties of eleven years ago. And it does not even mention the new disintegrating forms of aggression of one nation upon another through propaganda and fifth columns. The Regional Organization, the methods of review of outmoded treaties, and the lack of commitment to relative reduction of armies and navies leave much to be desired. Most of these vital questions are referred to in terms of hope or permission, not in terms of positive undertakings or agreements. But these weaknesses point the directions in which there should be amendment over the years to come.

REGIONAL ORGANIZATION OF THE WESTERN HEMISPHERE

There is a step that should be taken at once, after the Charter is ratified. The Western Hemisphere should be immediately organized as a region under the permissions of the Charter. This hemisphere could thus settle its own troubles without interferences from the outside. In any event our troubles are not the kind that have ever led to world wars. The long development of the Monroe Doctrine, the Pan-American Union, the recent session and declaration at Mexico City, all point in this direction. Our ideas of personal liberty and self-government, our opposition to domination of other nations, to imperialism, to fifth columns from Europe are common to all the nations of the Western Hemisphere. This hemisphere is the only great region in the world where unity in these vital foundations of lasting peace is universal to us all. Were we thus united into a regional council we would present a much more effective force in the rest of the world than if we rest simply on the individual influence of each nation in the Security Council and the Assembly of the Charter. Such an organization could give immediate strength in the presentation of Western Hemisphere ideals. The Western world could become in time the voice of freedom to the whole earth.

POWERS OF OUR DELEGATE SHOULD BE DEFINED

From an American point of view, ratifying the Charter involves little commitment beyond those that may be entered into by our representative on the Security Council. Somewhere along the line there must be a definition by the Congress of the powers of this delegate. While there need be little worry about our representative using our military forces for minor police incidents, yet the Congress should never part with its powers to declare war. It should be understood that the structure of our government differs from those of the other principal powers. The British and French are parliamentary governments where there is no division of power between the executive and the legislative branches. Their executive is a committee of the legislative arm and constantly responsible to it. Therefore the authorized vote of their representative will be the view of the legislative arm. Russia is a totalitarian government where the vote of their representative will be determined in Moscow. Our delegate will represent the executive. We alone have such a separation of the powers of government that ours is the only delegate on the Security Council who might commit his country to war without the consent of the legislative arm, as the Constitution requires. His authority should be defined so that the delegate is in some way responsible to Congress before our country is committed to war.

PEACE RESTS UPON CONTINUED COLLABORATION OF WASHINGTON, LONDON AND MOSCOW

The plain fact is that the making of political and economic peace settlements among the United Nations themselves and between the United Nations and the enemy states and the preservation of lasting peace still rest upon the successful collaboration of the three centers of power—that is, Russia, Britain and the United States. And it will rest there for many years to come. But lasting peace cannot be based upon the dominance of three or four or even five powers forever. The Charter will offer a forum for world opinion and advice to these responsible powers. The retreat from the Atlantic Charter, the ambitions and emotions of war, the omissions from the San Francisco Charter emphasize that these three great powers are really the trustees of world peace rather than the Charter itself. There must be a transition period where this collaboration will require much patience, it will require great firmness. It will take time and much good will to find lasting settlements after the high emotions of war, of national ambitions, of differing national purposes. In any event, for twenty years after the victory over

Japan, all of the nations of the world will be absorbed in restoring their internal economy and in reestablishing their standards of living. During this period the world should be able to work out the problems of lasting peace and to build greater strength in the Charter.

I have said we will require great patience if a peaceful world shall emerge from this most gigantic explosion since civilization began.

Civilization on the continent of Europe will survive but it is dreadfully ill. Millions of her best have died. Scores of cities have been reduced to rubble. Her industrial life is paralyzed. The peoples are hungry and destitute. But even more important, men's minds are distorted by suffering, by hate, by the desire for revenge. Governments are weak from destruction, from exhaustion and bitter factionalism. This is the soil in which revolution will thrive and civil war will arise. Revolutions do not end when the firing of war ceases and liberation comes. That is just the time when they begin. We shall indeed need patience and resolution while these storms blow themselves out.

THE ROAD TO LASTING PEACE

But gradually war emotions will cool after this period and it should be possible with time to re-establish the only basis upon which the world will have peace. That is, the relations between nations and men must be founded upon positively agreed political, moral and spiritual rights.

The most fundamental of these rights are plain. And I do not use the term "shall be" but the term "must be":

No annexations of territory;

No territorial changes without the free consent of the people therein;

Full sovereignty of people without domination;

The right of all peoples to choose freely their own form of government and their own officials;

Equality of trade and freedom of the seas;

The right of minorities to protection;

The right of fair trial before conviction;

The prohibition of deportations, of slavery or compulsory labor in and disguise;

And finally the greatest rights of all, that is, free press and free worship.

And there will be no peace unless these rights be applied to those peoples who have been deprived of them during this war or who have not yet attained them. This is more important to-day than ever before, because liberty and freedom have shrunk in great areas as a result of this war.

We have many millions of people whose parents came to us from Poland, Finland, Latvia, Lithuania, Esthonia, Czecho-slovakia, Yugoslavia and Greece. In America's First Crusade for liberation of these peoples of 25 years ago we established them in independence, in representative government and in personal liberty. Not only these millions of our citizens from these countries but all Americans are today uncertain of their fate. Questions arise as to whether this, our second crusade of liberation of these and other peoples, will not be lost in the peace-making of this war. I may say at once that peoples who have had independence and freedom will not forever remain suppressed and that lasting peace cannot be assured on this basis. America cannot guarantee or hope an unjust peace will last.

Profound questions affecting lasting peace arise in our treat-ment of the enemy states. They cannot expect to have all the rights of free men given to them until they have proved their worthiness of them. But still other questions arise in peace-making which bear upon lasting peace. Is Germany to be par-titioned? What sort of government is to be erected over the enemy states?

Peace can come only if we differentiate between the common people of the enemy nations and their criminal leaders, so that we do not transform stern justice to war criminals into general vengeance. The Germans, Japanese, Italians, Bulgarians and Hungarians must, sooner or later, govern themselves. While they cannot again be trusted to bear arms, yet they must be allowed to restore their productivity in peaceful industry if they, and indeed the rest of the world, are to recover decent living and to have enduring peace. Our purpose must be to lead them into the paths of peaceful contribution to civilization for our sakes as well as their own. The Charter cannot hope to succeed unless the nations successfully solve these questions.

These are the problems with which President Truman is dealing in Berlin today. And all America wishes him success in their solution.

THE TESTS

The preamble to the Charter contains a list of vital objectives. This preamble is an expression of hope. It is not a binding agreement. The test of the war-settlements and indeed of the Charter itself will be whether these ideals are applied to all peoples. If the nations fail in these particulars we shall have explosions which no Security Council can control. But if the ideas of this preamble be followed in the political and economic settlements of the war, the wounds of war can be healed, liberty restored in the world, the Charter strengthened and lasting peace can come to mankind.

PART II

ORGANIZATION OF THE HOME FRONT

Organization of War Economic Controls

WASHINGTON, D. C.

[*December 16, 1941*]

I FEEL honored by your request to advise upon the proposed price control. I have read as much of the hearings upon the Bill as time permitted. I wish to say at once that the problems and economics of war prices have been presented by Mr. Henderson and his assistants in a most able fashion. The evidence of many other witnesses and the nature of their examination by the Senate and House members have shown a penetrating understanding by Congressional Committees of the forces and needs involved.

I will not, therefore, take your time to discuss economic questions, but rather will draw from my own experience in formulating and administering commodity control laws during five years of World War No. 1 and the Armistice, from 1914 to 1919. I mention this only as I wish to make suggestions of somewhat wider action than purely price questions.

PART A

I agree fully with Mr. Henderson's statement that with the declarations of war against us during the past ten days the whole situation has shifted greatly from that of when this legislation was formulated. The problem has moved from the limited area of preparedness to the direct field of total national

mobilization to fight a desperate and long war. This change makes even a wider degree of controls imperative. We must now take more men from production, yet we must produce more for war purposes. Some of our supplies from overseas will be imperiled or reduced. We must reduce civilian consumption to a greater degree for the enlargement of war needs. The degree of inflationary forces will be increased by the larger measures of finance now necessary.

However, actual and desperate war gives one advantage in that it is now possible to secure a far greater degree of willing sacrifice and cooperation from business and the public than in peace or semi-peace time. I believe this greatly modifies and facilitates our approach to the whole problem. All our people are united to prosecute the War. They realize the necessity for self-sacrifice, and are seeking for cooperative service. Almost anything can be asked of our people at this time and under this influence.

PART B

The emphasis of the pre-war drafts of this legislation was upon price control. I should like to suggest to the Committee that the problem now moves into the much wider field of commodity control of which price control is but one segment.

I wish to state at once that I agree wholly with the general objectives of this Bill. Price controls are absolutely imperative to win the war; to lessen suffering of our people during the war; to take profits out of the war; they serve to protect the social and economic system as much as possible from destructive aftermaths of the war. But the problem now becomes much wider than price alone.

So far as price control is concerned, obviously when we abstract commodities from civil consumption for military use, and at the same time increase civilian buying power by war expenditures, we are going to create shortages, and when we finance, as we must, some part of the war by inflationary methods, we are creating double pressures toward price increase. Mr. Henderson has pointed out that it is impossible to stay all price rise,

that there will be increased cost of living, no matter what brakes are put on, and that wages will move with the increased costs of living.

And we must not have too much confidence that maximum prices by law are wholly effective. Any maximum price tends to become the minimum at once, as it becomes the moral price to be charged by traders. Moreover, if there is a real shortage, bootlegging will set in. Thus any price fixing is a brake on price rise—it is not a full control. I do not know of any particular rigid mandatory prices that held for long in the last war. The problem is therefore rather one of stabilization and orderly movement on the whole economic front. But in order to secure even price stability other measures of commodity control must be included.

PART C

I would list the measures required for commodity control in somewhat the following order. Many of them affect price and are inseparable from it. These measures are:

1. To increase the production of needed commodities wherever possible by new manufacturing facilities or increased acreage.

2. To increase production of some commodities by simplifying diversity in styles, varieties and dimensions of products, by simplifying methods and processes, by securing full seven days' operations of machinery and by avoiding cessation of work.

3. To conserve industrial uses of some commodities.

4. To induce the use of substitute materials for some commodities.

5. To reduce consumption of some commodities by reduction of activities not essential in war, such as public works and some building and similar trades.

6. To avoid the non-essential uses of material equipment, capital and labor where needed for war purposes.

7. To increase supply and avoid profiteering by prevention of hoarding and speculation.

8. To reduce consumption by organized voluntary civilian conservation.

9. To put price ceilings upon some commodities.

10. To put price floors under some commodities in order to secure production, or to do justice to producers such as agriculture.

11. To give stability in price or supplies or incentive to production of some commodities by government purchase and sale.

12. To give stability to price by complete coordination of governmental and allied purchasing agencies for each commodity.

13. To give priorities.

14. To provide for rationing if that becomes necessary.

Many of these actions result in increased supply and decreased demand, and thus contribute not only to supplies for war and civilian purposes, but decrease pressures upon price.

All of these items have been pointed out by Mr. Henderson and his assistants. Many of these measures have already been started in the Government. But with the shift in our situation to desperate war the emphasis has changed, and I believe has somewhat changed in the form of organization and authorities now required.

I suggest at once that all these 14 measures, or such of them as may be applicable to any particular commodity or some grouping of commodities, must be administered by the same government agency. In other words, unless there be administration of all measures affecting a commodity in one hand there will be great confusion in this commodity, for all these measures affect price as well as supply. I will, however, discuss this more fully later on.

The authorities needed to carry out these measures are in the main:

(a) Authority to make voluntary agreements with trades and groups as to price, conservation and distribution.

(b) Authority to establish wise cooperative measures to bring about industrial and civilian conservation.

(c) Authority to enforce regulations against a minority who may not comply.

(d) Authority from time to time to fix floor and ceiling prices and margins in business transactions.

(e) Authority for government buying and selling of commodities.

(f) Authority in priorities and rationing.

Some of these authorities have already been given, but some of them may require enlargement.

PART D

The actual administrative problems will come down at once to the economic setting of each particular commodity. Some commodities can be excluded from control such as certain luxury goods. In many essential commodities there will be no shortage. The degree of shortage of other commodities will vary. Except as a check against inflationary pressures from financing of the war, the commodities in ample supply will need no measures of control. On many of the other commodities, the pressure to higher prices can be relieved by more extensively organized use of methods I have listed.

PART E

I should like to emphasize the necessity of more organized voluntary cooperation to effect these ends now that we are actually in war. Nothing affects so many people and requires such delicate handling if morale is not to be impaired as these control measures. It is a job of steering between the rocks of economic disturbance through rising costs of living; legitimate and stimulative prices to producers; avoidance of the appearance of dictatorial action which creates resentment and trespasses upon the accepted freedoms of men as little as possible.

It seems to me that every industry, trade and calling involved in war action that is not already organized (and some are already set up) should be organized by calling upon such groups to appoint their own committees, whose leadership they will accept, freely to represent them. Before any of these measures are put in action, effort should be made to come to voluntary agreements covering many of these problems. The industries and trades can invent and put into action far more increased production and conservation measures than any governmental agency can think of. They can in most cases be brought to agree upon prices, margins and other measures in this category. They can do a large job in rationing, especially of industrial commodities, among their members where that is necessary. The only force necessary in such cases would be upon the small fringe that will not comply.

I need scarcely mention that this was the fundamental basis of our actions in World War No. 1. And I may mention here that the Commodity Control Act in that war contained the following provision:

"That in carrying out the purposes of this Act the President is authorized to enter into any voluntary arrangements or agreements, to create and use any agency or agencies, to accept the services of any person without compensation, to cooperate with any agency or person."

We availed ourselves of this authority every hour of the day, and 90 per cent of restraint on prices and the other measures was accomplished in this fashion.

That a large measure of controls as to price and other measures can be effected by voluntary agreement and cooperation is therefore not conjecture. And in many fields the powers to enforce were rarely, if ever required. The whole Food Administration, the War Industries Board, and the Commercial Economy Board, under Mr. Arch W. Shaw, which subsequently became the Conservation Division of the War Industries Board, from the first relied upon agreement and persuasive powers, although always conscious of the fact that there was authority behind them.

At once our great industrial raw materials, which are produced and distributed by limited groups, can be controlled by voluntary agreements, with a modicum of legal authority to compel some minor dissenter to go along. It is more difficult in the widespread consumption industries, but it can be done to large extent.

We have to remember also that we have 130,000,000 people widely spread and in varying economic surroundings in which cooperation is far more flexible than forced regulation. Our basis of action in the United States during World War No. 1 was entirely different from the formulae applied during that time in France, England and Germany. They were all pretty hard and fast mandatory systems. Often enough these systems were accepted as a challenge to a battle of evasion and ingenious violation. They required elaborate and exasperating policing that resulted in large expense and a great waste of energy. Their effect on the popular morale was most demoralizing and the results were not as effective as our American methods.

Our experience in the Food Administration has some interest in this particular. In World War I prices had already, because of foreign buying, risen greatly before we came into the war. The Food Administration came into being in August, 1917. Farm prices had already moved from 100 up to 204 on an index number. Wholesale food prices stood at 180. During the rise prior to the Food Administration it moved about 5 per cent a month in farm prices, and about 4 per cent a month in wholesale prices. Effective control ended just before the Armistice. That was because the people knew the war was over and voluntarily restraints weakened. Moreover, we did not wish to elaborate force machinery after the war was obviously over. And after the Armistice all prices rose sharply for various reasons.

However, during the period between August, 1917 and October, 1918, about 14 months, we greatly flattened out the movement, especially to consumers. We were deliberately stimulating farm production by increases and floors under farm prices. Their index moved from 204 to 219—or between 8 and 9 per cent. Wholesale prices of food moved from 180 to 200 and thus were held behind the advances in farm prices. This was a rise in wholesale prices of something over one-half per cent a month. Clothing, which was not controlled, moved from 180 to 253 in this period or at the rate of over 5 per cent a month. We stabilized prices by floors, by ceilings, by purchases and sale. We did conservation and stimulation of production. We did it largely by cooperation.

It must be borne in mind that we were steadily increasing our shortages by increases in exports at the same time. We increased our exports from a normal of 5 million tons to 16 million tons. At least this experience proves that price control can be of great value and that it must go hand in hand with other measures.

I dwell upon this subject of voluntary agreement for reasons which I believe are of the first importance. I may repeat that we are 130,000,000 ingenious and intelligent people. Our fundamental sense of freedoms makes force measures most irksome. We are naturally suspicious of all governmental interference even in war. Yet, on the other hand, ours are the most cooperative people in the world and the most willing to make sacrifice. It is this spirit which I hope will be invoked in the formulation and administration of these measures. Moreover, nothing will more greatly give confidence that our social and economic system will be preserved than cooperative action.

PART F

I wish to emphasize another phase of organization. I am a convinced adherent of a single-headed responsible administrator for all executive functions. Likewise I believe we should use Boards or Commissions for quasi-legislative and quasi-judicial functions and should separate these functions sharply from administrative functions and personnel. Boards and Commissions cannot do sound administration, especially under war pressures. Because no one had experience with total war organization before World War I, we had all these functions badly mixed at that time. In that war every single administrative Board blew up in disagreement and delay sooner or later. President Wilson finally solved these troubles by, in effect, making the Chairman the whole Board. That was the case of Mr. Baruch in Munitions, Mr. McCormick in War Trade and Mr. Hurley in Shipping. On the other hand, in the case of the industrial raw materials and munitions, it was finally necessary to separate the price question under a Board headed by Mr. Brookings. The Food Administrator had all the functions of administrator, quasi-legislator, and quasi-judge. I dissolved many of these conflicting functions by creating advisory committees from among the citizens, who checked upon regulations and who determined prices. We got by, but experience showed that these functions should be separated.

Nevertheless, in war emergency the Commodity Administrator or Administrators should have power to formulate regulations and prices and put them into temporary action. But there should be an independent Board for final decisions, for review, and for appeal in these fields.

PART G

It seems to me also that it is critical that all the 14 commodity control measures I have mentioned or such part of them as are applicable to any particular commodity should be directed by one Administrator over a group of commodities. It seems to me that it would be impossble to prevent confusion to secure supply, to stabilize prices, or secure distribution unless the same directing head applied stimulation, conservation, price, priorities, rationing, purchase, etc. of that particular commodity. It also defines responsibility. In this line of organization, I would assign certain groups of commodities to a separate Administrator or existing administrative agency and give to that Administrator or agency the direction of all the fourteen measures I have already mentioned.

Price administration is, as I have said, one implement among others. The major thing is commodity control. In the last war we divided these commodity functions into Munitions (The

War Industries Board), Food, Fuel, and War Trade. The emphasis has changed in this war. I may be traveling into unsafe ground, but it is my belief that at this moment Munitions should have direction of all the fourteen measures I have mentioned in respect to the commodities of which they are the dominant consumers; that they should make the agreements with trades as to prices, supply, conservation, issue the preliminary regulations, etc., with review and appeal in price and regulation to the central Price Board. For the present I would suggest three administrators or agencies divided upon a commodity basis. That is Munitions Commodities, Agricultural Commodities, and a third comprising other commodities which need control. The heads of these agencies to have the administrative powers in this Bill delegated to each of them by the President. That is, there should be no Price Control Administrator running crosswise and conflicting with the other functions of the administrators. As I have said, that price appeal Board could be made to serve all agencies. I have never believed that Munitions can be handled except under a single-headed administrator with, as I have said, a check review by a Board on quasi-judicial price or regulatory questions. If all nations learned one thing in the agony of the last war, it was precisely that. And as things now are, the Secretary of Agriculture (a single head) should control all these functions including price fixing in his field.

It seems to me there needs to be other separate agency or agencies or administrators dealing with commodities not in these two groups and likewise administer all the fourteen measures applicable to their fields. I know that the line between different groups of commodities is difficult to draw. But it is less difficult and less confusing than for one agency to fix price and another to buy and sell, etc. In any event, great cooperation is vital.

As a long war goes on, the needs of a control in commodity groups will shift. As an instance of this, in the last war food was one of our great economic problems. We had to carry the food deficiencies of 220,000,000 British, French, Italian and neutral people mostly on our backs. In this war the burden is largely the 50,000,000 British. In the last war our constant increase of exports created a shortage all along the food line. Today there appears to be ample supplies in sight, and the farmer needs price floors more than price ceilings. We cannot, however, know what the situation may be a year or five years hence.

PART H

In Mr. Henderson's original bill of last August, that these authorities and the duties to set up administrators or administrative agencies be given to the President, I suggest that that should be restored. The Congress can provide for confirmation of important officials by the Senate. My reason for this is that no one can see what form organization is going to be required one year or other years hence as the war moves on. Moreover, wise administration may require that these administrative authorities which I have mentioned be split at once among the existing or new war agencies. The President should have the widest latitude in organization.

The Price Reviewing or Appeal Board should, however, in my view, be made universal to all administrative agencies dealing with price, and can, of course, be set up definitely by the Congress.

PART I

I should like to suggest that it is important that the country be convinced that these drastic and necessary encroachments upon the freedom of men are going to be ended when the war is over. It will contribute to that confidence if every emphasis is put upon voluntary cooperation. It will contribute further if there is provision in this Act that these powers end not later than six months after peace.

REPLY TO QUESTIONS ON LICENSE PROVISION

The Food Control Act of World War I contained this licensing power. When we were engaged in drafting that Act, I sought for some method by which we, having come to an agreement with a trade as to price regulation, conservation, etc., could enforce such an agreement against a possible small margin who would not cooperate. The legal advisors of that time did not believe we could constitutionally regulate intra-state commerce even under the so-called war powers. We invented the license as a method of getting by. I never liked it. The penalty was too drastic. To take away a license was like hanging a man and all his family for stealing two dollars. We, in fact, never really got much use out of it for this reason. My recollection is that we issued about 250,000 licenses—that we cancelled only about 200 and these for repeated and most grievous violations. We had, as I recollect, about 8,000 cases, but most of them we did nothing about, and the others we dismissed upon their making a contribution to the Red Cross. That is bad and arbitrary government. Moreover, our license authority extended only to businesses whose sales were in excess of $100,000 per annum. Nor did we spread the licenses over all the food trades. But an almost insuperable administrative difficulty appeared at once. It required so many clerks to handle the licenses and would have required so many people to police them that we practically threw up our hands. Today there are about 1,250,000 food, drink and apparel manufacturers, wholesalers and retailers alone. And that does not cover all the other trades. It is a stupendous administrative job.

Of more importance, since the last war the whole interpretation of Federal control of intra-state commerce has changed, the concept of war powers has enlarged and I am advised that any regulation could be effected by straight statutory enactment, where penalties can be varied to the crime and imposed in the courts.

I am opposed to any such powers as the license implies. It

is unnecessary now. It puts a practical death sentence of a man's living in the hands of an administrative officer. It gives a power which can be used for punitive purposes. If I were administering these agencies I would not want such a power.

I believe Mr. Baruch's proposal of freezing prices and wages was sound if it could have been introduced early in this war. But great price and wage distortions have now occurred. Farm hands get $40 a month and board still, while munitions mechanics get $400 a month. Fuel and light are up only 10 per cent, while farm prices are up 50 per cent. Cotton is up 93 per cent, lead 13 per cent. Some prices must go through the ceiling to get production. Agricultural prices were too low at any time early in the war and would have had to be moved through the ceiling. I believe a large part of the value of Mr. Baruch's proposal could, however, be secured by an amendment to Section 2 of this Bill. At this place the prices existing between October 1 and October 15, 1941, are set out as a sort of advisory base for price fixing. The expressions "so far as possible," "give due consideration to" are used. I suggest it would give greater understanding to the public and a more definite system if these prices were made the actual base of the law. The other provisions of the Act enable prices to be varied from this base in any direction. That would embrace in part Mr. Baruch's suggestion.

The Limitations on Freedom in War

NEW YORK CITY

[May 20, 1942]

I T IS a pleasure to speak before this Association whose service to business, to agriculture and to labor these many years is so established and so esteemed.

The Conference Board has asked me to say something on the theory and practice of personal liberty during the war. However when you are riding an earthquake there is a tendency to less interest in the theory of geology than to the more immediate practice.

We are in this war and the only road out of it is victory. There will be no liberty anywhere if we lose the war.

Inside America we are vibrating between two poles. We are fighting to preserve personal liberty in the world. Yet we must suspend part of it at home, in order to win. And suspension creates grave dangers because liberty rapidly atrophies from disuse. Vested interests and vested habits grow around its restrictions. It would be a vain thing to fight the war and lose our own liberties. If we would have them return we must hold furiously to these ideals. We must challenge every departure from them. There are just two tests: "Is this departure necessary to win the war?" "How are we going to restore these freedoms after the war?"

The exploration of these questions calls for a calm and philosophical disposition. And we have no right to complain. Our soldiers and sailors are deprived of all their freedoms except the right to grouse a little. But they will expect their freedoms back when they come home.

OUR PREVIOUS EXPERIENCE

But at least in this war we are not on strange paths. The World War of 25 years ago was also a total war when there was total mobilization of the civilian population. It was a strange phenomenon in American experience. We had to pioneer suspensions of liberty. We had to march through strange swamps of total mobilization of civilian effort. We had to find our way in unknown and ambushed forests of peace-making and through the unrevealed and precipitous mountains of economic disorganization and restoration of liberty after the war. After that war we had to carry the burden of saving all Europe from the greatest famine of all history. No one had trod these human wildernesses before. We were lost many times. We made many mistakes. The problems of organization are today more intense as we have a larger part in the war. But there is nothing in essence of organization that differs from the last war. We then got some experience in what not to do. And we did some things successfully, including winning the war.

LIMITATIONS ON ECONOMIC FREEDOM

We may first contemplate the limitations on economic freedom, for here are the maximum restrictions. To win total war President Roosevelt must have many dictatorial economic powers. There must be no hesitation in giving them to him and upholding him in them. Moreover, we must expect a steady decrease in economic freedom as the war goes on.

We must start our thinking with a disagreeable, cold, hard fact. That is, the economic measures necessary to win total war are just plain Fascist economics. It was from the war organization developed by all nations, including the democracies, during the first total war, that the economic department of Fascism was born.

But there are two vast differences in the application of this sort of economic system at the hands of democracies or at the hands of dictators. First, in democracies we strive to keep free speech, free press, free worship, trial by jury and the other personal liberties alive. And second, we want to so design our actions that these Fascist economic measures are not frozen into American life, but shall thaw out after the war.

LIMITATIONS ON FREE SPEECH

While economic freedom must suffer most by the war, we can, if we will, and we must, keep the other great personal freedoms and their safeguards alive. Live free speech, free radio and free press are the heat that can thaw out any frozen liberties.

That there must be restraints upon speech and the press against information to the enemy needs no discussion. But there is left ample room to free speech and free press through pep-oratory and criticism of the conduct of the war. The only limit on pep speech, so far as I can see, is endurance of the audience. The use of free speech in criticism requires some limitations in war. Criticism is the higher art of protest. The vocal chords of democracy are well trained for this purpose. We start the practice of protest in the cradle and never let up.

LIMITATIONS ON CRITICISM OF THE CONDUCT OF THE WAR

And criticism of the conduct of the war is necessary if we are to win the war. We want the war conducted right. The margins between victory and defeat in our foreign campaigns are so narrow that if pressure groups are to take advantage of war to advance their interests, or if we make blunders, or keep incompetent men in office, or allow corruption, bad organization and bad strategy, they can bring about defeat. Democracy can correct mistakes only through public exposure and opposition to them.

The President has unbelievable burdens in war; he deserves

every support in this task. We cannot expect him to watch and direct the host of war agencies and officials that we must have to make war. The Congress and the people have to watch them.

The enemy may get mental comfort by reading these exposures and criticisms. But he will not get comfort from the remedy.

Nor should Congress or citizens be criticized for exposing mistakes and wrong-doing in the conduct of the war on the ground that such exposure lowers morale. It is not the action of the Congress in exposing these things that lowers morale; it is not the action of criticism by citizens that lowers it. It is the terrible stuff that is exposed which lowers morale. However, the confidence that there is a vigilant public opinion builds up morale.

But in these exposures and criticisms, we must remember that democracy is not created for war. It is not a war machine. It thrives only in peace. When it goes to war, it has to transform itself all over. In each of our wars the Administration has made many mistakes and had to find competent men by trial and error. The Administration must have time and a chance to create these new war organizations and for men to learn their strange duties. Nor should these incidents bring discouragement. We know that spiritual strength, intelligence and initiative inherent only in democracy finally make their arms irresistible in war.

Criticism of the conduct of the war may rightly lead to criticism of public officials. In a democracy even the President is not immune from rightful criticism. I ought to know something of the theory and practice of that subject. The President is not the spiritual head of the people. He is not sacrosanct like the Mikado. Patriotism is not devotion to a public servant. It is devotion to our country and its right aims.

No public servant can be free of criticism if democracy is to continue to live. But the first rule of criticism is that it must not take the form of personal detraction and abuse. We Americans have pioneered in the sadistic and higher art of abuse— that is smearing. The great officers who lead our people in war must have respect. We may not agree with them, but they are patriotic Americans, giving the utmost devotion to their tasks. The moral limitations on the liberty to smear should be increased drastically as a war measure.

Generally, there are three tests of criticism of the conduct of the war. That is, it should be decent; it should be directed to those things that hinder winning the war and that undermine free men in America both now and after the war.

I could say a good deal in criticism of the conduct of this war. But having been through one total war as a member of the American War Council, I know, probably better than most people, the difficulties of organizing democracy for total war. Although I have at times wanted to cry out yet knowing the time needed to overcome difficulties I have suppressed that craving. Nor am I going to criticize the conduct of the war now, although I may be permitted to grouse just a little between some constructive suggestions.

REFORMING DURING THE WAR

My first suggestion is that we adjourn trying to reform freedom and to make America over anew socially and economically during the war. This war is dangerous enough to require one single undeviating purpose on the part of the Government. Most of our social and economic gains will have gone by the board anyway, if this is a long war. After all, the great social gains of the last century were a mixture of liberty, compassion, unlimited sugar, automobiles and washing machines. These are at least getting scarcer.

There will be plenty of time to exercise the spirit of reform after the war is over. The world is passing into different forms and shapes which no man can foresee. The things to reform will be far different from what they now appear. Just now such efforts divert the energies of the government and the people, they dislocate war effort and above all they create a thousand frictions, a thousand controversies, suspicions and disintegrating currents which destroy unity in the people.

I have, however, felt that we must be philosophical on these questions, for every generation discovers the world and its tasks as being all new and strange to the human race. And it is a good thing that they do—or we would grow too old and lose our race vitality.

But I would like again to suggest that total war is not new. I venture the further idea that we generally have a little too much of the word New around about. In trying to get out of the age of misery imposed by the last world war we have somewhat overworked this word New. It has become a signpost to some easy way to escape.

We have had in the last 25 years the New Freedom, the New Day, the New Era, the New Outlook, the New Epoch, the New Economy, the New Dawn, the New Deal, the New Proposal and the New Liberty. I coined one of them myself, but a newer thing came along. Now we are fighting against Hitler's New Order and Tojo's New Asia. This war seems to revolve around the word New. The New Testament being often omitted.

That word applies better to physical things than to human forces. Indeed when the sun rises in the morning we hail it as a new day. We cheer the passing of the night. But it is a false analogy in the march of civilization. Our chores for the new day were assigned the night before. Our abilities to perform them were formed not only last year but over centuries or even geologic time. If the new day has no link with yesterday there will be chaos.

I wish sometimes we could change words once in a while. We might give some relief to the word New by substituting such ideas as advance, progress or recovery. They would not only connote forward movement but they would also connote that there were values in the past. They would connote stability instead of violence.

In any event, there is no need to take on the load of a new social and economic order in the middle of this dangerous stream. It does not help us to get across.

I will give you one of many instances of such added burdens. In the New tax bill there is a New proposal which most seriously affects our educational institutions and our public charities. That

New Proposal would ultimately undermine the independence of our great universities and colleges. It would render them dependent upon political subsidies. It will decrease the income of our hospitals and charities. In the meantime, it will make more war on the home front than it will pay for in foreign parts.

SOME EXCESSES AND PRIVATIONS IN FREE SPEECH

From the regions of the Past, I would like to make a constructive suggestion on both certain excesses and certain privations in free speech.

INTOLERANCE

A few years ago in speaking from experience in the first World War, to the students of one of our universities, I said:

"One of the emotions arising from that total war was rabid intolerance. National unity was essential in the face of national danger. But impatience of some people ran to intolerances which themselves brought limitations not only on free speech but on other liberties. The democratic governments did not need or did not want such violences. Intolerance did it."

Our histories of that war teem with regrets over those attitudes and proofs that intolerance brought many material and spiritual losses. And above all that intolerance did not contribute to national unity.

I suppose it is asking too much that we would profit by this experience of the last war. But today intolerance at the hands of some self-appointed persons and organizations has already, in five months, risen to great heights. Perhaps it is because the radio has multiplied the voices. Perhaps it is because the logic of the new intolerance is mostly made of name calling.

There are a number of varieties of intolerance. One cult undoubtedly believes that outside the obvious alien enemy agents and crackpots, who are in charge of the Attorney General, there is a great group of Americans somewhere in some dark corner who want defeat. I have not heard of a single sane American who wants defeat. They want victory.

But the national gunning for this phantasmagoria has taken in too much ground. The high priests of this cult have concluded that all those who were opposed to war before Pearl Harbor cannot possibly be patriotic Americans ever. Or at least they are under suspicion as being appeasers, compromisers, various obnoxious bipeds, reptiles, and Cliveden sets, Nazi sympathizers and Sixth Columnists. Yet 75 per cent of the American people were opposed to war before the attack on Pearl Harbor. Nevertheless this 75 per cent who are now in outer darkness are willingly sacrificing their sons, their brothers, their husbands, and they are working and paying without murmur. And no man can give a greater proof than this. Certainly he who offers his life for his country is not to be condemned as unpatriotic.

FREE SPEECH AND NATIONAL UNITY

But is all this name calling the way to national unity? To have unity we need the healing of our prewar differences, not this pouring of acid into the wounds.

However, as I have said, this war has naturally been discovered as new—so we must be philosophical at new discoveries in intolerance.

From a philosophical viewpoint, I would like to see the Sixth Columnists given a little more liberty. They are defined as the ones who discuss the war or speculate or even criticize in private conversation.

To a person who is reminiscent of American life, it would seem that particular restraint is too drastic. The American people have always been a debating society. They get immense satisfaction out of gossip. They always have views. They always speculate about events. They are profoundly anxious over the fate of their loved ones, and the welfare of their country. And all this cannot be stamped out of them by a hob-nailed heel. They will debate and speculate on this war around every corner grocery store, every logging camp, every machine shop, every family table, at every party, whether it serves beer or tea, lemonade or cocktails. Even if it is not specifically mentioned in the Constitution, it is part of Americans' inalienable right. All this is the stuff that makes free men. This is the way democracy resolves its problems. It is not sedition. It comes from concern to win the war and they ought to be allowed to grouse and gossip a little without being Sixth Columnists. That puts too great a weight on our national safety valve.

Nor does this create unity. Unity is not to be confused with uniformity. When uniformity comes we will have ceased to be free men. Those who would reduce us to a collection of parrots do not know the meaning of America. It is from our diversity that we sharpen our wits, gain in initiative and strength over regimented peoples. That is the whole distance between the spirit of America and the spirit of totalitarianism. We have Unity on the only issue that counts now.

After all, what counts in war is—are the people willing to fight and die for their country? Are they willing to suffer the greatest griefs that can come to people in the loss of loved ones? Are they willing to work and work and work to pay and pay until they are exhausted? The American people today are willing and doing just that.

ARTIFICIAL LIFTING OF OUR MORALE

And I would like a ticket to grouse a little over one other use of free speech. Just for mental comfort we could use a little less quantity of free speech in some particulars. Some of us are getting a little sensitive over having our morale artificially lifted. Especially more often than once a week. Our people can take defeat after defeat and keep at this job. Our people are not complacent or apathetic about this war; they are getting pretty mad at being told that they are unconcerned and that "this is war" as if they do not know it with aching hearts at every fireside.

We folks at home and our boys in the camps can take anything that comes in this war—and take it standing up—except being told our morale is too low.

OUR FOUR TASKS AND FOUR SUGGESTIONS

I have indicated we have four major tasks before the nation. We must win this war if we would preserve liberty. We must secure recovery after the war of our suspended liberties. We must secure lasting peace if liberty is to live. We must again be prepared to meet famine after the war is over if life is to be saved and peace preserved. I have four more suggestions to these ends.

ORGANIZATION TO WIN

First, to win the war we need develop the most effective organization of it. Before the last war ended there came out of the swamps of the war organization of all principal nations the same formation—the establishment of a National War Council. Every nation came to it—American, British, French, Italian and German.

In this present war the British, the Germans, the Russians, the Italians, and I expect the Japanese, have such Councils. I believe the time has come when America should have a more definite War Council embracing in its members the civilian heads of the great war agencies. It should sit directly with the President as many times a week as is necessary. Within such a body a vast amount of coordination, overlap, and conflicting policies, which are the inevitable consequence of war, could be planed out. Perhaps also it could detour a little of these reforms in liberty until after the war.

PREPAREDNESS FOR RECONSTRUCTION

Second. In the last war we made little advance preparation to cross the precipitous mountains of afterwar disorganization or of methods to recover the lost freedoms. We were then ignorant of what lay ahead. We know more about it this time. We need to think out economic reconstruction. We must think out the recovery of freedom. And that preparedness can come only from organized objective research and public debate. It must come from many sources and many places and not from the government alone. It is a safe area for vigorous speech.

PREPAREDNESS FOR PEACE MAKING

Third. The last time we did not prepare for peace-making. We were told: "Destroy the Kaiser first. Discuss peace afterwards." Today, again, it is "Hitler, Mussolini and Tojo must be first destroyed; we cannot discuss peace until that is done."

We went to the Peace Conference in 1919 animated by the loftiest and most disinterested ideals, but we were totally unprepared for the specific problems and the ambushes that had to be met at the peace table. We did not secure much peace.

There must be just as much preparedness for peace making as there is for war. And in many ways it is a more difficult job. Preparedness for war deals mostly with tangibles, men, guns, ships, planes, money, and with tactics and strategy. Preparedness for peace deals largely with intangibles, the setting up of moral, intellectual, economic and political forces over the whole world which will produce and hold peace.

Nor is this alone the job of the several government departments now engaged upon it. If we are to make a better job of the peace this time than last it will be because intelligent public discussion develops more ideas and better ideas and because a public understanding of the problems is prepared to accept the solutions made.

Fourth. Unless we are to see again the aftermath of the Thirty Years' War, when one-third of the people of Europe fell before the Horsemen of Famine and Pestilence, we must have preparedness, not alone in America, but in every surplus food producing country, and unless there be food there will be no foundation for peace.

FINALLY

And finally during the last war I ventured a paragraph which attained considerable circulation, and I may be pardoned for repeating it, although it does belong to a bygone age and no longer has the stamp of New. It was apropos of some folks who wanted more mortification of the flesh than even the war itself necessitates. And they become more depressing to cheer and mirth when they get time on the radio. I said then, "Go back to simple food, simple clothes, simple pleasures. Pray hard, work hard, sleep hard and play hard. Do it all courageously and cheerfully. We have a victory to win."

Today again we have a victory to win in war, in making peace and in restoration of freedom. And again as before it must be won by our united effort, by the heroism of our men in the field, and by the eternal vigilance of a free people.

Some Principles of Civilian Economic Organization in Total War

NEW YORK CITY

[December 3, 1942]

I PROPOSE to discuss some principles of civilian organization in modern war. In total war the first necessity is to put forth the maximum military strength. The only limitation on the size and equipment of military forces is the number of men that can be spared from the two jobs of producing arms and keeping the civilian population alive and the spirit strong on the home front. Obviously the utmost work, the energy, the talents of every adult civilian are involved.

Failure in organization and strategy on the home front may be as disastrous as failure in organization and strategy on the military front. To squeeze out the maximum armed men and supply them, the civilian population must be directed to the maximum production of necessities and reduction of non-essentials.

Those who participated in the sleepless nights and the sweaty days of organizing civilians in the First World War naturally look at the organization of this war somewhat through the spectacles of that experience. The organization of the last war was not perfect. It had to pioneer its problems without a previous World War to refer to. This war should be easier to organize than the last one by virtue of that experience and the lanterns it affords for dark places. Young men are needed for the administrative jobs of war. And each generation has to learn not to touch hot stoves and has generally to discover the world. If it did not believe its problems were new, and much greater than ever before, it would be a sign of decadence. And time makes us philosophical. For democracy moves by incessant trial and error.

Not as a criticism of the present organization, but as a compliment to the generation of Americans who organized the last war and who are now mostly passed beyond, I give you a statistic.

Seventeen months after passing the Conscription Act in that war 4,400,000 men were in arms, largely trained and largely equipped. About 2,000,000 of them were transported overseas. That war was organized by increasing the Federal civilian employees by about 435,000. It is now twenty-seven months since the Conscription Act of this war was passed. The present armed forces are about six million men. Less than one million are overseas. And we have increased the Federal civilian employees by over 2,000,000 to do the job in this war. I know the differences in the two situations, but there remains a residue of tribute to Americans now mostly passed beyond who have led their country in other periods of trial.

From our own experience and the experience of all other countries in the last war and from the experience of this war, we can distill some principles or policies of organization of civilians. I shall give here what I believe are sound conclusions from that experience. I do not offer them as criticism, but as recommendations for adoption where they have not been applied in this war.

Nor am I going to illustrate these principles by horrid consequences that have come from failure to adopt them or successes that have come when they have been followed. You can lay them up against your own many experiences with the war organization and test them out for yourselves.

(1) The first of these principles for democratic countries is that all civilian activities should be directed by civilians and

within limitations laid down by the legislative body. Otherwise we shall be a military dictatorship with all its implications.

(2) The second principle is that civilian activities must be directed by single-headed administrators. In every country in the last war—and in this war—the United States, Britain, France, and for that matter Germany, all boards, committees, or commissions proved a failure except in advisory or judicial functions. Especially in war do we need leadership, and leadership comes from individual men. That basis of organization is in fact inherent in our Federal Government itself. It is the experience of 150 years in the whole productive economy of the United States. We can no more administer civilian activities in war with a committee than we could direct a battle with a committee.

(3) The third principle is that all functions and authority in respect to a particular activity must be concentrated into the hands of one administrator. We can no more have an administrative job divided over several independent men than we could conduct a battle with several independent generals. The problems of production, distribution, conservation, and price fixing in any particular material are interlocked. The same single head must direct all these functions. Otherwise we have infinite confusion, conflicts, and waste. For instance the Munitions Administrator, whatever his title, must of course have many subadministrators, but each should have all the authority and all the functions that relate to his particular job. Likewise, there should be head administrators of food, labor, fuel, shipping, transportation, and finance, as well as the Secretaries of War and Navy.

(4) The head administrators of such major groups should comprise a War Council sitting directly with the President. Here alone the general economic and civilian policies should be determined, the conflicts and overlaps planed out, with the President present as the final umpire. There was a War Council or a War Cabinet in every principal nation in the last war. There is one in every principal nation in this war, except in the United States.

(5) The first civil necessity of total war is the maximum production of war essentials. Increased production is the best answer to shortage, and all the mechanisms of price and controlled distribution must be focused toward increasing production. If maximum production is to be secured, the high-cost producer must be brought into action. And, with drastic taxes on excess profits, the low-cost producer does not get away with anything consequential.

To secure maximum production there must be no rules of labor that restrict or retard effort or output beyond those which safeguard health.

(6) There are some principles or policies in assignment of manpower. We can better appraise our manpower if we calculate the male manpower available and assume that women can do the rest. There are certain jobs that only men can do. There are jobs that are beyond the physical strength of women. There are jobs that require long training and skill for which there is no time to train women. The number of males between 18 years and old age is a positive number and there is a considerable number who are unable to work. If we compute the males necessary to carry on the government, the professions, the farms, the transportation, the mines, the skilled crafts, and to fight, we shall find certain limitations on what we can do.

We have undertaken seven major jobs: To raise military forces; to equip them; to build transport ships and a navy; to fight a war overseas; to furnish our Allies with ships and arms; to furnish food to our Allies; and, finally, to support our own civilian population. We have to divide our available manpower among these fields. And we must choose which of these jobs we will give priority for the long-view winning of the war.

(7) The seventh principle relates to control of inflation and justice in distribution of short commodities. That involves price fixing, wage fixing, controlled distribution, conservation, and rationing, all of which are inherent in the administration of total war.

In general there are two methods of price fixing. The one is by fixing general price ceilings over retail and wholesale prices.

The other method is to fix prices of a given commodity or raw material at as near the source of production as possible and to regulate the subsequent percentage addition for processors and the mark-up for merchants. General price ceilings (or legal maximum prices as they were called in the last war) were tried out by every nation in that war and proved a failure. All nations came to the alternative method. Theoretically, if all prices were frozen before the economic structure was disrupted by war, they might work. But to fix them after war begins, with price and wage relations distorted, only leads to a million conflicts and confusions.

As war proceeds the confusion gets worse because of the constant shifts in production costs, transportation, and sources of supplies. Under these shifts generalized price ceilings either require constant bulges upward for special commodities, or require subsidies where they fail to cover costs. Subsidies come from the taxpayer. It is about the same thing in war economy, whether the citizen pays his money in taxes or in the small increase in price.

Another objection to general price ceilings is that they too often stifle and delay production, and they stimulate black markets. The subsidy phase offers large opportunity for blunder and favoritism. The alternative method is just as effective in retarding price rise; it avoids stifling of production; it is a lesser burden upon conduct of the trade; it is easier to police; it requires a far less number of government officials to police and direct it.

Fixing of wages is not wholly determinable by the cost of living. There enter into it the comparative wages in other trades. Otherwise men naturally drift to the highest-paid calling and production is stifled in the lower-paid industries. To freeze men to their jobs is a violation of the constitutional freedom of men from involuntary labor.

(8) The eighth principle of war organization is to do no more regulating than is necessary to attain the major objective. Fixing of prices is necessary only upon things that the Government uses or that comprise the essentials of the cost of living.

To the great mass of people 95 per cent of the cost of living lies in less than 40 staple raw materials. Price control starting near the source avoids a host of price fixing and policing of non-essentials.

(9) The ninth principle relates to the necessity to change from the normal bid and contract peace practice of Governmental purchases of commodities and services. That safeguard cannot be made universal in war. But a great measure of successful alternative was found in the system of allocations first developed in the last war. Where Government purchases or uses are from the existing industries, such as canned goods, steel, or copper, and a host of others, this system avoids a multitude of priorities and it sustains much small business.

(10) The tenth principle is to secure the enthusiastic co-operation of the civilians with the Government in order to mobilize their abilities, skill, and sacrifice with the least bureaucracy and force. A given industry will function infinitely better with an Advisory War Board to its Federal Administrator if it be elected by the industry itself. We can have confidence that leaders of a given industry when so organized and given responsibility will serve patriotically just as we can expect of government officials. The American people respond better to a statement of the need under the words "please" and "serve" than they do under the word *"verboten."*

(11) The eleventh principle applies to the concentration of every governmental energy upon winning the war. Reforms or making America over, no matter how attractive, cannot but dislocate the war effort. If we lose or delay the winning of the war, social gains will be scarce for a generation. If we win it, there will be plenty of time to reform our way of life. And there will be plenty to do.

(12) And, finally, a major principle is to organize all these activities so as to assure the return to economic and personal liberty the moment the war is over. Civilian war organization is economic Fascism itself, and if Democracy is to live these measures must be dissolved. In peace times we must think in terms of preparedness for war. Likewise in war times we must

think in terms of preparedness for peace—and of return to freedom.

Nor can I end without tribute to the men of this day who are struggling with these gigantic problems. Our civil officials are patriotic men. But they could function more effectively with a better foundation in organization in several spots. Industry is doing the magnificent job which only an industry born of free enterprise and directed by men who have risen by merit could do. The Army and the Navy are proving to have the full courage and skill of our race—and will prove that by victory in this war.

The Home Fronts and Global Strategy

Six Articles Appearing in Press
[January 11-16, 1943]

ARTICLE I

SO IMPORTANT is the home front of the enemy in its bearing on our military strategy that by its correct or incorrect appraisal the lives of hundreds of thousands of American boys might be saved or lost. And healthy home fronts in the United Nations are essential to win the war.

The strategy in global war is not solely a military question. In total war between great nations, the home front is, in many ways, as important as the military front. Wars can be lost or won on the home front. Germany lost the last war by exhaustion and collapse of the home front which weakened her army. France would have collapsed on the home front in the third year of that war had it not been for American support to the civilian population.

There have been explosions of Western civilization into world wars before but total war was new in 1914. Great nations in total war, in addition to military forces, now pit against each other their total resources, the total emotions, the skill, the sacrifice, the work of every adult civilian. It becomes a contest of strength, spirit and endurance of civilians against civilians, as well as between armies and navies. Today the only limitation on the size of the military forces is the number of men who can be spared from the two jobs of producing arms and supplies for the military front and keeping the civil population alive.

And total war is not alone combat between armed men. It is also war between armed men and civilians. Since the last total war the improved airplane and submarine have immensely increased the power of attack upon civil populations and their war efforts. The improved submarine through its intensified sinking of ships increases the power of blockade; the plane works to relieve and intensify it. The improved plane and the improved tank have increased the power of land offensive and made the blitz possible. On the other hand, the airplane has immensely increased the power of defense against invasion by sea, making it practically impregnable if the sea is wide enough or there are land-based planes enough. And the radio has increased the power of propaganda.

The United Nations have now closed iron rings around the European and the Asiatic Axis. But both of them still have tremendous powers of defense through their powerful armies with interior lines of communication and their air and submarine protection from overseas' invasion. Japan has, in addition, great naval strength.

With the occupation by the United Nations of bases in North Africa and the Pacific, with the growth of our naval, air and ground strength, the ring around them grows closer and closer. But for some time to come the war is obviously a war of aggressive attrition and the creation of conditions favorable for major combat blows. That attrition is just as vital on the home front as on the military front. And our powers of attrition and combat are increasing more rapidly than the Axis.

This process of wearing down the strength of their home fronts is not solely a matter of military attrition, through blockade, sinking of ships, or air attacks or even through propaganda. There are implacable internal forces which contribute.

Experience both in the last war and in this war shows that after a certain period steady economic degeneration sits in on the home fronts of all nations engaged in total war.

In the earlier years the military strength of each nation grows steadily. Production of arms increases. But at some stage, probably about two years, the military strength reaches its maximum size and from there on it diminishes. Likewise, at some point, industrial production reaches its zenith. Even more rapidly than armies waste away after their zenith, the industrial machinery, the resources and the productive capacity of the civilian population wear down.

On the home front of all nations, shortages in food and other consumption goods grow progressively due to diversion of manpower. Armed men consume more than when they were civilians. The people must work longer and longer hours at harder and heavier labor. Movement is restricted. Rationing, price and wage restrictions are inevitable. Regimentation becomes steadily more onerous and economic dictatorship grows increasingly as war goes on.

On the spiritual side grief stretches into every family; emotions become more fragile and intolerant; criticism, freedom of speech become more and more frozen.

All these forces are multiplied in civilians by terror of attack from the air and destruction of their industries.

In the end the multiplication of civilian hardships—in some degree universal to all nations—becomes a race between them toward exhaustion. The Germans are in the fourth year of war. We have had one year.

And in this race of exhaustion, the home front of the greatest staying power, of the greatest resources, of the greatest will to endure and fight is a vast support to the military arm. The weak home front becomes a disintegrating liability to its military arm. That was the case of the Allies versus the Central Powers in 1918.

ARTICLE II

GERMANY'S HOME FRONT

All is not well upon the German home front today. The blitz and terror which were to have won a short war have in a large sense failed. Germany has abandoned the hope that she can bring the war to a swift conclusion.

Warned by the collapse on the home front in World War I, the Germans this time made great preparations in expanded agriculture, in stored food, metals, textiles and in synthetic production of oil, rubber, explosives. Upon invasion of Norway, Holland, Belgium, Jugoslavia, France, Poland and the Ukraine she seized their accumulated stores.

In consequence of this advance preparation and this robbery, Germany was not substantially short of supplies during the first two years of the war. But she has consumed her stocks and there is much less to be taken from the invaded countries. The tide has now turned on the home front, and all the forces of internal degeneration are now in action.

By working millions of prisoners and imported labor they have kept up the bread, potato, and vegetable supplies. The so-called normal bread and cereal ration amounts to a rate of about 260 pounds per person per annum against the 200 pounds the American people eat.

But the story in meats and fats is far different. The blockade has greatly reduced her imports of vegetable and fish oils and feed for her animals. Her animal products have greatly diminished.

All calculations of meat and fat supplies are very involved, but the following represent an approximation and indicate the trend. In 1936 the Germans consumed at the rate of about 165 pounds of combined meats and fats of all kinds per person per annum. In 1939 the "normal" ration was at the rate of about 105 pounds, in 1940 about 91 pounds, in 1941 about 81 pounds and in 1942 it was about 70 pounds per annum. Hard workers get more. This does not indicate any substantial meat or fat supplies from the Ukraine.

At my direction after the last war, an investigation of the food experience during the war indicate that the present amount of fats in their ration is below the full health level to the ordinary consumer.

But equally important is the degeneration of practically all other supplies for civilian use, including clothing and coal. The people suffer from cold in winter. Overcrowding is adding its miseries.

The wear and tear on the railways and machine shops and their destruction by air attack are creating difficulties in transportation and manufacture. German manpower on the home front is weakening steadily despite forced labor from the occupied countries.

A work week of 60 hours is the minimum in factories compared to our average of under 44 hours. The workmen are feeling the pressure of overwork. She is making frantic efforts to secure skilled manpower from the occupied countries.

Mentally the people have retreated from confidence of victory and have fallen back upon resolutions of defense. They now realize that they are an island in a sea of 200,000,000 invaded and starving people who hate them with an irreparable bitterness. And thus the Germans know the dream of the new order in Europe has vanished. The terrors of aerial bombardment and the losses in battle are having a depressing effect upon the spirit of the people.

That the home front is far from contented is indicated by the Nazi fortifications of strategic buildings in preparation to quell civil disturbances and by the placement of Nazi generals in command of the armies over the older staff.

Further degeneration cannot be stopped. However, I do not believe the Germans will collapse again internally at the end of this their fourth winter in this war. But it is impossible for them to withstand indefinitely these pressures on the home front.

There is, however, at once a major reservation to this statement. Germany is still potent for offensive, and she is under tremendous pressures from the home front to break somewhere the ring which surrounds her. The only direction she can gain substantial relief for the home front is to the southeast. If her armies could effect junction with the Japanese in the Indian Ocean by defeat of the United Nations in Persia or Egypt and India, they could open a new economic area from which great relief would come—rubber, metals and oil. She could get food, particularly fats, fruit and sugar. She could lift her whole standard of living, and in such an event the home front would stiffen for an indefinite number of years.

ITALY'S HOME FRONT

The Italian armies have been so repeatedly defeated in Africa that they have long passed their zenith. Her navy has been beaten in every first-class encounter. Her submarines are not so effective as the Germans'. Her airmen have proved inferior. Like Rumania and Hungary she is only a military appendage to Germany.

Italy is suffering greatly from air raids and seems to have little resistance. She is short of many materials due to the blockade. In food, with a much lower normal standard of living, she is more nearly self-supporting than Germany. But with poor administration many of her people are suffering. She has no coal or oil except such as the Germans give to her. Her clothing is in bad shape from lack of textiles. The coming winter will be the worst she has experienced. Thus on the home front, Italy has degenerated more than Germany. Her zeal for this war has never been extravagant. It is weakening despite stiffening by German personnel. Attrition is likely to produce results on Italy sooner than upon Germany.

ARTICLE III

JAPAN'S HOME FRONT

Japan is an entirely different problem from the European Axis. Her home front at this time is the reverse of the European home fronts, for her civil population is very well supplied with necessities and generally in high spirits. She is still in the ascendent stages of total war.

Japan also differs from our European enemies on the military front. The European Axis is depending mainly upon land war for victory. Japan's ultimate destiny depends mainly upon sea warfare. Germany's conquests are over land, and Japan's are basically conquests over sea.

Japan with Manchuria is normally about self-supporting as to food. Her conquests have given her far more rubber, oil, tin, lead, zinc, copper and hardening metals, rice, and vegetable oils than she needs. She has a possible shortage in iron. Her people are far better off in standard of living than before Pearl Harbor.

The spirit of her people, depressed during some years by costly and inconclusive fighting in Asia, has been given a fresh impulse by apparent victory over the white races.

Her great weakness is that all her conquests are like beads on a string. And the string is her merchant marine and its air and naval protection. Through that alone can she, for the present, maintain her garrisons and her many supplies to support the home front. If that merchant ship lifeline should be cut by adequately based airplanes, all the southern arms of the octopus would be paralyzed.

The Japanese airplane, ship and tank output is not one-fourth what we can produce. Her ships, planes and men are under steady attrition from the British and ourselves. With every growth of our air and sea power and our advancing bases, this destruction becomes more severe. Merchant shipping is the Achilles' heel of her "co-prosperity order" in Asia. And if her sea transport be steadily crippled, she will start degeneration in munitions and raw materials on the home front.

THE HOME FRONTS IN OCCUPIED DEMOCRACIES

The Axis armies have overrun twelve independent democratic countries and part of Russia. Over 200,000,000 people have been ravished, their men murdered, their women and children starved. Many of these countries have always lived partly upon food and feed for their animals imported from overseas. As the result of the blockade, they have had to slaughter their animals down to those that could be fed. Their ground crops are decreasing. Their fertilizers have greatly diminished. Their agricultural machinery is run down. Each winter the food is less and less. Theirs is not food shortage. They are starving.

The "normal" ration of meats and fats combined in these countries ranges from two to four pounds per month. Compare this with the American consumption rate of about 20 pounds per month. I have a survey of a number of Belgian industrial areas which show that 35 per cent of the children are suffering from scurvy, rickets and tuberculosis. Most of the city schools are closed because the children are too weak to do their work. The mortality is appalling. The same stories come from other cities.

During the last eighteen months I have repeatedly insisted that the blockade should be opened to allow an experiment in supplies for their soup kitchens which feed the women, children and unemployed men. I proposed that the experiment should be conducted by the neutral governments of Europe after agreements with the Germans that both the imports and the native food should be unmolested and that the whole should be supervised by agents of these neutral nations.

Six months ago, under the pressures of the Turkish, Swedish and Swiss Governments, this plan was adopted for Greece. Greek lives are being saved, although the amounts are insufficient. Our State Department now reports that the Germans do not benefit and our Government encourages support to the Greek Committee. The arguments against my proposals have now proved to be wrong by the Greek experience.

Is there now any reason why the Swedes and Swiss should not be allowed also to save the children in Belgium, Holland, Norway and Poland? They are willing to undertake it; they have ships that cannot be placed in Allied war service. They can get food in South America. Most of the invaded countries have financial resources in the hands of their exiled governments to pay for this food.

The Germans can save their people from famine by surrender. These people are helpless.

Food for the small democracies has a bearing on the whole future of freedom. These people are the only centers in Europe of fidelity to democracy. It is not a pleasant prospect if they are to bring up a generation of children stunted in body and embittered in mind. Nor are promises of food after the war of much avail to people in the cemeteries.

Hitherto this has been considered a problem for British decision. But it is now also an American responsibility. And I dislike to contemplate the verdict of history upon our default in that prime foundation of Christianity—compassion.

ARTICLE IV

THE RUSSIAN HOME FRONT

When Russia was invaded she dropped the mental garments of Communist Internationalism and took on the fighting armor of nationalism. The Russian people rose as of old to defend the soil of Holy Russia. She still holds fast, after the loss of probably 5,000,000 soldiers, 70,000,000 of her population, with a considerable part of her industries and food sources. It is a magnificent defense by a people of unlimited courage. And now she bids fair not only to hold her segment of the ring but to even strike telling blows. From her untapped manpower and her vast hinterland, she will still be formidable in 1943.

Russia will suffer greatly on the home front. But with the spirit of nationalism reawakened, with the furious hates against an enemy on her own soil cruelly butchering her people, she will keep fighting. But she will need help in food, clothing and arms.

CHINA'S HOME FRONT

I have lived in China in years gone by. It is only in the last 25 years that she has developed a national spirit of independence. That spirit has been fiercely inflamed by the invasion of her soil and barbaric treatment of her people.

The living standards of the great mass of Chinese are always at bare subsistence level. Famine is the experience of every Chinese village. At present she cannot be reached with much-needed supplies of food or arms. Yet she holds half of her hinterland from the Japanese.

When we try to assess China's spirit, we must remember that Asiatic peoples are less sensitive to death and more stoic in misery than the Western people. The spiritual strength of their home front seems strong, but every possible help must be given to lessen her sufferings.

THE BRITISH HOME FRONT

For three years the British have made magnificent defensive war. They have lost many battles on the military front. Yet, with a nucleus of 65,000,000 white population, they have held their Empire of a half a billion people intact except for Burma, Malaya and the Chinese cities.

The Battle of Britain was the greatest home-front battle of history. They won by the greatest display of organization, magnificent courage and fortitude on the part of a civilian population that has ever been witnessed.

The people on the home front in Britain are the great heroes of this war. Despite air destruction they have reached the highest point in their industrial production.

In a military way the British Isles are now apparently safe from invasion by land. German tanks will never see Trafalgar Square. Her industries are turning out proportionately more materials than ours.

Britain's greatest problem is the submarine. Her survival on the home front depends upon convoys of materials and food from the United States. If her civil population can be protected from a degree of privation which might undermine its physical strength, they will fight endlessly. There can be no question of their determined spirit.

THE AMERICAN HOME FRONT

On our home front we are in a more favored position than our Allies in one great particular. The airplane has rendered the Atlantic and Pacific Oceans wider instead of narrower. No effective sea attack against the Western Hemisphere is now possible against adequate land-based planes and our navy. We need have no fear that enemy armies will march through the United States in this war. If we hold our outlying bases we do not need to fear the destruction of systematic air attacks. While we are discommoded, we do not need fear being starved out by submarine blockade.

Our task on the home front is different from that of any other nation in the war. We must not only raise large military forces, equip them and transport them overseas but we have an enormous further burden. We must furnish finance, food and munitions to the other United Nations. We must do this in the face of the Axis submarine blockade and the Japanese conquests, which reduce our normal supplies of many commodities from overseas. And we must support our civil population in such a fashion that their physical strength and spirit are not exhausted.

If we are to perform these tasks so as to get this war over without delay, we have no margins for the waste of blunders or mismanagement on our home front.

Our job is production, production and more production. And it is production of planes, ships and arms, and food right now, if the United Nations are to aggressively tighten the rings around the European and Asiatic Axis, and if we are to compel their continuing internal degeneration by effective attrition.

We could wish for better conduct and organization of our civilian front.

Our fighting forces have availed themselves of every experience and every lesson from World War I in building their organization. But these experiences and these lessons have been largely ignored and even repudiated on our civilian front.

All nations in that war, Britain, France, the United States, and even Germany—had to pioneer the way to total civilian organization. In the end, they all arrived at certain common principles of organization. Our initial and continuing mistake in this war was ignoring this experience and these principles.

Only in the past few months has their validity been recognized and only yet partially adopted.

ARTICLE V

AMERICAN HOME FRONT—CONTINUED

The first principle in organization of the home front distilled by all nations from the last war is that civilian activities must be directed by single-headed responsible administrators. The second principle is that all functions and authority in respect to a particular activity must be concentrated into the hands of one administrator. We can no more administer civilian activities in war with committees, boards or commissions than we can direct a battle with a committee. And we can no more have divided authority over one function than we can have independent generals in command of a battle.

Yet it was 19 months after we started large preparedness, before munitions was given a single head; it was over two years before oil, food, rubber and manpower were given single responsible administrators. There are still important executive functions under committee control. And of the administrators appointed, none of them have full control in their field.

The third principle is that the head administrators of such major groups should comprise a war council sitting directly with the President. Here alone the general economic and civilian policies should be determined, the conflicts and overlaps planned out with the President present as the final umpire.

There was a War Council or a War Cabinet in every principal nation in the last war. There is one in every principal nation in this war except in the United States.

There are other principles as to co-operation with the public and the trades, the methods of price-fixing, removal of labor, restraints on production, allocation of supplies, etc., in which hard-won experience has been ignored. That there is delay and confusion and enormous bureaucratic interference needs no proof. It lies all around the landscape.

There are some policies that should be determined at once by a National War Council. We have two bottlenecks; one is manpower and the other is ships. In view of these bottlenecks, certain home front policies suggest themselves for immediate determination. And they need be related to global strategy itself.

For instance, to carry on a war of aggressive attrition we need give full emphasis to fighting planes. They can mostly transport themselves. We will be short of ships for another year. To transport American armies overseas requires three times the tonnage that is required to arm and support the manpower of our Allies. We are endangering the food supply to ourselves and our Allies by excessive drafts of manpower from agriculture.

It is entirely possible that a realistic revaluation of our manpower, our bottlenecks and priorities in need would result in temporary release of soldiers already trained into producing food, ships and planes, or alternatively, in the import of Mexican labor for our farms and the lengthening of the work week in our shops.

A realistic revaluation of our whole economic home front would reenforce some conclusions as to military strategy which I suggest in my next article.

We must admit that so far our spiritual front in this war is not as united as it was in the last war. The weakness today is not complacency or apathy. There is a great deal of bewilderment and confusion of purposes.

This is contributed to by the confusion in administration; by criticism of the divergent ideological purposes of our Allies; by the lack of confidence in the news of the war; by tiresome repetition of radio propaganda; by exceeding powers granted by the Congress and by the widespread conviction that the purposes of our administration are not alone to win the war, but to use the war to change fundamentals of American life without submission to the people or their representatives.

Despite all this, the American people are united upon the defense of America from attack and are grimly determined to defeat the Germans and Japanese. I believe they are united upon securing lasting peace this time even if they have to use airplanes to garrison it. No enemy need believe because we exercise our blessed right to debate, discuss and differ between ourselves, that we are not united upon his defeat.

On the military front we have magnificently courageous sons. We can have every confidence in our Generals and Admirals. Men and officers alike are performing stupendous deeds. They merit everything we have got.

We have the blessing of huge industrial equipment and managerial initiative created in the mills of private enterprise. It is equipped with skilled workmen and farmers. Failures in administration interpret themselves in delay of the war; in unnecessary hardship on civilians and increased problems after the war. But we will win the war.

ARTICLE VI

The first deduction from this survey of the Home Front situations is that the degeneration upon European Axis home fronts will be continuous from now on. It will be disastrous unless they can break through the aggressive ring with which the United Nations have surrrounded them. The internal pressures on their home fronts are so great that if they are to have relief they must, through their enormous land strength, break the ring in some direction. Global war is full of surprises and no one can anticipate all that can happen.

The European Axis can apparently try in any one of four directions:

(a) Against Russia. The fanatical resistance of the Russians and their superb tactics in turning the cities into fortresses indicate that another great attack will so further increase the huge Axis losses as to finally weaken their whole military structure. The present advances of the Russians give every confidence that with support on their home front they cannot be overcome.

(b) Against Britain. Here they have to cross the water

against the enormously increasing British-American air and naval strength, and American-supported land defenses. This seems futile to attempt.

(c) Against Northwest Africa. Here again they have to cross the water. It seems unlikely that they can hold the bridge head in Tunis and Tripoli that they already possess. Even if they succeeded in holding it and extending their operations to include Spain, Gibraltar and Morocco there are no supplies in North Africa in amounts that would relieve their home front.

(d) Against the southwest, either through Greece, Crete and Syria, where again they have to cross water, or through Turkey, or through the Caucasus and Persia. In this the South-East movement alone, in conjunction with successful Japanese invasion of India, can the European Axis secure sufficient relief for the home front to assure long continuation of the war. With the full British-American occupation of North Africa and the Mediterranean route under possible protection, it would seem that such a movement could be stopped.

The degeneration upon the European Axis home fronts has another bearing upon military strategy. Their armies of six to seven million men behind their control of the whole European seaboard and with their interior lines are exceedingly powerful. They greatly exceed any land force that the United Nations could bring to bear in 1943. The European sea coasts have been enormously fortified. For the British and Americans to attack their central position on land, during 1943, will be a bloody business. On the other hand, if the Axis for some time yet be held within Europe and constantly compelled to guard this enormous coast line, the decay on their home fronts from internal degeneration, from shortages of supplies by blockade, and from aggressive attack from the air will weaken them enormously and their defeat less costly in life.

One conclusion seems certain. The European Axis military strength will be less in 1944 than in 1943. Ours will be greater in 1944 than in 1943. The European Axis home fronts will degenerate in 1943 and 1944 while the United Nations' home fronts grow in strength.

The whole Axis fabric will be much easier to crumple with blows on land later on. And there is the possibility that Italy, especially, may crumple up without the blows.

The Japanese home front is not under interior pressures as yet. They have aggression still within them. They might go in three directions:

(a) Against the United States. Their experience at the Coral Sea, Midway and Guadalcanal would seem to dampen any such notions.

(b) Further action against China to prevent the establishment of large air bases there by the Allies. Owing to enormous spaces they did not succeed in overwhelming China when they had only China for an enemy.

(c) Against Russia through Siberia. This would no doubt aid Germany, but in that case the Japanese will have the danger of terrible destruction on their home front from American air fleets via Alaska and Siberia. And an invasion of Siberia could bring no conclusive ending of her war with the United States and Britain.

(d) Against India in the hope of joining the Germans, moving to the Southeast. It would be some job to overrun India, but it is not to be discounted.

Japan's great weakness is merchant ships with which to keep her castle of conquests supplied and to bring products to her home front. She is today losing ships faster than she can build them.

In conclusion, the bearing upon military strategy of the progressive situation on the home fronts both of the United Nations and the European Axis at this moment, and probably for all 1943, seems to point to (a) aggressive sea and air attrition of the Axis; (b) tightening the ring around them; (c) extension of adequate bases for offensive action; (d) further building of American air, naval, land, merchant marine and food strength; (e) supplies to our Allies. The result should be undoubted weakening of the Axis, guaranteeing decisive blows against their central citadels later on without uncertainties and with the saving of enormous loss of lives.

Until the European situation is on the way to disposal the United Nations do not have sufficient naval and air forces to make direct attack upon the heart of the Japanese ring. With the European Axis disposed of or weakened the destiny of Japan is certain.

Food Production, Manpower, Machinery

Senate Committee on Appropriations

WASHINGTON, D. C.

[February 8, 1943]

THE American manpower problem involves the coordination of wide issues of global strategy and strategy for the conduct of our home front as well as our military front. If we attempt too much on the military side, we may commit the fatal error of overstrain on the home front and thus damage our effectiveness in ultimate victory. It seems to me there are three *immediate* factors in the problem.

FIRST FACTOR—THE HOME FRONT

There is a limit to our capacities and resources great as they are. And in our planning we must at least prepare for a long war. Including the defeat of Japan, we must envisage at least three more years of war and a prudent nation would possibly envisage five years.

With one year of war strains on the home front are already evident. We have impending decrease in production of meats and fats. Yet a great increase in this production is imperative if we are to support our own people without destructive hardship and at the same time support the home fronts in Britain and Russia. And beyond that to expand production to meet postwar famine. And if we do not do the latter, we will have no peace after victory. The definite assurance of manpower and machinery to agriculture must not even be second to ships and planes.

There are evidences of future decrease in the production of oil due to lack of advance drilling. We should increase instead of decrease or the whole war machine may be hurt. Similar strains are in metal production by insufficient labor for development work.

No one can doubt the strain in this program of one hundred billions annual war expenditure. To continue that rate at the present purchasing value of money over three or five years will make dangerous strains. Reduced to our proportionate populations we are spending 8 billion dollars to every 4½ billions of the British and every 4 billion of the Germans.

If we overdo these strains, we will find exhaustion and delays upon our home front. Total war is inevitably a race of exhaustion between nations. And we must make a strong finish.

SECOND FACTOR—THE WAR FRONT

The United Nations now have a ring around the European Axis and the Japanese. From these rings we are doing an effective job of aggressive attrition to their home fronts. Germany and Italy have passed their zenith and are steadily degenerating on both the military front and the home front. They will be weaker in 1943, and still weaker in 1944. Japan cannot grow stronger; she is losing more tonnage and planes than she can construct. Russia has demonstrated her ability to at least produce a stalemate on that military front, and with aid in food and materials from us, will do more. The British and ourselves are steadily growing stronger on the military front. Time runs in our favor in this war. We do not therefore need try to do everything all at once. The knockout blow to Germany can be delivered more certainly in 1944 than in 1943.

THIRD FACTOR—THE SHIPPING BOTTLENECK

But overriding any generalizations, we have for the next year, and possibly two years, a bottleneck upon our military front. That bottleneck is shipping, both freighters and tankers. It would seem that its limitations should be exhaustively investigated for it may present a controlling base from which many of these home front manpower questions may be determined.

The official statements are that submarine sinkings were such that we made no net gain in the United Nations' tonnage in 1942. During 1942 we transported about 1,000,000 men and their equipment overseas. Obviously, in this task and in supplying our Allies, we used our 1942 tonnage to the utmost as witness the necessity of almost dangerous reduction of our coastal movement of oil, imports of food, etc. In addition to transporting more men, additional tonnage must be devoted to furnishing supplies to every hundred thousand sent over.

Our enlarged shipbuilding in 1943 will exceed even the present rate of submarine sinking by an amount of freight and oil tonnage we can call X. With increased escort vessels and other methods, we will decrease sinkings and thus gain a further amount of tonnage in 1943 which we can call Y.

It seems to me it is possible to roughly estimate this X tonnage and this Y tonnage both in freighters and tankers. We know how much tonnage it takes to transport and service each additional million men. A rough schedule of the amount of men, equipment and supplies that can be transported month by month for 1943 and 1944 is possible for a minimum case based on X gain of tonnage and in the maximum case based upon Y tonnage.

The military authorities announce the intention to call 11,000,000 men to the armed forces by the end of 1943.

I do not have the full information upon which the shipping bottleneck can be estimated but from such information as I have, it does not seem that it is necessary to call up all of these

11,000,000 men in 1943 either to provide the men that can be shipping, or to be trained for 1944. Nor do we have to manufacture munitions faster than can pass the shipping bottleneck to our Allies and to our armies and to provide reserves against 1944.

Necessarily there were many unknown output factors in building production facilities and letting contracts for our munitions. We are probably producing more of some items of munitions than can be used by the men whom we can transport or that we can transport to our allies or provide reserves. If investigation develops such items, they could be slowed down, and both materials and labor devoted to other purposes, such as agriculture and mineral production. If this be the case, we can also probably greatly reduce the proposed expenditure for 1943.

THE THREE FACTORS ADDED

If we put all these three factors together of the obvious strains on the home front, that time runs in our favor in the war, the possible overfast production of some munitions, and the shipping bottleneck, it would seem at least warranted to study a revision of our whole program of national production and supply based on the bottleneck limitation. It is possible that this would reduce the financial as well as the mineral, the agricultural, the food and other home front strains. In any event we must have more labor in these fields if we are to maintain full national strength.

Such a program might not meet the views of the Generals or Admirals, who, of necessity, look only to the maximum military activity, but it is a serious consideration that we might break the back of our people on the home front and start internal degeneration, such as is now the fate of Germany. We should not imperil it by doing too much too fast. Especially when time runs in our favor.

A Typical New Deal Smear and Distortion

Report by Ralph H. Lutz, Professor of History, to Chancellor Ray Lyman Wilbur, Stanford University, California

[April 17, 1943]

IN NOVEMBER, 1942, and subsequently, former President Hoover gave the first and repeated warnings to the country of a dangerous food crisis unless there were reform in government organization and aid were given to the farmers in manpower, machinery and methods of price control.

On February 8th, at the request of the Senate Appropriations Committee, Mr. Hoover came to Washington and gave the Committee advice and views for meeting the growing problem. He presented constructive suggestions based upon his unparalleled experience in this field. He uttered no criticism of the Administration.

On February 23, Vice President Wallace made a statement, subsequently elaborated upon by Senator Green of Rhode Island on February 28th, which presumably originated in one of the prominent Administrative Departments. This statement was placed in the Congressional Record. It offered no solution of the food crisis but was a personal attack on Mr. Hoover based upon complete misrepresentation of a private memorandum of Mr. Hoover's, that was written 25 years ago in the previous world war. It was a discussion of shipping priorities at that time.

Senator Green must have known, or he should have known, when he spoke that he was stripping phrases and sentences from paragraphs of the original text, rearranging their continuity, omitting vital parts, and thus the historical meaning of Mr. Hoover's memorandum of 1917 was being altered. If Senator Green did not know, he could have found out.

After Senator Green spoke, President Wilbur of Stanford University asked Dr. Ralph Lutz, Professor of History at that University to examine the Senator's report in the light of the information in the War Library at Stanford and to report the facts.

On March 23rd, Senator Holman of Oregon, believing these misrepresentations should not stand uncorrected in the Congressional Record, offered Dr. Lutz's report for inclusion also. Senator Green took refuge in the Senatorial rules and objected to the refutation of his statements being officially recorded.

On March 28th, with hunger threatening the larger cities, President Roosevelt promised every one of Mr. Hoover's proposals—even those Senator Green had attacked.

The Republican National Committee considers it to be one of its functions, whenever it can, to expose such actions and such attacks against any Republican leader. It becomes the more important if decency is to be sustained in our public affairs and character assassination is not to be substituted for public discussion of vital issues. We therefore produce Dr. Lutz's report on Senator Green's statement.

This report also constitutes a contribution to the history of the last World War.

REPUBLICAN NATIONAL COMMITTEE

REPORT BY RALPH H. LUTZ, PROFESSOR OF HISTORY,

STANFORD UNIVERSITY

Dear President Wilbur:

In response to your request I have examined the statement of Senator Green of Rhode Island of February 28, 1943, so far as it refers to Former President Hoover. I have examined it in the light of the full information in the files of the War Library and I agree with you that such a distortion of American history should not stand uncorrected.

Senator Green's statement says:

"There are those who would so jeopardize the winning of the war by substituting their military judgment for that of the Combined Chiefs of Staff; who are willing to risk a protracted war or stalemate rather than take the steps necessary to mobilize ourselves for early and conclusive defeat of the enemy; who believe that we are not economically strong enough to wage total war on the same scale and at the same rate as our enemies. Foremost among these is the Honorable Herbert Hoover. He twice has attempted to predict the military future of the United States. . . . Once was on October 27, 1917, in a memorandum of which I have a copy. He did it again on February 8, 1943. . . . If the country had heeded his advice in 1917, it would have lost the first World War beyond peradventure of a doubt."

I deal with this statement in two parts. First is Mr. Hoover's press summary of February 8, 1943, and second his supposed memorandum of October 27, 1917.

PART I

MR. HOOVER'S STATEMENT OF FEBRUARY 8, 1943

The Senator to prove his assertions lifts paragraphs from the context of Mr. Hoover's statement in a manner that can be defended by no fair-minded person nor that gives any warranty for the Senator's assertions. For example:

1. Mr. Hoover stated that we were threatened with severe degeneration in agriculture, oil and metal production unless manpower and machinery be found for them. That is a public fact agreed to by all.

2. Mr. Hoover said there is a shipping bottleneck which limits the rate of shipment of men and materials abroad "for the next year and possibly two years." He suggested to the Senate Committee that the shipping bottleneck should be ex-

haustively investigated since it supplies the key to many of the homefront manpower questions. He said that, if it were found that men ready to go abroad or in training could not be sent for lack of ships, then the draft could be postponed for others who could be used in the manufacture of munitions and machinery and in argicultural and mineral production. He said that "it would at least seem warranted to study a revision of our whole program based upon the bottleneck limitation." He added that we should not imperil the war by doing too much too fast.

3. Mr. Hoover at *no* point suggested reduction of the ultimate size of our military forces.

No statement of his even remotely warrants: "risk protracted war or stalemate" or "not take the steps necessary to mobilize ourselves for early and conclusive defeat of the enemy" or belief that "we are not able to wage total war on the same scale and at the same rate as our enemies."

4. Mr. Hoover did not make an "attempt to predict the military future of the United States" except that we would win the war.

It is seldom in history that there has been so great a distortion of a public statement. The proof of distortion requires only the presentation of the entire document of February 8, 1943, with the sentences abstracted by Senator Green underlined which I attach to the Appendix.

PART II

THE SUPPOSED MEMORANDUM OF OCTOBER 27, 1917

Some days ago our Library staff reported that they could not find in our files the memorandum which Senator Green claimed had been written by Mr. Hoover to Colonel House in October, 1917. The memorandum was not in the general files, but I have found it among earlier materials in the confidential files with notes on the submarine losses and discussions with Amer-

ican and Allied leaders on shipping, food, and military operations.

DATE OF THE MEMORANDUM

The memorandum is undated. From the material in Mr.
Hoover's confidential files it is clear that the date was the end
of July and not in October, 1917, as purported by Senator
Green.

I have seen a copy of the typewritten memorandum in the
Edward M. House Collection in the Yale University Library.
It has no original date but is marked "Oct. 27, 1917," in Colonel House's handwriting. There is another memorandum in
our files which was sent on October 26, 1917, to Colonel House
at Magnolia, Massachusetts. This memorandum discusses food
and shipping problems and the appointment of Dr. Alonzo
Taylor as a member of the House Commission, then about to
depart for Europe. This document makes no reference to military questions. The original of this memorandum in the House
Collection is also marked "Oct. 27, 1917," in Colonel House's
handwriting. Such memoranda were usually sent by a secretary. Colonel House must have detached the covering notes at
some time and subsequently dated the memoranda himself. It
would not seem likely that Mr. Hoover would have written on
the same day two separate memoranda on food supplies and
transportation. In any event, the notes in Mr. Hoover's files
fix the real date of the memorandum quoted by Senator Green
as about the end of July, 1917.

There are numbers of memoranda between Hoover and
House, but the only other one referring to American military
action as related to food and shipping questions is of February,
1917, over two months before America entered the war.

QUESTIONS OF ETHICS

How did this memorandum of July, 1917, come into Senator Green's hands? It appears to have been supplied by the
custodian of the House Collection at Yale University to an offi-

cial of the War Department. Arthur Krock of the New York Times says: "(March 2, 1943) Since Mr. Green had the unlimited assistance of the War Department in preparing his report—in advance of the conclusions of the Senate Appropriations Committee . . ."

It certainly is not customary nor considered ethical for private memoranda to be published without the consent of the writer. As a matter of fact it probably is not legal to do so. This was acknowledged at least in respect to President Wilson's letters, which still remain confidential. President Lincoln's papers in the Manuscripts Division of the Library of Congress are still completely restricted. White House Correspondence of President Coolidge, also in this Manuscripts Division, will remain under seal for twenty years. *(cf. *The American Archivist*—January, 1943—p. 62.)

DISTORTION

The distortion of the whole meaning and intent of this memorandum is serious by the Senator's setting up of sentences and paragraphs for "comparative" purposes. It is true that the full text was attached to the Senator's "report," but it was the distorted version which was used in his discussion and conclusions.

(a) This memorandum of Mr. Hoover's is also given an entirely different meaning by part sentences and paragraphs lifted from the context and then rearranged as to their sequence. I attach the text of the original memorandum with the abstracted sentences underlined and the rearrangement of paragraphs indicated in the margin.

(b) This was a confidential memorandum from one government official to another. It was not a statement published to the world, or intended for publication. It represented the necessary day-to-day free thought between men of responsibilities. Its purpose was the suggestion of subjects for further discussion and consideration, as witness the phrases: "needs to be critically searched"—"I feel apprehensive"—"subject to revision"—"matter which commands attention"—"it should be seriously considered." The whole is written in obvious anxiety concerning our decisive victory in the war.

(c) The omission of the whole major premise of the memorandum in the Senator's version completely obscures the fact that this was a discussion of priorities in the decreasing available shipping as a result of the unrestricted submarine war not yet overcome. The opening paragraphs which were omitted were as follows:

"There are some phases of the international problem which impress me very strongly. The first is that the curtailment of food shipments from more remote markets is, in itself, a complete sign of decadent transportation and the narrowing volume of transport available to the whole of the Allied cause. Therefore, the whole transportation program needs to be critically searched from the point of view of the available shipping and its agreed priority use.

"It appears to me—

"*First*, that priority by all transportation must be given to the movement of food, and upon the inward movement to the various manufacturing nations of materials which form the foundations of munitions and the outward movement of these munitions to the front.

"*Second*, the movement of special services such as aeroplane forces, engineers, etc., across the Atlantic.

"I feel great apprehension that a proper coordination and statesmanlike handling of this whole situation does not permit of the third undertaking."

(d) Mr. Hoover goes on to say that the figures of shipping he possesses do not warrant any hope of such transportation of armies if future losses are allowed for, and adds controlling lines which Senator Green omits, that is, *"these figures are of course subject to more drastic revision as to the use to which ships are to be placed."* This refers to the use of ships to carry food and materials by the long voyages to the Southern Hemisphere. As a matter of fact, as shown later, it was this "drastic revision" in the use of ships which enabled the transport of American armies overseas.

(e) A further distortion is obvious in the sentence: "It

should be seriously considered as to whether we make any addition to armies in France" by the omission of the words "*except to the special services I have above referred to.*" (The air forces, engineers, etc.)

(f) A fairly typical distortion is in reference to possible excessive financial burden on the American people. The governing sentence is omitted wherein he says "The subject should have attention". . . .

MR. HOOVER GAVE AN ACCURATE PICTURE OF THE SITUATION
THEN EXISTING

What was the shipping and food situation when this memorandum was written? Now, twenty-five years after, with the inside facts available, and not influenced by oratory directed to scare the Germans, we can examine what the situation was which caused "apprehension" to Mr. Hoover and warranted his suggestion that there must be remedy to the shipping situation or no large army could be sent overseas. Mr. Hoover knew the inside facts. They were:

(a) The submarine sinkings, from the time we came into the war in April, 1917, until the end of July of that year when the memorandum was written, were over 2,700,000 tons, or nearly 700,000 tons per month. They continued to be very heavy until the following November when the American system of convoys began to have an effect. It was not until one year later that the total Allied construction became equal to the sinkings. The total American ship construction for the whole year 1917 was only equal to the sinking in the one month of April.

(b) The 1917 American grain crop had suffered great damage. There was not a bushel of wheat in stock or surplus beyond normal American consumption. Theoretically it looked as if the European Allies would need go the long journeys to the Southern Hemisphere for food. No one knew how much food Mr. Hoover could squeeze out of the scant supplies of the American people. And the British were adamant against diverting their tonnage to transporting a large American army upon the proposition that Mr. Hoover could produce the food. He did, however, soon begin large shipments, the total for the year after the crop failure being 160,000,000 bushels of bread-stuffs and over four billion pounds of meats, dairy products and fats. Thereby he himself greatly contributed to the remedy of the shipping situation. But all this was unknown when this memorandum was written, and the situation well warranted "apprehension."

(c) The British effectively controlled all world shipping except American and a few vessels in neutral ports for refuge. They controlled the French and Italian tonnage not only by the need of the French and Italians to borrow 2,000,000 tons from the British and they controlled neutral shipping also through bunker coal. For the first eleven months of our participation in the war, the British, in the face of the shipping situation, did not believe that any large American army could be transported to Europe. They wanted the American Navy, food and munitions. Until the military debacle in March, 1918, they did not believe such an army was necessary anyway. They repeatedly and continually refused any consequential tonnage for American Army transport. And no large American army could be transported without British-controlled ships.

(d) At the time war was declared in April, 1917, American officials had no notion of sending large armies to Europe. The whole idea was naval support, food, and munitions. It was not until the French Mission arrived in late April that the subject arose. Then only a "token" division was decided upon.

The whole story is amply clear from the statements of the principal American officers, Generals Pershing, Bliss, March, and Harbord, and are replete with confirmation of Mr. Hoover's "apprehensions."

General James G. Harbord says:

"In those April days of 1917, when French and British Missions descended upon Washington, our Government heard much of the desirability of sending to Europe thousands of laborers, railroad and otherwise, carpenters, miners, chauffeurs, foresters, nurses and doctors, and little about fighting troops. The military chief of the British Mission deprecated the prospect of an American army in France as making one more weakening joint in the Allied line. The French General Staff, as quoted from France, were 'not particularly interested in having American troops in France.' Marshal Joffre's principal staff officer thought it would be better if we gave money instead of men. The two Missions were a unit in believing we 'could not raise, train, and transport an army of sufficient size to have any effect in the European theater of war.' Marshal Joffre, however, asked for the immediate dispatch of one division to show the flag and added, 'It will cheer our people if you will send over some of your troops.'" *(America in the World War, pages 25-26.)

Major General Tasker H. Bliss said on May 28, 1917:

"General Pershing's expedition is being sent abroad on the urgent insistence of Marshal Joffre and the French Mission that a force, however small, be sent to produce a *moral effect*. We have yielded to this view, and a force is being sent *solely to produce a moral effect*. . . . Our General Staff had made no plan . . . for prompt dispatch of re-enforcements to General Pershing, nor the prompt dispatch of considerable forces to France." *(My Experience in the World War, Pershing, Volume I, page 78.)

There is little doubt that the formation of an American Army was not looked upon with favor by the Allies.

General Bliss again says, speaking of this time:

"There was no definite plan in any mission. Some individuals urged that what was wanted from the United States was not men, not an army, but money, food, munitions, supplies of all kinds; others said, send men, trained or untrained, and send them quickly; still others, send one small division to France to show the flag and inspire the hope that others will follow quickly, but then take a year, if need be, to train those others." *(The Evolution of the Unified Command in Foreign Affairs, Vol. I, Number 2, pp. 3-4, December 15, 1922.)

General Harbord again says:

". . . When General Pershing went to France not even the Allies believed that we should ever land and support an army of sufficient strength to be a factor in determining the war." *(*The American Expeditionary Forces, Its Organization and Accomplishments*, page 10.)

". . . The American public at first found our participation in the War almost as incomprehensible as it had found the original outbreak in 1914. . . . The Chairman of the Senate Appropriations Committee, Thomas S. Martin, of Virginia, dealing a few days later with greatly enlarged requests for appropriations in one of the supply departments of the Army, was astounded when told that the articles to be bought were intended for use in Europe. He said: 'Congress will not permit American soldiers to be sent to Europe.' " *(*The American Army in France, 1917-1919*, pages 17-18.)

On July 6, 1917, General Pershing cabled asking for 1,000,-000 men and urged that transportation be arranged with the European Allies. The General says:

"The question, in its finality, was therefore, one of sea transportation, but so far all efforts to get the Allies, especially the British, to consider giving help to bring over men and supplies had been futile. . . . They seemed to regard the transportation of an American Army overseas as entirely our affairs. This apparent indifference also gave further color to the suspicion that perhaps an American army as such was not wanted." *(Pershing, Vol. I, page 95.)

General Pershing again says, after a visit to London in this period:

"Underneath the surface of seeming cheerfulness there was more than a suggestion of serious apprehension. . . . It was easy to conclude that if the destruction of British shipping continued at that rate there would soon be none left either to help transport an American Army to Europe or to supply it after arrival. Under the circumstances, the apparent unconcern of the British as to our need of shipping is not difficult to understand. They were seriously alarmed regarding their own food situation." . (Vol. I, pages 54-55.)

It seems clear from the above that not only the British but General Pershing also had apprehensions identical with those of Mr. Hoover.

General Pershing further says, with reference to American assistance:

"I gave [to the Conference of Allied Military Leaders, July 26, 1917] in detail the situation. . . . A cablegram had just been received in response to mine of July 6th. . . . This message, indicating that the War Department foresaw small chance of securing the necessary tonnage, was read to the conference:

"By using all shipping which is now in sight for the purpose and which will be available after month of November, the plan proposes to transport to France by June 15, 1918, 21 divisions, . . . making a total of 634,975 men." . . .

"Although short of my recommendations, even this schedule could be carried out only by a large increase in tonnage. The other members of the conference were of the opinion that if new adjustments could be made, there might be shipping for nine or ten of our divisions before Spring." (About half of the 635,000.) *(Vol. I, page 118.)

"About this time (July, 1917) further disturbing reports were submitted to me . . . sent by Admiral Sims. They were based upon tonnage losses for May, June, and July, and seemed to confirm the conclusions of a month previous that there would soon be insufficient Allied shipping left to bring over an American army of the strength required and that the Allies (European) would find it difficult to keep up their supply of food from overseas and provide material necessary to carry on the war." *(Pershing, Vol. I, page 120.)

The hope was the convoys being inaugurated by the American Navy. Mr. Hoover had the same report from Admiral Sims.

General Pershing says (in the latter part of September, 1917):

"In conference . . . with Lord Derby, the British Minister of War, I was told that his Government could not be counted on to furnish us ships as transports." *(Vol. I, page 171.)

On October 11, 1917, as a consequence probably of General Pershing's urging, Balfour cabled House:

"England now considers it important to clearly state that she sees no possibility of carrying on her military and naval part in the war, transporting civilian and military supplies in British bottoms and continuing to furnish her [European] Allies with as many ships as in the past." *(House, *Intimate Papers*, Vol. III, p. 191.)

The conclusion is that England could give no ships. America must build her own.

General Pershing relates (November 18, 1917):

"Our estimate of tonnage required to transport and supply the twenty-four combat divisions and S. O. S. troops which it was considered essential to have in France by the end of June [1918] showed that the amount then allotted to us would have to be increased up to May by 2,000,000 tons. No one seemed to know where we were to obtain this additional shipping. It appeared certain then that should disaster befall the Allied armies under these conditions we would be left in an almost hopeless situation." *(Vol. I, page 242.)

The situation drifted on with constant British refusal to furnish consequential tonnage. By end-January, 1918, six months after Mr. Hoover's "memorandum" there were only about 150,000 American combat forces in France and in addition about 65,000 service troops.

Then came April 1, 1918. At this moment a great reversal took place in Allied attitudes on the question of transporting a large American Force to France. It was based partly on the critical military situation that had arisen, but partly on the demonstration that Mr. Hoover could furnish the food from the short journey to North America, and partly upon Admiral Sims' success with the convoy system in combatting the submarine danger.

The military situation and incidents of reversal of Allied policies are given by General Peyton C. March:

"The debacle of Russia in 1917, followed by the signing of a separate treaty of peace with Germany by the Bolsheviks on March 3, 1918, by Finland on March 4, 1918, and a preliminary treaty of peace by Rumania on March fifth, had released many German divisions from duty on the Eastern Front for service on the Western, so that Hindenburg was able to strike with a clear numerical superiority at that point.

The Allies at once turned to America, the only source of manpower left, to make up the deficiency. They were bled white and could put no more men on the firing line.

"The premiers of Britain and France, therefore, united in a cablegram to President Wilson [April 1, 1918] emphasizing the crisis which had arisen, and asking him to send to France, if possible, 120,000 men a month for four months.

"Every request [page 82] which we had hitherto made of the British Government for additional ships had been met with statements that all her ships were imperatively needed to bring food and supplies of all kinds not only for her armies in France, including Canadians, Australians; and others, but for civilian population at home; that they had rationed their people and had given us every available spare ship they had. Their losses from German submarines were set forth, and the impossibility of doing anything further in the way of furnishing us ships had been asserted and reasserted." *(*The Nation at War*, pages 79 and 82.)

MR. HOOVER'S PUBLIC ATTITUDE IN 1917

Mr. Hoover made very few public statements during the last war. Two quotations are enough to cover the period under discussion—that is, July, 1917. Mr. Hoover wrote in *The Independent*, New York, June 23, 1917, page 568:

"We must enter a period of sacrifice for our country and for democracy. *Many must go into battle* but many can only remain at home."

In the *Engineering and Mining Journal*, July 21, 1917, page 125, he said:

"We must adjust our minds to a long-continued war. . . . In order that we may contribute our share to this and to secure our ultimate objective, we must bring to bear every possible national resource. We have got to build ships to supply munitions and food, *and ultimately we will have to supply soldiers at the front to maintain the strength of the Allied ranks.*" (Italics are mine.)

A fitting conclusion to this recitation of events is an unpublished tribute in the files of the War Library:

"For Herbert Hoover, whose contribution to the success of the Allied Cause can hardly be overestimated. John J. Pershing."

OTHERS THAN MR. HOOVER HAD SERIOUS APPREHENSIONS ALSO

It may not be out of point to give a few instances of leaders, other than those already mentioned, who summed up the situation with as serious "apprehensions" as Mr. Hoover.

Franklin Delano Roosevelt, Assistant Secretary of the Navy, said at Speakers' Training Camp for Education in Patriotic Service at Chautauqua, July 7, 1917:

"I am a distinct optimist on the result of the war, but let me tell you it is an optimism that comes more from my heart than from my head; it is an optimism that we all have, that you can't down the American people.

"But when I weigh facts, when I weigh the difficulties of transporting our troops, our munitions, our grain, to the theater of the war, I am not quite so sure. The other day—on the Fourth of July morning —we woke up with the pleasant news that all of our first expeditionary force had been landed in France without the loss of a man—but do you realize how much the elements of luck came into that? You know that torpedoes were fired at our transports; you know that those torpedoes missed those transports by a very few feet, and it isn't doing the raven act, it isn't croaking, when I tell you that we are bound to have losses of transports, when I tell you we are going to have ships torpedoed, probably with troops on board; that we are going to lose munitions, going to lose grain, and we are going to have big casualty lists. Perhaps then the country as a whole will really have the war brought home to our own individual hearthstones, even though we may not have any of our own family at the front. We will have it brought home to us with full realization for the first time that we are at war. It is one of the penalties of war and it is one of the reasons that make me hesitate to say that I am an optimist because of my head. I wish I could tell you seriously enough so that you would take it home and think it over and stay awake all night thinking it over, that this German submarine campaign has not yet been solved; that we have not yet the means of stopping these sinkings. I would like to have you think over the fact that they are sinking a great many more ships, a great many more of our ships and the Allies' ships, every day than we can possibly build. Yes, and we haven't yet found an invention to take care of it." *(Patriotism Through Education Series No. 12, page 10.)

Paul Painlevé, French Minister of War, March-September, 1917, ended a telegram to the French Military Attaché at Washington with:

"A last paragraph which envisages 'the possibility of sending volunteer contingents to France. There should not be any question at present of preparing a considerable number of large units whose organization would be a long process and whose equipment would absorb the industrial resources which the Allies need.' But on the contrary, in view of the shortage of Allied man power and above all of French man power, 'it is desirable to send in a short time small units, companies, or battalions of volunteers as numerous as possible." In other words, one would ask America for men but not for an army." *(Lieutenant Colonel Jean Fabry: *Joffre et son destin,* pages 237-238.)

Frederick Palmer stated:

"I turn back to the records of late April and early May, 1917, illuminated by the memories of our officers. We learned how completely British methods of training differed from the French. Both Marshal Joffre and General Tom Bridges of the British Mission at first told our staff people that they realized that we could not raise, train and transport an army of sufficient size to have any effect in the European theater of war. The extent of our military aid would be a gesture to strengthen the morale of the people and the soldiers of the Allies. . . . It would make two more joints in the trench line, and it had been found that joints were always weak spots. . . .

"Colonel Fabre, of the French Mission, thought that we could contribute very little military support; instead, we should give our money." *(Newton D. Baker, *America at War,* Vol. I, 152-153.)

André Tardieu, French High Commissioner in the United States, 1916-1918, writes:

". . . When I assumed responsibility for it, I knew that even those in whose name I was acting had no faith in its success. My Government, in bidding me Godspeed, had said: 'Do the best you can.' Our generals had confided to me that they did not believe it possible to create a great American army in a few months. General Foch said: 'Send me American regiments to be incorporated in our brigades.' General Petain said: 'Recruit volunteers to fill up our losses.' Our Air Service said: 'Don't let the Americans try to build aeroplanes and motors. Let them specialize in raw materials and parts.' Every one looked upon the United States as a vast reservoir from which European forces and supplies could be fed. No one believed it capable of creating a new army to be added to those already in line. Every one believed it would be dangerous to make the attempt." *(France and America, page 218.)

Frederick Palmer further states:

"In the Baker files is a confidential report of a conversation with Colonel Johannet, Comptroller of the French War Department, in charge of the purchase and supplies in the United States, and with M. Bloch, representing the French Minister of Finance in the United States. This said that France primarily needed credit to purchase supplies, and then their prompt transport. An American army in France was deprecated. There were soldiers enough. Transporting an army would clog the transportation facilities and take away men needed in our fields and shops to produce supplies. Canada and Australia each had a hundred thousand trained and equipped men who were waiting for transport. England had a large number of men who had not seen service."

" 'As far as this country is concerned,' according to the report of the conversation, 'this should be a war af finances, supplies, and transportation, and the best protection we have against foreign aggression is the soldiers of France and England and the navies of the Allies, ably assisted by our own Navy.' " *(Newton D. Baker, 1, 108.)

Finally I quote from a published letter of Colonel House to President Wilson of March 19, 1917:

"Dear Governor:
. . . It has seemed to me that we should constitute ourselves a huge reservoir to supply the Allies with the things they most need. No one looks with favor upon our raising a large army at the moment, believing it would be better if we would permit volunteers to enlist in the Allied Armies." . . .

*(Intimate Papers of Colonel House, Vol. III, page 6.)

(Signed) RALPH H. LUTZ.

APPENDIX

The texts of the original MEMORANDA with the sentences abstracted by Senator Green underlined and his rearrangement of paragraphs indicated in the margin are as follows:

MEMORANDUM OF JULY, 1917

I feel great apprehension that a proper coordination and statesmanlike handling of this whole situation does not permit of the third undertaking. The figures which I possess on the available shipping in the world certainly do not bear any hope of such consummation if future losses are allowed for. These figures are, of course, subject to more drastic revision as to the use to which ships are being placed.

In the particular of the use of shipping for the movement of food, I want to impress upon you the critical necessity of moving food from the more remote markets in preference to the movement of armies. I feel apprehensive of a great danger overhanging this country, if we should place a million and a half men in the front, that the shipping left after they had been provided for will drive the Allied countries wholly to this market for their food supply, and that it may turn out over a lengthened period to be entirely insufficient.

In connection with this event, it is useless to sit like children and say that so long as our Army can be fed, all is well. We have absolutely to feed not only the Allied Armies, but the whole of their civil populations, or our Army may be enveloped in the social cataclysm in Europe and its retreat absolutely cut off.

There is another feature to this whole matter which I think commands attention. The drain upon the credits of this country is to my mind at present running to greater dimensions than the saving capacity of our people, and that we sooner or later must have relief from some portion of this charge.

2 { Furthermore, the assembling of millions of men under arms here is undermining the foundation of our productive capacity, and it is in our productivity of food and munitions that the safety of the world must rest. Therefore, I venture that from the point of view of proper conservation and use of the whole world's food supplies, of the maintenance of the proper productivity in munitions and their transport, and in the guardianship of our financial resources, that it should be seriously considered as to whether we should make any addition to the armies in France except to the special services that I have referred to.

5 { I have no right to speak from a military point of view, but two years of fairly active mind on both sides of the front have impressed me with the fact that if the western line is impregnable to five million men, it will be no more pregnable by the addition of another million.

5 { The problem is solely one of artillery action and thereby the attrition of Germans, of our ability to outlast in the food struggle, and in the use of the new aeroplane reinforcements.

6 { I feel that we are not in this war to create the glory of soldiers, but in the defense of the whole world, and that we should submit ourselves to the place as farmers and mechanics if it is necessary for us to do so in order that we should win.

Mr. Hoover's Press Statement at the Senate Hearings of February 8, 1943. The underlined sentences are those extracted by Senator Green.

"The American manpower problem involves the coordination of wide issues of global strategy and strategy for the conduct of our home front as well as our military front. If we attempt too much on the military side, we may commit the fatal error of over-strain on the home front and thus damage our effectiveness in ultimate victory. It seems to me there are three immediate factors in the problem.

"First Factor—The Home Front.

"There is a limit to our capacities and resources, great as they are. And in our planning we must at least prepare for a long war. Including the defeat of Japan, we must envisage at least three more years of war and a prudent nation would possibly envisage five years.

"With one year of war, strains on the home front are already evident. We have impending decrease in production of meats and fats. Yet a great increase in this production is imperative if we are to support our own people without destructive hardship and at the same time support the home fronts in Britain and Russia. And beyond that, to expand production to meet post-war famine. And if we do not do the latter, we will have no peace after victory. The definite assurance of manpower and machinery to agriculture must not even be second to ships and planes.

"There are evidences of future decrease in the production of oil due to lack of advance drilling. We should increase instead of decrease or the whole war machine may be hurt. Similar strains are in metal production by insufficient labor for development work.

"No one can doubt the strain in this program of one hundred billions annual war expenditure. To continue that rate at the present purchasing value of money over three or five years will make dangerous strains. Reduced to our proportionate populations we are spending 8 billion dollars to every $4\frac{1}{2}$ billions of the British and every 4 billions of the Germans.

"If we overdo these strains we will find exhaustion and delays upon our home front. Total war is inevitably a race of exhaustion between nations. And we must make a strong finish.

"Second Factor—The War Front.

"The United Nations now have a ring around the European Axis and the Japanese. From these rings we are doing an effective job of aggressive attrition to their home fronts. Germany and Italy have passed their zenith and are steadily degenerating on both the military front and the home front. They will be weaker in 1943 and still weaker in 1944. Japan cannot grow stronger. She is losing more tonnage and planes than she can construct. Russia has demonstrated her ability to at least produce a stalemate on that military front, and with aid in food and materials from us, will do more. The British and ourselves are steadily growing stronger on the military front. Time runs in our favor in this war. We do not therefore need try to do everything all at once. The knockout blow to Germany can be delivered more certainly in 1944 than in 1943.

"Third Factor—The Shipping Bottleneck.

"But overriding any generalizations, we have for the next year, and possibly two years, a bottleneck upon our military front. That bottleneck is shipping, both freighters and tankers. It would seem that its limitations should be exhaustively investigated for it may present a controlling base from which many of these home front manpower questions may be determined.

"The official statements are that submarine sinkings were such that we made no net gain in the United Nation's tonnage in 1942. During 1942 we transported about 1,000,000 men and their equipment overseas. Obviously, in this task and in supplying our Allies, we used our 1942 tonnage to the utmost as witness the necessity of almost dangerous reduction of our coastal movement of oil, imports of food, etc. In addition to transporting more men, additional tonnage must be devoted to furnishing supplies to every hundred thousand sent over.

"Our enlarged shipbuilding in 1943 will exceed even the present rate of submarine sinking by an amount of freight and oil tonnage we can call X. With increased escort vessels and other methods, we will decrease sinkings and thus gain a further amount of tonnage in 1943 which we can call Y.

"It seems to me it is possible to roughly estimate this X tonnage and this Y tonnage both in freighters and tankers. We know how much tonnage it takes to transport and service each additional million men. A rough schedule of the amount of men, equipment, and supplies that can be transported month by month for 1943 and 1944 is possible for a minimum case based upon X gain of tonnage and in the maximum case based upon Y tonnage.

"The military authorities announce the intention to call 11,000,000 men to the armed forces by the end of 1943.

"I do not have the full information upon which the shipping bottleneck can be estimated but from such information as I have, it does not seem that it is necessary to call up all of these 11,000,000 men in 1943 either to provide the men that can be shipped or to be trained for 1944. Nor do we have to manufacture munitions faster than can pass the shipping bottleneck to our Allies and to our armies and to provide reserves against 1944.

"Necessarily there were many unknown output factors in building production facilities and letting contracts for our munitions. We are probably producing more of some items of munitions than can be used by the men whom we can transport or that we can transport to our Allies or provide reserves. If investigation develops such items they could be slowed down, and both materials and labor devoted to other purposes, such as agriculture and mineral production. If this be the case, we can also probably greatly reduce the proposed expenditures for 1943.

"The Three Factors Added

"If we put all these three factors together of the obvious strains on the home front, that time runs in our favor in the war, the possible overfast production of some munitions, and the shipping bottleneck, it would seem at least warranted to study a revision of our whole program of national production and supply based on the bottleneck limitation. It is possible that this would reduce the financial as well as the mineral, the agricultural, the food and other home front strains. In any event we must have more labor in these fields if we are to maintain full national strength.

"Such a program might not meet the views of the Generals or Admirals, who, of necessity, look only to the maximum military activity, but it is a serious consideration that we might break the back of our people on the home front and start internal degeneration, such as is now the fate of Germany. We should not imperil it by doing too much too fast. Especially when time runs in our favor."

The 5th Freedom

The Rotarian

[April, 1943]

T HE President of the United States on January 6, 1942, stated that we seek "everywhere in the world" the four old freedoms: freedom of speech and expression, freedom of religion, freedom from fear, freedom from want.

Soon thereafter I called attention to the fact that there is a Fifth Freedom—economic freedom—without which none of the other four freedoms will be realized.

I have stated many times over the years that to be free, men must choose their jobs and callings, bargain for their own wages and salaries, save and provide by private property for their families and old age. And they must be free to engage in enterprise so long as each does not injure his fellowmen. And that requires laws to prevent abuse. And when I use the term "Fifth Freedom," I use it in this sense only, not in the sense of laissez faire or economic exploitation. Exploitation is the negation of freedom. The Fifth Freedom does not mean going back to abuses.

Laws to prevent men doing economic injury to their fellows were universal in civilized countries long before the first World War. In the United States, for example, the State and Federal Governments had established regulation of banks, railroads, utilities, coinage; prevention of combinations to restrain trade; government support to credit in times of stress; public works; tariffs; limitations on hours of labor and in other directions.

The key of such government action to economic freedom is that government must not destroy but promote freedom. When

Governments exert regulation of economic life, they must do so by definite statutory rules of conduct imposed by legislative bodies that all men may read as they run and in which they may have at all times the protection of the courts. No final judicial or legislative authority must be delegated to bureaucrats, or at once tyranny begins.

When Government violates these principles, it sooner or later weakens constitutional safeguards of personal liberty and representative government.

When Government goes into business in competition with citizens, bureaucracy always relies upon tyranny to win. And bureaucracy never develops that competence in management which comes from the mills of competition. Its conduct of business inevitably lowers the living standards of the people. Nor does bureaucracy ever discover or invent. A Millikan, Ford, or Edison never came from a bureaucracy.

And inherent in bureaucracy is the grasping spirit of more and more power. It always resents criticism and sooner or later begins directly or indirectly to limit free speech and free press. Intellectual and spiritual freedom will not long survive the passing of economic freedom. One of the illusions of our time is that we can have totalitarian economics and the personal freedoms. Ten nations on the Continent of Europe tried it and wound up with dictators and no liberty.

The first trench in the battle for the five freedoms is to maintain them in America. That rests upon fidelity not only to the letter, but to the spirit of constitutional government. Failure of Congress to assert its responsibilities or for the Executive to take steps beyond the authority of Congress is a direct destruction of the safeguards of freedom. We badly need a complete overhaul of our governmental relations to the Fifth Freedom if it is to be preserved.

The Fifth Freedom in no way inhibits social reforms and social advancement. In fact, it furnishes the increasing resources upon which such progress can be built. And itself flourishes upon the advancing social aspirations of our people. Social advancement was part of the whole American concept during the whole of our national life. The greatest of all social advances was free education. Next came concern for public health. We have always held it an obligation to prevent suffering from misfortune, to care for widows, orphans, and old age, and those upon whom disaster falls.

The methods have gradually improved from the ancient work-house, the asylum, and the county hospital to more systematic and more inclusive action. And that more inclusive action has only been possible with the growing wealth born from the Fifth Freedom. For many years in the United States our States and the nation have been gradually developing protection to children, to women, limitation of hours, and safeguards of health in industry. From these 48 laboratories we have seen the development of such actions as public health control, hospitalization, care of children, workmen's compensation, unemployment and health insurance, old-age, widows', and orphans' pensions. They are not new ideas. As we expand in these purposes, there are safeguards to liberty that can and must be preserved.

One of these safeguards is where personal insurance for any purpose is given by the Government it must be contributory. Even where subsidized by the Federal Government it should be administered by the States to limit the growth of centralized bureaucracy and political action.

Liberty has its greatest protection from local not centralized government.

Another concept in all social insurance or pensions must be that the responsibility of the people as a whole is to provide only a reasonable subsistence basis. Beyond that the citizen must look after himself if initiative and self-respect are to be maintained. Today our measures in these matters badly need vigorous overhauling to make them comport with these fundamental principles; to put them upon a "pay-as-you-go" basis; to make them inclusive of everybody; and to make them synchronize and not destroy private institutions and efforts.

A system devoted to development of individuality and personal freedom is a complicated business. It can destroy its own purposes by foolish action.

Today we are faced with the relation of personal liberty to total war. Our people must be mobilized for that immediate purpose.

We must sacrifice much economic freedom to win the war. That is economic Fascism, for Fascist economics were born of just these measures in the last war. But there are two vast differences in the application of this sort of economic system at the hands of democracies or at the hands of dictators. First, in democracies we strive to keep free speech, free press, free worship, trial by jury, and the other personal liberties alive. And, second, we want so to design our actions that these Fascist economic measures are not frozen into life, but shall thaw out after the war.

Even the temporary suspension of economic liberty creates grave dangers because liberty rapidly atrophies from disuse. Vested interests and vested habits grow around its restrictions. It would be a vain thing to fight the war and lose our own liberties. If we would have them return, we must hold furiously to the ideals of economic liberty. We must challenge every departure from them. There are just two tests: "Is this departure necessary to win the war?" "How are we going to restore these freedoms after the war?"

We have no right to complain of necessary sacrifices. Our soldiers and sailors are deprived of all their freedoms except the right to grouse a little. But they will expect their freedoms back when they come home.

Under the stress of reconstruction after the war, our liberties will be slow in coming back, but the essential thing in this sort of questions is the direction in which we travel. We must establish the direction now.

A Preliminary Program of Reconstruction

Collier's Magazine
[February 5, 1944]

WHEN these men, whom we fondly call boys, come back from the wars, what sort of a country will they find? What sort of a country do they want to live in?

They will, under the experience in this war, have increased individual initiative, dignity and skills. They are the self-reliant. They want the security and self-respect of a job, not a dole. They want to be free to choose their own jobs and to prove their own worth. They want the rewards of their own efforts. They want to be free to plan their own lives. They want to be free to undertake their own adventures.

They want the pleasure of creative work and the battle of competition. They want the joy of championing justice for the weak. They want to tell every evil person where he can go. They want a government that will keep the channels of opportunity open and equal. They want a government that keeps down economic abuse and crime. That is the social and economic climate they are looking for.

If I am right as to what these men will want, then we know our social and economic goal from the start.

We know that we must organize the Transition Period from war economy to a peace economy so as to rebuild an America of free men. And it is only from free men that the initiative of our people can be summoned to the effort necessary to overcome our difficulties. If we organize a Transition Period in such an economic and social climate, these homecoming men will rebuild a greater and finer America.

Unless the character of the social and economic climate is set at the beginning, no effective organization can be created and no organization can succeed. A clear determination of our objectives and the methods of attaining it becomes doubly important, for we have ardent groups in government and private life busy designing a frame of bureaucracy with a background of force and coercion for America. We have already a large number of Trojan Horses labelled falsely "Liberalism" and "Freedom" but whose insides are stuffed with a mixture of totalitarian economics, spiced up with special statistics. The very proposal of such plans from influential quarters produces exactly the economic climate which freezes individual initiative in our people.

We will have a hundred immense problems to overcome in the Transition Period. Demobilization both of armies and war workers, conversions, obsolescence and depreciation in our plants, debts, dangers of inflation and unemployment. And we shall have from the war new ideas, new inventions.

On balance in material things we shall be much poorer as the result of the war. There is no more cruel illusion than that war makes a people richer. The time it will take us to recover will depend on how much harder and more efficiently we are willing to organize and work.

It is possible in so short a space to deal with only few of these problems.

COOPERATION OF LABOR AND INDUSTRY

One of our oldest and most urgent problems in providing a right economic and social climate lies in the relation of industry and labor. The responsibility of labor is no less than the employer and the technician. Their fate is equally involved as is also the stockholder whose savings are in the business.

There are great fields of mutual interest. If we are to come through this Transition Period a better America, it will be from cultivation of such fields instead of the fields of conflict.

To expand production by every scientific discovery and every labor saving device is one of the fields of mutual interest. We cannot come through this post-war period to the Promised Land unless labor leaders use their immense power to remove all restrictions on the use of new devices and the effort of the individual worker that do not injure health and proper leisure.

It means constantly lowering the cost of living. It does not mean more speed up of workers, longer hours or lower wages. Its effect is just the reverse, as can be proved by our whole industrial history. Today, twenty men are employed in the garage to every one in the livery stable at double the wages and shorter hours.

There is mutual interest that business have a chance to make a profit. That is the proof that products commend themselves to the consumer. Without profit there are no advancing wage levels, no increase of capital, no increase in jobs.

It is to the interest of the employer as well as labor that labor have the right to organize, to negotiate and to enforce their bargaining. But the men coming home must have the free right to join the union or, alternately, we must have complete open shop and no fooling. The men coming home must not be excluded from a job.

And there is a mutual ground in recognition that labor is not a mass, not a commodity, but is made of individuals each with his own ambitions, urges and attitudes.

One of the claims of arm-chair intellectuals is that managers and labor are inherently at war. All of them—managers, technicians, workers and labor leaders—are specialists in their own fields. Efforts to create class division are the most insidious destruction of American life and the certain destruction of jobs and recovery.

Organized labor and employers have a mutual interest in keeping the government out of business or dictating to business. Labor should not be blind to the fact that trade unions are shorn of all real freedom when government becomes their employer or dictator.

There is a ground that neither the employer nor labor can occupy. Neither of them can for long dictate to the American people.

TAXES

After the war we shall need from 18 to 20 billion a year of Federal taxes to meet our debt, veterans' pensions, unemployment and other services of the Government.

There are two ways these Federal taxes can be secured. One, by inflation of prices and wages so that the national income in dollars rises and we are able to collect more dollars. This inflation route would be strewn with the destroyed savings of life work. The other route by which we preserve the savings of our people is by increasing the initiative, the efficiency and the productivity of America by every device known. By the production of more goods we can pay more taxes.

And one of the greatest of all fields in which the initiative of our people can be stimulated and the brakes taken off their energies and jobs created is in reform of taxation. I do not refer to war taxes although these are unnecessarily killing small business. Obviously we shall reduce taxes from war levels. But we need more than just horizontal reductions.

Long ago I suggested that our whole peace Federal tax system should be revised to accomplish definite social and economic objectives. To those who believe taxes should not be designed to promote economic or social objectives, I would remark that this Republic has been doing it ever since the first tax bill was signed by George Washington.

We need four consequences from taxes. We want revenue for the Government. We want no inheritance of great power either from money or birth. We want to protect savings for old age and we want reasonable protection to the family. We want the maximum of enterprise and production of our people.

Our major varieties of taxes are excise, luxury, estate, income, corporation and capital gains taxes. Excise and luxury taxes have least damaged the relation to initiative and stimulation of enterprise. We can well hold to high estate taxes in the upper brackets to secure revenue and at the same time prevent inheritance of economic power and the breeding of more playboys. We tried to eliminate them at one time by doing away with primogeniture. There is a stimulant, however, to the living by their efforts to provide in proper inheritance for protection to family and other dependents after death. And we have need to increase the exemptions and decrease the lower brackets.

Our greatest reconstruction problems in taxes lies in the corporation, income and capital gains tax fields. Herein lies the whole problem of savings against old age and for protection of the family. And in this category lies the major problem of the formation of capital to carry on the country and to make jobs.

At the beginning of all new production and distribution there must be "venture capital," for great risks must be taken in establishment of new inventions, new mines, new business of all kinds. Then there must be capital for expansion and jobs. Most of this capital arises from plowing back profits. As business gets bigger, it can secure capital from savings of the public. But these avenues are not open to the small businessman. He needs both relief and encouragement.

To assure reconstruction and expansion of jobs I suggest several directions of thinking in relation to income and corporation taxes.

First. Lower all income taxes and especially those in the middle and lower brackets. Restore the differential of lower taxes on earned incomes.

Second. To encourage "venture capital" we should take all taxes off all "capital gains" taxes. Such taxes stifle new enterprise.

I am aware that capital gains taxes were intended to take something from the market speculator. But he also has the right to deduct losses. His memory is better upon losses than profits. I have been long convinced that over a period of years the net to the Treasury from him is about nothing. This tax clogs desirable trade in real estate and securities. Its removal would aid men to secure capital to start small businesses. Otherwise we are driving the development of inventions, mines and venture business generally into the hands of the great corporation who can take on ten ventures and write off the losses on nine against the usual one winner and pay little or nothing. The small business man with his one enterprise is taxed if he wins.

Fourth. There are other directions in which small business could be helped. He often must have some outside capital to begin with. In consequence he usually has to form a corporation in order to limit the liability of those who supply his capital. They won't supply it and take the unlimited liability of partnerships. But the moment his business is put into corporate form he must pay double taxes. That is, he pays corporation taxes and then income tax on the balance, if any. If his business were a partnership, he would pay income taxes only.

Therefore, if corporations of a capital of, say less than one million dollars, and with, say less than a dozen stockholders, were allowed to pay taxes as a partnership it would avoid double taxation. And this is the more important because small business must grow from plowing in capital while big business can get it from the market.

Third. The corporation taxes will no doubt be decreased with peace. Today all corporation taxes constitute double taxation to those who save their money and invest in them. Moreover, it is a double tax that totally ignores "ability to pay." The widow with ten shares of stock pays the same rate as the person with a million shares. Corporation taxes should be drastically lowered and then the government should collect its needs from the income of the individual stockholders.

Be this as it may, I suggest that at once that the corporations should be allowed to set up tax-free reserves for reconversion and war obsolescence purposes. Otherwise manufacturers are not likely to have enough working capital to convert and make more jobs in the Transition Period. If after a term of years it was found that these reserves had not been used for the specified purposes, they could be returned to the original tax status.

Worth considering also is that all corporations should be

given a peace-time exemption from taxes on all capital plowed in to increase efficiency and to expand employment.

In many of these ways, and others, the small business, so sorely hurt by the war can be restored. Small business is the major employer of labor and the school for training in bigger business, the start of most new enterprise and the very home of individuality.

CANCELLATION OF WAR CONTRACTS

The first problem of Transition is liquidation of war contracts. With the enormous sums involved in these contracts the ability of industry to convert quickly to civilian production will depend on how rapidly they can get their working capital out of war production. Unless they get the money fast there will be millions of people needlessly out of jobs. To all concerns of financial responsibility the government should pay 95% of their claims over the counter and settle any mistakes afterwards.

BEGINNINGS OF CONVERSION

The timing of conversion does not need await until the complete ending of the war. Already producers of some raw materials are getting ahead of war requirements. We have some surpluses of copper, lead, zinc, tungsten, chrome, aluminum, magnesium, wool and some chemicals. However small the surpluses are, they should be quickly released for civilian purposes. That would especially aid the survival of small business. The war seems likely to end in Europe before the war with Japan. After Hitler is beaten we will have armed forces, munition workers, raw materials and shop capacity that can be released. We might reach some stage of return to plowshares before the defeat of Japan.

ABOLISHING REGULATION AND REDUCING BUREAUCRACY

Immediately when firing ceases Congress should set up a joint committee to liquidate war restrictions. There must be some authority wholly independent of bureaucrats to abolish them. No bureaucracy will ever abolish itself. Some restrictions can be relaxed after the defeat of Hitler and without waiting for that of Japan. Some restrictions will need to be gradually but firmly relaxed over the Transition Period. They cannot be relaxed until a supply of labor and goods overtakes demand if we are to retard inflation.

In this field of bureaucracy we must have drastic reform of that phase of government known as administrative law if men are to be free again. We must have regulation to prevent economic abuse. But gradually we have endowed these government commissions with all three powers of government. They combine the functions of legislator, executive prosecutor, judge and jury. And from many of them men do not have full appeal to the courts. Congress should do its duty and set up the rules of conduct so clearly that men can understand without a lawyer. The prosecutor must be separated from the judge. The citizen must have the right of full review of the courts.

DISPOSAL OF GOVERNMENT OWNED INDUSTRY

Except for those plants and raw material reserves needed for national defense the whole of Government war property, factories, land, raw materials and everything should be placed in the hands of a nonpartisan liquidation commission under requirement that government operations cease and all such facilities be disposed of back to the people.

The removal of the threat of government competition in the production of commodities and services must be the first step in restoring the economic and social climate where industry can operate.

In handling our government war plants there is an opportunity for a great step in national progress. The Government has a mass of new machine tools. Where adaptable, they should be used to replace the obsolete and worn out tools in every industry. The Government could well afford to trade new tools for old ones and sell the old ones in foreign trade. The war investment could thus fructify all production and could quickly repay the government losses by increased employment and taxes.

AGRICULTURE

Agriculture offers less immediate transition problems than industry. Due to the destruction in Europe the world is likely to be short of food and textiles for some years after the war. It will take time to restore their fertility, machinery and animals. People may do without gadgets but they cannot do without food and clothes. Thus our farmers are likely to have a foreign market for any surplus they produce for at least two years after the war.

After that several forces will operate, the sum of which is difficult to assess. The synthetic fibers will further invade the products of the land. The prewar surplus of farm products was partly due to gradual mechanization and thus less farm products consumed by animals. That transformation is about over and the increase in our human population will tend to produce a better balance. With wise protection we could increase our acreage of vegetable oils in substitution of imports and, likewise, our acreage of sugar. What the farmer badly needs in the long run are more crops for industrial uses instead of food.

In any event the farmer seems to be resolute on securing his independence from bureaucratic dictation and he will not likely be stopped.

FOREIGN TRADE

The first necessities for the development of foreign trade are stable currencies, abolition of governmental trading, cartels, quotas, and excessive tariffs.

The outlook in restoration of foreign trade is very obscure. It is obscure because we do not know the economic philosophy which will prevail in other parts of the world. We do not know how much the trade of foreign countries is going to be conducted by governments or by government fostered cartels. There will certainly be many cartels about it.

Except for relief, when governments engage in or direct the exchange of commodities then governments become the higglers in the market with other governments. And all the frictions of the market place and all the emotions of competition are transferred to Foreign Offices and become frictions between nations. It is the most dangerous of roads toward war.

Either government trading or cartels inevitably drive toward domination of domestic industry by the government. It means some sort of totalitarian economy. If a large part of the trade of other countries is to fall into these channels, we will need to set up many defense mechanisms if we are to preserve freedom in America.

Foreign countries should not count on American promises of gigantic post-war capital from the United States during our transition period beyond such credit as we can establish for the export of goods. We are going to be short of real capital for ourselves for some time.

MERCHANT MARINE

We are now getting over the hump of the submarine losses. We have been building crude cargo ships which will have little chance of competing with modern deisel-engine ships after the war. At the earliest possible moment we should change to the construction of the most modern cargo-liners, although they may take longer to build. Otherwise we Americans will not be able to hold our own in merchant marine.

AIR TRANSPORTATION

We will see a large development in air transport after the war. The improvement in the plane and the great stock of engines we will have on hand assure that a large part of the world's long distance passenger and express traffic will go by air. Heavy goods and local traffic will still be handled on the ground and on the sea. Nevertheless, the expansion of air transport will aid over the Transition Period. Much of such expansion will depend again on what the attitudes of governments may be toward international transport. There are jobs at stake.

MAKING JOBS

We will be faced with the demobilization of 30,000,000 people from the war effort.

But demobilization of the armed forces is not so titanic as some people think. Probably 75% of the men know exactly to what farm, to what firm, to what home they can return and get their own start in life. The veterans who need it should have jobs, vocational training; the injured and war dependents must be provided for.

A large number of the war workers will be absorbed by conversion back to civilian goods. Many of our women in war work will return to their homes. A healthy economic and social climate will produce a lot of new jobs. But there will be a margin left who must be looked after.

Our business associations through their national committees are making a great contribution in organization to take care of this marginal group. Their work represents statesmanship and courage. But these other controlling factors of taxes, liquidation of government property, abolition of bureaucracy, the revitalizing of freedom, and the economic climate will determine whether the business world will fail or succeed in this task.

GOVERNMENT JOBS

Government cannot find jobs of any great numbers, unless it is going to transform industry into a full socialized state. That could be done, but it means a standard of living about the present Russian level. And that level is as low as any city slum or any agricultural slum in our country.

The Government can make some jobs by public works.

But it is an illusion that government public works are a great remedy for unemployment in slack times. I was possibly the first to advocate their use for this purpose. It did help in the mild depressions of 1921 and 1930. But when we came to the deep depression of 1931, several new things turned up. The volume of useful permanent government works that can be instituted is a small proportion of the construction industries generally. Probably one billion dollars per annum of Federal works and another billion of State and local works could be inaugurated and might be a useful supplement to aid employment. But after all this would not represent more than 15% of the normal construction industries alone. We were spending about seven hundred million a year on Federal works in 1932 and the succeeding administration found they had to do boondoggling if they were to give substantial employment on this route. This is not the place to discuss the social and economic effects of those programs but their results were just as bad and much more expensive than direct relief administered by the local communities.

HOUSING

The segment of the construction industries to help across the Transition Period is housing. With some Federal grants in aid to municipalities and a lot of common sense and an enforcement of public health laws, we could really wipe out slums. But the Federal Government should get out of direct construction and management.

We could use tomorrow six million detached family houses of five rooms with gadgets. If labor would cooperate with the manufacturers and contractors so as to take restrictions off of erecting factory-built houses, if vicious municipal building codes manipulations were removed, and if credit were organized for home builders, it is the most certain of all aids to employment in the Transition Period.

Anybody ought to be able to buy a house on the installment plan as easily as an automobile. A set-up in the Home Loan Banks by which anybody could deposit 20% in government bonds, and then borrow the money necessary to build with repayments in installments over 20 years together with a removal of unnecessary restrictions would produce more jobs than all the public works in the nation several times over.

REAL SOCIAL SECURITY

If we are to have recovery from our losses and at the same time an increasing number of jobs and a rising standard of living, we must have a constantly expanding production of goods and services. We cannot secure this expansion unless we constantly invent new articles and new services and constantly decrease the cost of producing the older articles and services. Thereby more people can buy more things. But all this can come only from constantly increased efficiency. That is, more scientific research, new inventions, new labor-saving devices, new methods, new skills.

It means constructive competition must be maintained in order to make sure that decreased costs will be passed on in lower prices to the consumer. From that restless pillow of competition we will get more progress in economic life than from all the governmental action that can be dreamed up.

We must rid ourselves of the idea that there is any other real security for self-reliant people than a job and our own savings. Truly, through government, we must tide over a margin of self-reliant people who, through no fault of their own, cannot be at once fitted to jobs. And we must provide for the unfortunate and the aged. No American can be allowed to starve if he is willing to work. But we cannot make a great America on a concept that this is a chronic illness.

EXPERIENCE TO BE HAD FROM WORLD WAR I

We can gather some useful experience from the last war. It was the first total war. After that war we were pioneering these same difficult problems. Some of the difficulties were greater at that time, many of them were less than now. But we had then to grope through unexplored swamps and precipices of reconstruction with no light from previous experience. Out of those mistakes and successes there is much to learn.

The country then said, "We will return to normalcy." There is no such a thing as return to "normalcy" after such gigantic upheavals as total war. Our spiritual, moral, economic and political life will be changed in many directions. In any event, American life is vibrant with change from new ideas, advancing invention and scientific discovery. War speeds up these forces. But there are certain eternal principles of liberty, certain realisms in human behavior and certain economic experience which American life must adhere to or all recovery and progress will go onto a long night.

THE MORAL AND SPIRITUAL CLIMATE

We should pay attention to not only the experience with the economic aftermaths of the last war, but also to our experience in other fields. Between these two wars we have seen throughout the world an unparalleled slump into agnosticism, defeatism, intellectual dishonesty, growth of crime, the "debunking" of courage and decency, and ridicule of the very virtues which won the last war and must win this one—to say nothing of signs of the degradation of good taste. Fortunately this degeneration did not penetrate the great mass of our people, or we would not be winning this war. A climate of high moral standards are even more important to national progress than economic or social standards. Therefore, we have a job of regeneration of morals and of spirit in some quarters as well as economic reconstruction. However, this article is not a sermon and is mostly concerned with the economic problems of the Transition Period. Unless we succeed in rebuilding our economic foundations we have little hope of reaching these other vital goals.

Fortunately in America we have the best human material on earth to work with. Both from the natural selectivity of our immigration out of persons of initiative, and from the opportunities America gave succeeding generations we have the greatest proportion of self-starters of any nation. It was their driving spirit that made this country. It is to them we owe the highest standards of living ever attained by any country and at any time in history. They are the men fighting on the front, working our farms and moving planes, tanks and munitions from our factories. They are the people who can lift this country from the mire of war destruction if they are given a chance.

THE SOCIAL AND ECONOMIC CLIMATE

We should explore this question of economic and social climate further for that underlies the successful solution of all our problems. It is essential that we be realistic about the impulses in human beings that make the economic wheels go around in war and peace.

These dynamic forces which make for initiative, hard work and production lie deep below the surface in human behavior. They lie in a mixture of selfish and altruistic instincts. The self-interest impulses include acquisitiveness, ambition, rivalry, desire for glory and power. Fortunately, they are tempered with other and unselfish desires. The altruistic group of impulses comprise love of family and of country, compassion, desire to create, desire to be free, faith, and the mystical yearning for spiritual things.

In war, the altruistic impulses rise above all others and they mainly drive the economic machine. But regrettable as it may be, the self-interest group are the dominant drive force in peace.

It is this impulse that makes the difference in war. In war our people are willingly the servants of the State, but in peace they want the government to be the servant of the people.

Out of all these complex instincts and impulses, we must fashion our economic life. Even the squirrels have an acquisitive nature.

Whatever these impulses may be it is certain we cannot get the 100% initiative and productivity from our people in peace times unless they are unshackled in mind and spirit. And men cannot be free in mind and spirit if government is either to operate or dictate their economic life. Nor can we have a mixture of government operation and dictation. Economic life is interlocked in a myriad of impulses and deeds, the slowing down of any one of which affects a hundred others.

Freedom requires that government keep the channels of competition and opportunity open, prevent monopolies, economic abuse and domination.

PEACE

Above all contributions to a regenerative economic and social climate is the building of a lasting peace—and confidence that it will be rightly built.

These are by no means all of the backgrounds or methods needed to restore America. American life is not all tangible things. And we must demobilize many intangibles. We must repair many moral standards. We must restore faith. And for these things we need the aid of Almighty Providence.

Freedom in America and the World

CHICAGO, ILLINOIS

[*June 27, 1944*]

Delegates and guests of the Republican Convention:

W E MEET at a difficult time for a political convention. Millions of sons of both Republicans and Democrats are fighting and dying side by side for the freedom of mankind. But it is the part of freedom for which they fight that we should carry on at home. Nothing could be a greater shock to freedom than for us to suspend the national election or the soul-searching criticism which will make the more sure that the war will be won and freedom preserved.

Tonight I propose to speak to you upon some larger forces which are contending in this world convulsion. And the direction our country should take if freedom of men is to be preserved.

You will, I am sure, permit me to claim some personal experience with these larger forces which are today dominating mankind.

Like most of you coming from forebears to whom hard work was the price of existence, I worked with my hands for my daily bread. I have tasted the despair of fruitless search for a job. I have seen the problems of labor both as a workman and as a manager of industry. Long before the first world war professional work took me to many lands under many governments, both of free men and tyrannies. I dealt with the poverty and squalor of Asia and the frozen class barriers of Europe. I participated on behalf of my country in the first World War.

I saw the untold destruction and misery from that war. I dealt with famine among millions. I dealt with violence and revolution. I saw the degeneration and regeneration of nations. I saw intimately the making of the peace treaty of Versailles.

And in all those years of travel to every corner of the earth I landed a hundred times on the shores of my country. Every time it was with deep emotion and gratitude. Emotion, because here was the sanctuary of real freedom. Here was a land of opportunity; a land of wider-spread comfort; a land of greater kindliness; a land of self-reliance and self-respect among men. And gratitude, because I had been born in this land.

During another twelve years I was placed by my countrymen where I had to contend with peace and war and where I had to deal with the hurricanes of social and economic destruction which were its aftermaths. I have had to deal with explosion of Asiatic antagonism to the West. I have seen the rising tide of totalitarianism sweeping over the world.

Why do I recite all of this? Because the experience that has come to me, the honors that have been given to me demand of me, that I contribute whatever I can to preserve freedom in America and the world.

THE 170 YEARS OF STRUGGLE FOR FREEDOM

Over long periods the deep-rooted forces in the world move slowly. Then from accumulated pressures have come explosive periods with wars, convulsions, violent change and a train of stupendous problems. And always a part of the complex forces in these gigantic explosions has been the quest of man to be free.

The first of these gigantic explosions which was to shake the modern world began 170 years ago with the American War of Independence and the French Revolution. After those world wars there followed a hundred years of comparative peace in which the will to freedom spread widely over the earth.

Then came the gigantic explosion of the last World War.

Again among the forces in that convulsion was the death clash of free men and dictatorship.

Men inspired by freedom were victorious twenty-five years ago and freedom spread to additional millions of mankind. But victorious men failed to lay the foundations of lasting peace. And from the destruction of that world war came unemployment and poverty over the whole world. And in its wake also came instability of governments, lowering of morals, frustration of ideals and defeatism. Out of this desperate aftermath despotism rose again in the grim shapes of Fascism and Communism. By them the freedom of men was defeated over a large part of the earth.

Now we are in the midst of the greatest explosion in all the history of civilization. Again free men are fighting for the survival of human liberty.

FREEDOM PERMITS NO COMPROMISE IN THIS WAR

By whatever failures of statesmanship the world were brought to this ghastly second world war, the realistic fact is that we are in it. There is only one way out of war—that is, to win it. And victory will come again to our armies and fleets for the sons of America do not quit. By winning the war I mean absolute victory over the enemy armies. Any compromise with Hitler or Tojo will destroy all hope of either freedom or a lasting peace. That is our pledge to these thousands of our men who are dying in the islands of the Pacific and upon the fields of Italy and France.

We are fighting not alone for preservation of freedom, but also for the moral and spiritual foundations of civilization. And it is not alone these foundations under other parts of the world which concerns us today. We have need to look to our American house.

OUR MEN WANT FREEDOM WHEN THEY COME HOME

Recently a canvass was made among youth, both in the armed forces and on the home front, to learn what sort of a world they wanted after this war. I may tell you:

They want a home with a family, a dog and an automobile. They want the security and self-respect of a job. They want to be free to choose their own jobs and not to be ordered to them by a bureaucrat. They want to prove their own worth and have the rewards of their own efforts. They want to be free to plan their own lives. They want to be free to undertake their own adventures.

They want the pleasure of creative work. They want the joy of championing justice for the weak. They want to tell every evil person where he can go. They want a government that will keep down oppression whether from business or labor. They want a fair chance. They want peace in the world that their children never need go through the agonies and sacrifices they have themselves endured.

They want to be free Americans again. Unexpressed in all this there is deep in their souls a force that reaches back into a thousand generations. That is, the ceaseless yearning of human-kind to be free. Its advance is as sure as the movement of the stars in the universe. It is as real as the law of gravitation. It is as everlasting as the existence of God.

DEGENERATION OF FREEDOM IN THE UNITED STATES

At each of the great rallies of our party in 1936, in 1940 and today in 1944 I have been called to speak upon the encroachments and the dangers to freedom in our country. Each time I knew even before I spoke that our people would not believe that the impairment of freedom could happen here. Yet each subsequent four years has shown those warnings to have been too reserved, too cautious.

The reason why these warnings have been accurate is simple.

From the beginning the New Deal in a milder form has followed the tactics of European revolutions which have gone before. The direction being set, the destination is not difficult to foresee.

The violent forms of these European revolutions all have certain methods in common. They seek to destroy every safeguard of personal liberty and justice. Their method was to create centralized government and a single political party. Purge was their political weapon. Their economic system is regimentation through coercion by bureaucracy. Their faith is the negation of Christianity—that the end justifies the means. Their strategy is to make public opinion by falsehood and to destroy opposition by assassination of character through smearing.

Now I ask you a question. Do you recognize any similarity between these practices and the ten years of the New Deal?

Has not every distress, every sorrow, every fear of the people been used to further fasten some part of these totalitarian practices upon us?

With the blessing of the Attorney General, the Communists and the fellow travelers are spending vast sums to reelect this regime. Would they spend their money to support the freedom of men?

We all recognize that to win this war many liberties must temporarily be suspended at home. We have had to accept much dictatorship of bureaucracy. We must adopt some of the very practices against which we are fighting. In former wars we had no fear of such temporary suspension of liberty. Abraham Lincoln and Woodrow Wilson believed in freedom of men.

Long before the war, in an address on January 3, 1936, Mr. Roosevelt recounted how he had "built up new instruments of public power" which could "provide shackles for the liberties of the people" in any other hands. Freedom is not promoted by shackles in anybody's hands.

We now know the peace-time shackles they provided for the liberties of the people. They put shackles on our farmers. They put them on honest labor unions, on the freedom of workmen, on honest business enterprise. They have done more. These bureaucrats with these "instruments of power" fanned bitter hatreds between labor unions which divided the ranks of labor. And they fanned hate between employers and workmen. They built class conflict instead of national unity.

Can a regime which forged "shackles on the liberties of the people" in peace time be trusted to return freedom to the people from the shackles of war?

Our present rulers have now issued an abridged edition of the Bill of Rights and the other Constitutional guarantees of the citizens from oppression by government. They call the new version the Four Freedoms. The original edition, issued and perfected by the fathers, contains thirty freedoms, not four only. True freedom abides in the whole thirty. They have enriched the soil and the soul of this land for 170 years. Not one or four, but all of them together have brought the greatest advance in civilization in the history of mankind. In this time of crisis to freedom should we amend or abandon any of them?

The Constitution of the United States is a philosophy of government. It is not suspended even by war. But apparently some of these guarantees in our Constitution have not yet been approved by the O.P.A., the W.L.B., the N.L.R.B., the F.E.C., the F.C.C. and some other parts of the alphabet.

If you happen to get into the clutches of these agencies you will find a lot of the spirit of even the Magna Charta has been forgotten to say nothing of the Constitution. As an exercise in history you might read again some of those rights, such as, trial by jury; the right of appeal to the courts; just compensation for property taken for public use; the provisions against search and seizure, taking of property without due process of law and others.

These thirty freedoms guaranteed by the Constitution will survive only so long as their safeguards also survive. I need not remind you of the steady invasion of states rights; the packing of the courts; the dictation to Congress; the constant proof that executive officials arrogate unlawful authority.

Only by a change in administration will our returning soldiers find freedom preserved at home.

REGENERATION OF FREEDOM IN THE UNITED STATES

The price of freedom is not only vigilance as to rights and their safeguards. It also requires vision and action to keep freedom in step with social and economic change that would restrict it.

There is little real freedom for citizens, who, because of forces beyond their control, must go hungry, cold, sick or ignorant. From the very beginning the faith of America has been that we were our brother's keeper. In earlier time that responsibility was attended to by neighbors, by counties, by municipalities. Many years ago the state governments began to assume a larger part in these responsibilities. In recent years the Federal Government has assumed a part of the burden in education, public health and by various experiments in old age pensions and unemployment insurance. But if all these services are to bear the full fruit in freedom, they must be cleared of politics and discrimination. They must be placed upon expanded and firmer foundations.

For the past seventy years the American people have had to engage in battle for freedom on our own economic front. The fertile soil of freedom has grown gigantic business and labor organizations which have immensely increased our comfort and our standards of living.

The vast majority of both business and labor leaders are honest and patriotic. We cannot, however, permit even a small minority of arrogant and irresponsible business leaders to dominate the freedom of men through monopolies, unfair treatment of labor and manipulation of elections. Neither can we have even a small minority of arrogant and irresponsible labor leaders dominating the freedom of men, dictating who can have jobs and manipulating elections. The truly American concept is that we shall maintain freedom from such abuses by a government of law instead of by the whimsicalities of men or the regimentation of men. We do not need to burn down the house of freedom with the fires of totalitarianism to destroy a few rats.

An imperative problem in freedom is rising before us in the transition from war economy to peace economy. We must convert huge plants and find peacetime jobs in industry for thirty million men and women.

We must begin now to make the blueprints of this transition. But before the blueprints can even be commenced, the major question for America must be determined. That is, in what economic and social climate, under what sort of conditions is this transition to be made? Already the New Dealers have planned a large number of Trojan Horses labelled "Liberalism" and "Freedom" stuffed with a mixture of totalitarian economics and with doubtful statistics. The easiest task of government is to suppress individuals, subject them to bureaucracy and subsidize them to lean on governments—or a political party. If a government has enough power, it can always do that. The hard task of government, and the really liberal task, is to build self-reliance, stimulate initiative, and thereby create men and women of energy, of dignity and of independence. That is the motive power of America.

We will need every atom of this power in the nation, if we are quickly to convert from guns to plowshares in such fashion as to provide jobs and opportunity for all our people. That can never be had by bureaucratic curbing of initiative, class war, or any other mixture of this totalitarianism with freedom. The decision between these philosophies of government must be made now. For the plans must be established now. We cannot be without a peace program as we were without a preparedness program. We owe it to our fighting men that they find no delays in productive jobs.

Only by a change in administration will these gigantic problems be solved in a climate of freedom.

A WORLD IN WHICH FREEDOM CAN LIVE

We are faced already with the gigantic problems of making a peace where freedom can live. The world cannot go on like this. Science daily creates more dreadful weapons. Chivalry

and compassion have gone out of modern war. Women and
children are slaughtered and starved with the same ruthless-
ness as armed men. We cannot fail again in making peace that
sticks if civilization is to survive.

Already during this war we are making the mould in which
the new world will be cast. Some of these shapes are already
beginning to emerge.

1. It is obvious that the hot fires of nationalism are rising out
of the emotions of this war just as they do from every war.
The Communist internationalism of Russia has been driven out
by the nationalist aspiration to free Mother Russia and expand
the Empire. Other United Nations are demanding the independent resumption of their possessions. Mr. Churchill has
stated that he did not become His Majesty's Prime Minister to
preside over the liquidation of the British Empire. I am sure
that if the Republican Party comes to power it will not be to
liquidate either the economic welfare or the independence of
the United States.

2. It is obvious from the rise of nationalism that ideas of
world super-government, no matter how idealistic, are already
dead from these cold blasts of realism. Peace must be based
upon cooperation between independent sovereign nations.

3. It is obvious that three great dominant centers of power
will emerge from this war—that is, the United States, Great
Britain, Russia and possibly China as a fourth. And France
will someday return as a major power.

4. It is obvious that there must be some sort of world organization to preserve peace. It is proposed that, like the League
of Nations, it shall have a general assembly representing all
peaceful nations and a council in which the great centers of
power have a permanent part. If the general assembly is not
to be a mere debating society, it should be split into three divisions—one for Europe, one for Asia and one for the Western
Hemisphere. And each region should be given the primary responsibility for peace in its area before the central council is
called upon. Especially should that responsibility be imposed
on Europe where the dangers of world wars come from.

5. It is obvious that there must be a long transition period from war to stable peace. Before any organization to preserve peace can succeed, the foundations of political and economic reconstruction of the world must be laid in such a manner as to allay the causes of war. Unless these foundations are securely laid, any temple dedicated to preserving peace will be built upon sand. That was the disaster of the League of Nations. A good league has never cured a bad peace.

6. It is obvious that the great centers of power in Washington, London, and Moscow will dominate these vital political and economic settlements no matter what peace-preserving machinery is set up. Their approach to these settlements must be that of trustees for all nations not their selfish interests. They must not become a disguised military alliance or become the scene for power politics or balance of power. The whole history of the world is punctuated by the collapse of such methods into renewed wars.

7. It should be obvious that there can be no lasting peace unless the productivity of the world be restored. That can come only by exertion from within nations and from political settlements which give them a chance. The United States must furnish food to thousands of starving towns and cities ravaged by the enemy. We should have long since been feeding the undernourished children, for compassion is not dead in America. The United States can be helpful to all mankind, but it is certain we cannot finance a world W.P.A.

8. It is obvious the American people have but one purpose in this war. We want to live in peace. We do not want these horrors again. We want no territory except some Pacific island bases that will protect the United States. We want no domination over any nation. We want no indemnities. We want no special privileges.

But we do want the freedom of nations from the domination of others, call it by whatever name we will—liberation of peoples, self government or just restored sovereignty. We want it both in the cause of freedom and we want it because we know that there can be no lasting peace if enslaved peoples must ceaselessly strive and fight for freedom.

There are constants in the relations between nations that are more nearly to be found in their history, their surroundings, their ideals, their hearts, than in the declarations of their officials. Foreign relations are not sudden things created by books or speeches or banquets. The history of nations is more important than their oratory.

The ideal of freedom for other peoples lies deep in American history and the American heart. It did not arise from Woodrow Wilson's 14 Points nor from the Atlantic Charter. It was embedded in the hearts of the American people by the suffering and sacrifice with which they won their own independence. It was in response to the cry for liberation and freedom of peoples that we established the Monroe Doctrine, that we fought the Mexican War, the Spanish War, and the first World War. And now, after twenty years, we again sacrifice the sons of America to the call of freedom.

Without this spiritual impulse of freedom for others we would not have engaged in a single one of these wars. Had we not been concerned with the freedom of China, we would not have been attacked at Pearl Harbor. Only because freedom was in jeopardy in all Europe are we making this gigantic effort.

Therefore, the American people are not likely to welcome any settlements which do not include the independence of Poland as well as every other country which desires to be free from alien domination. Americans do not want this war to end in the restriction of freedom among nations. It is obvious that the United States will emerge from this war the strongest military, and thus political, power in the world. Our power to bring freedom to the world must not be frittered away.

SOME ROADS THAT DO NOT LEAD TO FREEDOM

During the past month Forrest Davis has published a circumstantial account of the Teheran Conference. It is said to have been authorized. It has not been denied. It relates to President Roosevelt's new peace method, called by him, The Great Design. A peace method under this same name, The Great Design, was proposed by Henry the Fourth, a French monarch, some 350 years ago. It has some similarities to Mr. Roosevelt's idea.

We are told Mr. Roosevelt had this Great Design in mind during his recent conference at Teheran.

So far as these published descriptions go this method is power politics and balance-of-power diplomacy. That is not the diplomacy of freedom. And worse still apparently the United States is to furnish the balance between Britain and Russia. If that be the case you may be sure that we will sooner or later gain the enmity of both of them. The basis of lasting peace for America must be friendship of nations not brokerage of power politics.

There may have been no political commitments at Teheran. But certainly since that Conference we have seen a series of independent actions by Russia which seem to be the negative of restored sovereignty to certain peoples. Certainly the Atlantic Charter has been sent to the hospital for major amputations of freedom among nations. The American people deserve a much fuller exposition of this Great Design.

And the Teheran Conference raises another question. Under our form of government the President cannot speak either for the Congress or the conclusions of American public opinion. The only way for America to succeed in foreign relations is by open declaration of policies. They must first have seasoned consideration and public understanding. These do not come by secret diplomacy. America cannot successfully bluff, intrigue or play the sordid game of power politics.

Nothing contributed more to the tragedy of Versailles than the suspicion and misunderstandings which arose when the heads of states sought to persuade and beguile each other in secret. Such unchecked bartering results in implications, deductions and appeasements will rise to plague us.

Direct Conferences by heads of State and their military leaders on military questions are useful. But under our institutions and our public opinion negotiation in political matters with our allies should be conducted by Secretaries of State. The President of the United States is far more influential delivering considered judgments from the White House. The voice from that pulpit is far more potent than any beguilement in private conversation in some foreign city, or any personal power diplomacy.

President Wilson also had a "great design" most of which was lost by the blandishments and pressures of personal negotiation. Every thinking American views with great apprehension a repetition of 1919. America needs a change in administration to get out of personal power diplomacy.

FREEDOM, THE JOB OF YOUTH

There is a force for freedom as old as life itself which will emerge with new vividness from the complexities of the times. Not only life but freedom itself must find regeneration from youth.

In every generation youth presses forward toward achievement. Each generation has the right to build its own world out of the materials of the past, cemented by the hopes of the future.

Older men declare war. But it is youth that must fight and die. And it is youth who must inherit the tribulation, the sorrow and the triumphs that are the aftermath of war.

This Convention is handing the leadership of the Republican Party to a new generation. And soon to support these younger men there will be an oncoming generation who will differ from all others. Twelve million young men matured far beyond their years under the supreme tests of war will be coming home. To them will be added the other millions of young men and women serving in the shops, on the farms and in the offices. They also, by the responsibilities they have shared, have had their minds and understanding advanced beyond their age. From the tremendous experience in this war this new generation will have grown in responsibility, in dignity, in initiative and skills.

And these young men who are offering their lives on the

beaches and in the mud, those who are fighting in the air, those who battle on the seas, will return to demand justification for their sacrifices and for the sacrifice of their buddies who have died. They will insist upon a reckoning and they will be stern and hardfaced. They will reject the easy language of politics, the straddlings and compromises, and the senseless phrases of skilled ghost-writers. And they will be watchful of political leaders lest they again be led into the giving of the blood and risking the future of their families from failures in international statesmanship. Today, more than any new generation that we have known, youth will demand a voice in its own destiny.

I rejoice that this is to be. Youth can bring the courage, the ideals and confidence which can erect a new society in America upon the debris of two world wars. We need their courage as never before.

We, the older generation, who have learned something of the great forces in the world, can advise and counsel. The issues are not new, and we can distill principles from the experience of the past. But youth must act and the past can never wholly point the way through the changing future.

And let me say this to the many younger Republicans in this Convention. On each election night, I read of able young Republican men and women who are chosen by their countrymen to positions of trust and eminence. I see men whom I have known since they cut their eye teeth in district politics, rise to state and city government, to the Congress, and to the Governorship in their state. From that I know that our party is a living institution recruiting from the oncoming generation its brilliant men and women and setting them to work for the good of our country. And it is through this living institution, the Republican Party, that I call upon the younger generations to take up the weapons for American liberty, to fight the good fight in the manner and according to the lights of their own time.

And may I say this to youth: You have a great material heritage. You are receiving millions of farms and homes built by your forebears. There have been prepared for you magnificent cities, great shops and industries. But you have even a greater heritage. That is a heritage of religious faith of morals and of liberty. There is no problem which confronts the nation that you cannot solve within this framework.

You in your own manner can lead our people away from the jungle of disorderly, cynical and bitter ideas, the topsy-turvy confusions, the hopelessness and lack of faith and defeatism that have haunted this nation over these dozen years. You can lead our nation back to unity of purpose again.

We of the older generation know that you will carry forward. We wish you to carry the torch bravely and aloft. Carry it with the dauntless assurance of your forebears who faced the chill of the ocean, the dangers of the forest and desert, the loneliness of the pioneer to build upon this continent a nation dedicated to justice and liberty and the dignity of the individual man. Watch over it. Vigilantly guard it. Protect it from foes, within and without. Make for this a sanctuary and dedicate it to God and all mankind.

Youth of the Republican Party! I, representing the generation of your fathers, greet you and send you forth crusaders for freedom which alone can come under a Constitutional Republic —a Constitutional America.

We who have lived long, turn our eyes upon your generation lovingly with hope, with prayer and with confidence for our country.

The Challenge to Free Men

LONG BEACH, CALIFORNIA

[*August 11, 1945*]

THE occasion today is dedicated to renewal of old acquaintances and recall of stories of happy days. Yet despite our will we cannot curtain from our minds the gigantic events which surround us. The specters of war and revolution stand behind every shoulder. They haunt every thought and our every word.

Today the fighting stage of the war is ending. We glory in the valor and courage of our Army, our Navy and our Air Force. They have performed their task. We now face the gigantic problems of peace. These problems have many visages —economic, moral and spiritual. They also involve the survival of freedom in the world. For freedom meets its greatest dangers from the aftermaths of war. Therefore may I on this festive occasion say a few sober and frank words upon the great decision that will confront us?

THE SWEEP OF COLLECTIVISM OVER THE WORLD

Today Communism and Creeping Socialism are sweeping over Eurpoe. They are beginning in Asia. The causes lie deep in the holocaust of misery from the war, from power politics, from the impulse for any change from the bitter years which have passed and from the years of propaganda of a new Utopia. A score of Fascist nations have shifted to Communism; and half a dozen nations once liberty-loving are shifting to Socialism.

The most recent chapter is the Socialist victory in Britain. Whatever the particular name of these European systems may be, whether it be Communism, Socialism or the decoy term Planned Economy, they are all Collectivist. They all have a common base in bureaucratic power over the liberties and economic life of the people. In the extreme form they leave little of free speech, free press, free assembly or independent justice. The less violent forms claim that government can dictate or operate economic life and still preserve personal liberty. But history shows over and over again that bureaucrats, to stay in power, and to enforce their ideas, must in the end dominate the making of laws, the press, the courts, and the police. Inevitably and invariably the totalitarian "liberals" find themselves whittling away the freedom of men. Their Utopia is a will-o'-the-wisp that leads implacably to the swamps of serfdom.

You have seen a form of collectivism in our own country. You are familiar with the pre-war growth of governmental power over our own citizens. To this are added the controls necessary to win the war. Have you not seen with your own eyes the flood of bureaucratic violations of liberty and the moral degeneration which comes with this collectivist process?

The Western Hemisphere is fast becoming the last hope of free men. We do not question the right of these other nations to decide for themselves. But equally we have a right to make our own decisions. And yet we shall be besieged by the missionaries, the propaganda, the Fifth Columns of these foreign bureaucracies. They are militant faiths that will seek to preserve themselves at home by expanding their ideas abroad, through poisoning our waters of free speech by their propaganda.

There are persons who talk of the middle of the road. The middle between what? Fascism? Communism? Socialism? Thinking American people are allergic to all of them. We should have none of them.

THE AMERICAN SYSTEM OF FREEDOM

Indeed the time has come when America should again proclaim our faith. We should proclaim our resolution to hold it. We should cease to apologize for it. Our first post-war purpose should be to restore it.

The American system of life is unique in the world. We made it. It started as a revolt against the curbing and suppression of the inalienable rights of men by the State. Our structure of government, our political, social and economic ideals and practices have, in all these centuries, been a vigilant defense of these rights against the power of the State, the power to use force, to enslave.

As we have over these three centuries built the American System from things of the spirit, it is not easy to define. The American way acknowledges the Fatherhood of God, the dignity of man. It knows no rank, no caste, no exclusions. It recognizes man's right to personality, to freedom of choice, to freedom of will and judgment; the right to think, to believe, to have faith, to dream, to speak, write. It insists that these inalienable freedoms of mind and spirit come from the Creator Himself, not from the state. It is the duty of the state to protect these rights, not to coerce them.

Our American system also holds to economic freedom. We hold that every man shall be free to choose his own job, plan his own life, to own his own home, his farm or his business, free to save for his old age and his children, secure in his savings. We hold that men shall be free and equal to adventure, to enterprise, to compete so long as they do not injure their fellows. The true American system brooks neither tyranny of bureaucracy nor tyranny of business. We do not defend economic freedom because of profit and greed. We defend it because we know that without economic freedom all the freedoms of mind and spirit will perish.

And we know that discovery, invention, competition and skills can never come from government officials. They come alone from the initiative of free men. We have proved the American system by raising the standards of life higher than any nation on earth. We have proved its power by winning the greatest war in history.

Our system has faults. It has lagged at times in discipline of business tyranny. It has lagged at times in provision for the unfortunate, the unemployed and the ill, although it has done more for them than any other system in the world. And their needs can be supported only from the productivity that arises from the initiative of free men and women. In any event reform and progress can come alone from free men.

If it be "reactionary" to be for free men then I shall be proud of that title for my remaining days. As a matter of fact it is the only genuine Liberalism.

BRITISH SOCIALISM

The British Socialist program should bring home to the American people that this is no academic question. While their program is a creeping socialism, their platform has been stated time and again—as ultimately to take over by the government "all the instrumentalities of production and distribution including the nationalization of the land." Whether the nation which was the mother of liberty in the Western world will take over for the government the title to every farm, every home, every business, and reduce every citizen to a servant of the government remains to be seen. But do you want to start on the impoverishment and servitude of such a system?

WE MUST PROCLAIM FREE MEN

We should proclaim again and again that the road to free men and to progress and prosperity is not to be found in the spread of governmental powers and bureaucracy, but in striving to set bounds to it. For these are principles of life from which no American dare depart, whatever the exigencies or even fears of the moment.

Today fifteen million boys have joined the armed services. They have gone into battle gladly and with courage because they believed they were preserving America for free men. A million have been wounded or have died that America may be free. Those who survive look to a return to the free America they have known.

I say to you that for three centuries, from Plymouth Rock to this very day, the American Way has moved men to deeds of daring, of unimaginable bravery. They crossed a perilous ocean for it; they traversed the desert and fought men and beasts for it; they labored and dreamed and invented and sweated and bled for it. They have fought four great wars for it.

Is it not a faith? Is it not a belief for which men die? Is freedom to be defeated by slogans, or foreign propaganda, or Fifth Columns? You and I must not be marked as the generation who surrendered the heritage of America.

PART III

ORGANIZATION OF THE FOOD FRONT
AND RELIEF

Organization for Food Supply

Farm Journal and Farmer's Wife

[December, 1942]

To the Editor, The Farm Journal:

I HAVE your request that I express my views upon the question now under discussion of a Food Administrator for this war.

At the outset, I may say I deem it imperative, in order to secure the maximum production and justice to the farmer as well as the consumer, that in this war the Secretary of Agriculture should be made Food Administrator.

The best service to the consumer in a food shortage is more and more production. Reduction in consumption comes second.

While our grain supplies are ample, there must be unified and strong action if supplies of meats, dairy products and fats generally are to be maintained in ample quantities to feed our own people, to feed the Allies, and to meet the extra demands of our men in uniform and of our munitions workers.

Our problems are, of course, increased by shortage of shipping and Japanese conquests, which combine to reduce materially our imports of vegetable oils, sugar and coffee. The most critical problem is animal products and vegetable oils. In the present world situation their greatly increased production is as imperative a munition of war as are guns and ships.

About a year ago I advised the Senate Committee on Banking and Currency that the functions of production, distribution, governmental purchases, prices, and rationing of food cannot be conducted under separate commands without confusion and disaster. The lack of co-ordination and the conflict between government bureaus are now limiting, and will even reduce, rather than increase, our animal products.

This division of authority and the consequent conflicts are apparent enough. At the present time the agencies under the Department of Agriculture control production policies, make purchases for the Surplus Commodity Corporation, and Lend-Lease, administer the farm guarantees, the floors and loans which affect farm prices. The Office of Price Administration fixes retail prices and makes the reduction in consumption through prevention of waste and rationing. The regulation of processors and dealers in food is now partly under the Department of Agriculture and partly under the OPA. The War Production Board, through its requirements committee, apparently determines the needs of the Allies, and also formulates some production policies. That Board controls the production of farm machinery. The Army and the Navy independently compete in the markets for their supplies. The Draft Director and the War Manpower authorities are, in effect, determining the labor supply of agriculture. The Federal Employment Service of the Labor Department and the Farm Security Administration of the Department of Agriculture are competing with each other in recruiting labor for farms. The Board of Economic Warfare apparently determines import questions in relation to food. The Economic Stabilization Office also determines policies that affect food supply.

Thus a squeeze of the farmer has been going on for some months between the price systems of the Department of Agriculture and the OPA and competitive buying by other government agencies, which has resulted in reducing the fattening of cattle on the feed farms, in sending less proportion of prime cattle into market, and these of lower average weight than last year.

The conflicts of manpower policies, by forcing wages up and draining men from the farms, are compelling farmers to sell dairy cattle. The proof is the widespread auctions and the greatly increased percentage of female cattle sent to slaughter.

Another of the consequences is that the increase which was hoped for from the admirable hog production program of the Department of Agriculture has so far been disappointing.

From these situations, and the extra demand of our allies and soldier for supplies, severe shortages are already developing. In addition, considerable ground crops are going unharvested in the southwest for lack of labor. Of even more importance, without immediate assurance of labor many regions will plant less next year. The first answer is more production.

No Food Administrator can hope to succeed unless he administers (a) production policies (as that is the major solution); (b) farm price policies (because they affect production); (c) wholesale and retail prices (as they affect farm prices); (d) control of processors and dealers in food (to prevent profiteering and hoarding); (e) all Federal Government, Lend-Lease, Army and Navy purchases (as by competition they affect prices to both consumers and farmers); (f) all rationing and conservation of consumers (for that affects price and justice in supply to general consumers as well as to farmers); (g) determination of the needs and supplies that can be given our allies and co-ordination with their supplies from elsewhere; (h) allotment of the use of import shipping space to food; and (i) has a large voice in manpower policies in respect to agriculture and in production of farm machinery.

Moreover, unless these functions are in one place and under one leadership, it is impossible to mobilize fully the voluntary action of the people, which is so necessary in food administration, and which alone can raise this phase of our war effort above the level of mere regimentation.

A further enormous production by the American farmer will be required to feed a starving world after fighting ceases. To do that we should, as in the last war, have price guarantees that carry over for some time after war.

At the time of the last war the Department of Agriculture was largely a scientific institution, and gladly left major production policies, price policies and farm marketing problems to the Food Administrator. The enormous increase in production which we secured is proof of its success. We so enlarged production and reduced consumption that we raised food exports to 17,000,000 tons per annum from our pre-World War I average of about 5,500,000 tons.

Since that time the Department has become a vast economic agency affecting both production, price and distribution. I do not believe these functions can now, or should be, taken from the Department. The solution seems to me to transfer to that Department the OPA and WPB functions in relation to food control, and to transfer to the Department the other administrative fractions of purchasing, etc., now scattered in many directions. Further, as I have said, the Secretary should have a large voice in determining the policies of other agencies I have mentioned—and otherwise make a single-headed administration and responsibility.

The Department of Agriculture already commands a great staff of expert men and women in every county in the United States, who could absorb many of the new duties. They could effectively organize public co-operation. Again may I emphasize that I am not discussing personalities, but organization.

Yours faithfully,

HERBERT HOOVER

New York, N. Y., Nov. 5, 1942

We'll Have to Feed the
World Again

Collier's Magazine
[*November 28 and December 5, 1942*]

A STARVING world must be fed after this war ends. That has been promised to the victims of the war again and again by President Roosevelt and Prime Minister Churchill. Even if it had not been promised, we would have to do it if we want to make a lasting peace instead of lasting anarchy. And we will need to do it unless we are willing to stand by and watch millions of human beings die after we have made gigantic sacrifices to give them a chance to live.

If this war stopped tomorrow there would be millions of permanently debilitated adults and millions of stunted children. But there will always be millions who can be saved. If European civilization is to live, they must be fed. And especially must this be done for the children, or we shall be faced with a generation of physical degenerates and potential gangsters.

But if these promises are to be kept we shall need to begin preparedness long before the war ends. That preparedness means some new direction and new strategy for American agriculture. It means preparation of supplies from South America. It means advance agreements with our Allies as to control of world supplies, finance, shipping and administration. It means creation of organization in advance, with an understanding of the huge volumes needed, the kind of food needed, the source of these supplies, their transportation distribution, and the economic, social and political problems which must be met.

There are more Horsemen that follow modern war than at the time the Apocalypse was written. In modern total war Famine and Pestilence are accompanied by four new recruits whose names are Revolution, Unemployment, Suspicion and Hate. These additional destroyers make the job harder to manage.

That there is and will be famine needs little demonstration. Already 148,000,000 people in the occupied democracies in Europe and Asia are short of food; millions of them are actually starving and our Allies are obviously running on very short rations.

The Nazi's food supply is sufficient for their evils of today. They are working hordes of prisoners on the farms and robbing some of the occupied territories. But their internal production will get worse as the war goes on and there is less to steal from the subjected peoples.

In fact the whole of Europe will continue to degenerate in domestic food supply. The reasons for that are simple enough. Europe in peace time—and by "Europe" I here mean Britain and all of Europe excluding Russia—has to import large amounts of food for human beings. That is now cut off by the blockade except to Britain and some small amounts to the neutrals.

On top of this, under the pressure of total war field crops decline year by year. Manpower and horsepower are increasingly drained to the war; farm implements cannot be replaced; fertilizers are diverted to explosives; planting is less effective and harvesting less perfect. Also the animals in Europe are in considerable degree dependent upon imported feed. In consequence of the blockade some part of the dairy and breeding herds must be slaughtered early in total war. And domestic feed for the remaining animals decreases because more fields must be turned to direct food for humans—and thus still more of the flocks and herds must be slaughtered.

In the last war the principal food animals of Europe, cattle, hogs and sheep, decreased by over 70,000,000 head and that is again going on. The invaluable chicken vanishes, and fishing is greatly diminished. Thus the stream of animal products steadily decreases. To all this must be added the ravages of armies and scorched earth policies.

Nor will famine this time be limited to Europe for these causes are also working in Asia and Russia.

THE MEANING OF HUNGER, STARVATION AND FAMINE

It is difficult for Americans to picture widespread hunger or starvation. We have not had such a thing in America.

Nation-wide hunger and starvation mean grim suffering, incalculable grief over wilting children, physical degeneration, stunted growth, distorted embittered minds and death. Its lasting effect is one of degree and time. Adults can recuperate from months of under-nourishment. Children can stand less. In fact, the undersized, rickets and the death rate among children are the sensitive barometers of starvation. Not even during our Civil War was there a town or city where these effects reached one-tenth of what they are in certain cities of the Occupied Democracies at this moment.

THE THREAT OF DISEASE

From all food shortages comes the danger of Pestilence. People do not often die directly from starvation. Their resistance is weakened and they fall easy prey to contagions. Moreover, people consume their available fat supplies and have little or none left for soap. Uncleanliness invites such scourges as typhus —which is transmitted by lice.

There is another vital peril in this question. Unless these masses of people in scores of nations can have food and be protected from pestilence there can be no social or political stability upon which peace can be built.

THE SIZE OF THE PROBLEM

We had a parallel experience with this problem after the first World War. In that famine America bore the major load of supplies, finance and administration. Except for American food preparedness, food strategy and American intervention there would then have been the greatest sacrifice of human life in all history—even more devastating than that which followed the Thirty Years War, when one-third of the population of Europe is said to have died. That America succeeded in its task is evidenced not alone by grateful statement of every government in Europe but by the statistical fact that their populations did not decrease during the period.

No nation had ever undertaken such a mission before. We had to pioneer through the thickets and swamps of governmental, social, financial, and economic problems, including human nature in the raw. From that experience we can make some estimates as to the need next time, the source of supplies and the strategy and tactics necessary to defeat both famine and pestilence and to set millions upon the road back to strength and health.

The nations in Europe, outside Russia, short of food after World War I varied in degree of need and again after World War II will vary in need, as all nations in any circumstance have some domestic supplies. After the last war we grouped them as to degree of hunger, and, for administrative purposes, into four categories.

There was the "Neutral group" of six nations of 43,000,000 people; the "Allied group" of five nations embracing 132,000,-000 people; the "Enemy group" comprising the four shrunken old empires with 102,000,000 people; and the "Liberated group" of thirteen states freed from domination having 98,-000,000 people. That was a total of 28 nations embracing about 375,000,000 human beings.

Although the positions of nations in the groups will be shifted after World War II, yet there will be about 390,000,000 people short of food. And this time Russia and China will need be added.

In the last war defeated Russia with roughly 140,000,000 people was famine striken in certain areas. We made an effort to furnish food but Russia refused relief because the Allies stipulated that she must stop fighting her neighbors. It was not until the renewed famine in 1922 that we were able to assist her on a large scale.

Russia will need food help during this war and afterwards, with lands despoiled and scorched by the Germans, there will be tens of millions to add to the prospective totals.

China's normal food supply is a bare subsistence level and therefore shortage spreads disaster even faster than in countries of higher standards. Despoiled and ravaged by Japan, she will have scores of millions to add to these totals.

Therefore it is possible to estimate over 500,000,000 people will be suffering from some degree of food shortage after this war, and that some European countries—Norway, Holland, Belgium, France, Greece, Poland, Jugoslavia and the Baltic States—will be much worse off than last time.

HOW MUCH FOOD WILL BE NEEDED?

Certainly the amount of food required to meet the emergency cannot be less than after World War I, even if the war should end tomorrow. The ultimate need will depend on the length of the war, as that controls the degree of the demoralization in domestic supplies.

The total amount of food for human beings imported from overseas into the European area during the acute period of twelve months following the Armistice in November, 1918, was about 27,000,000 tons (54 billion pounds). Of this between 4,500,000 and 5,000,000 tons (9 to 10 billion pounds) were animal and vegetable oil products, the balance mostly grains, rice, peas, beans and sugar. There was insufficient shipping to transport much feed for animals. The total value of this food at the prices of that time was roughly $6,000,000,000.

Something over 16,000,000 out of the 27,000,000 tons of food came from the United States, including about 2,400,000 tons of animal and vegetable oil products.

Of the American food which had a value of about $3,300.-000,000, we furnished about $2,400,000,000 on credit, about $325,000,000 in charity (mostly for children) and about $575,-000,000 was paid for in goods, gold and services. As the credits (our war "loans") were only about 6 per cent repaid the balance of that item can be written off as a gift also.

Of the 11,000,000 tons from other quarters, most of it went to the Neutrals and our Allies and was paid for in gold and foreign trade. The Allies and Neutrals also furnished $200,-000,000 of food on credits to the more desperate countries. Of this, the British furnished about $100,000,000; the French $30,000,000; the Italians $30,000,000; and the balance came from the neutral nations.

PREPAREDNESS OF ORGANIZATION

To be prepared to fight these famines and their inevitable companion of pestilence, we shall need to have great preparedness in supplies, but to lay some foundations of organization in advance.

After the present war the organization, the tactics, the strategy will not differ much from the last one. There are no new inventions in food except synthetic vitamins, and these do not reduce the need for food. The methods of determining the supplies needed, their sources, the methods of finance, of transportation and distribution will be the same. The area of famine will be greater and the need more intense.

Advance preparedness in 1918 was placed by the President in the hands of the United States Food Administration. We not only had great reserves prepared but we had accurate knowledge of all the other possible supplies in the world. In October, 1918, with the Armistice in prospect, I was able to lay before the President an estimate of world supplies. It showed a total of about 30,000,000 tons of essential food available for overseas

shipment, and as 27,000,000 tons of it was delivered the estimate was reasonably accurate. Ten days after the Armistice we
had cargoes headed for the famine areas and we had arranged
to turn over several hundred thousand tons accumulated in
France as a reserve for our armies as insurance against submarines.

FOUR FUNDAMENTALS

During the last war we demonstrated certain fundamentals
in organization to fight wide-scale famine that will repeat themselves again.

The first of these was that fighting famine is a gigantic economic and governmental operation handled by experts and not
"welfare" work of benevolent handing out food hit or miss to
bread lines. There must be no waste, no inefficiency.

The second was that when this mass of hungry people add
their demands upon world food supplies there will not be
enough fats to go around on a normal basis of consumption for
everybody. There will again likely be a shortage in shipping.
Therefore, the division of food among nations must be controlled, during the emergency period. To do this a large part
of the purchase, the overseas transportation, and the distribution
must be in the hands of governments. And with the economic
prostration of the famine area, the food must be largely financed
by the Allied governments. Restoration of commerce will be
too slow to meet such emergencies.

The third fundamental which developed was that the problem divided itself into two periods—the "Acute" period and
the "Reconstruction" period. The "Acute Period" lasted about
twelve months, from the Armistice in November, 1918, until
after the harvest of 1919. This is a period demanding fast work
and complete controls. The second, or "Reconstruction Period"
last time extended from the autumn of 1919 until the harvest
of 1921. Peace having been made, the harvest of 1919 being
in hand, the situation relaxed. Industry, exports and private
credits revived somewhat, and we abandoned control of shipping and control of distribution. The European shortage of

food during this second period was of large dimensions but was largely overcome by the initiative of European governments themselves. We were able to confine our activities in this period to the aid of those governments still economically destitute or to groups of destitute children and others which weak governments were unable to protect.

The fourth fundamental was that the problem of undernourished and diseased children had to be separated from all other questions and handled directly and independently of local governments.

The fifth fundamental was that some individual with great powers must direct and coordinate all this. Such an operation would be hopeless in the hands of international commissions or committees. In the last war, by the appointment of the Allied Governments and with the willing cooperation of all the countries short of food, I occupied that position—which is my justification for speaking on the subject.

Having been appointed by the Allied Governments to direct and coordinate these matters, I set up headquarters in Paris within two weeks after the Armistice.

For the American staff, I brought to Europe some key men from the United States Food Administration and in time added to them, through the co-operation of General Pershing and Admiral Benson, a magnificent staff of some 1,500 American officers. They were worthy pre-war civilians who had special skills, courage and single-mindedness. Aside from clerks, no civilian received a salary, some received expenses. The Army and Navy men received pay and allowances from those services.

To save time, avoid duplication and red tape we made as much use as possible of our existing American organizations, that is, the United States Food Administration, its subsidiary, the Grain Corporation and the Belgian Relief which had functioned during the war feeding the 10,000,000 people in Belgium and France.

SIMPLIFYING COMPLEX PROBLEMS

We created only one new organization—the American Relief Administration—which dealt largely with the charitable problems, chiefly children. We used the European branches of the United States Shipping Board, the Treasury and the Federal Reserve Bank of New York. We set up branches of combined organizations in each of the twenty-eight countries short of food and in eight countries which were major sources of food supplies.

Coordination with the other Allied Governments was worked through the Allied Food Council of which I had been a part during the war. This Council comprised the Food Ministers of the Allied countries. We cleared many joint problems through the Allied Blockade Council, the Allied Shipping Council and the Supreme Economic Council.

In order to co-ordinate the division of world supplies and to simplify the whole administrative problem, we divided countries short of food into four groups. That is, the "Allies," the "Neutral," the "Enemy" and the "Liberated" nations. We further separated out the special problem to under-nourished children.

The "Allied" countries—Britain, France, Italy, Greece and Portugal—comprising about 132,000,000 people, drew part of their supplies from the Far East, the Southern Hemisphere and Canada, and part from the United States. They did their own purchasing, shipping and finance for the supplies from outside the United States. We furnished their American supplies through the United States Food Administration as we had done before the Armistice.

Our European Allies provided the shipping for their American food and we financed their supplies through loans from the United States Treasury. The Allies restored their consumption to not far below normal. Their total overseas supplies during the acute period amounted to about 17,000,000 tons of which some secondary part was feed for animals.

The "Neutral" group—Denmark, Holland, Norway, Spain, Sweden and Switzerland—comprising about 43,000,000 people, were assigned their supplies partly from the United States, but mainly from other parts of the world. They furnished their own shipping and finance. They cooperated splendidly with us in co-ordination of sources of supply, and in chartering their surplus shipping to us. On many occasions they diverted cargoes and their own stocks to us with which to meet emergencies. We replaced these supplies to them later on. This group restored the consumption of their people to near normal by importing during the acute period about 4,300,000 tons of food.

In the "Liberated" and "Enemy" groups our administrative problems were enormously greater than the other groups. This was the area not only of acute famine but of economic prostration and our organization had not only to procure the food, finance, ships and organize the distribution, but we had to do it amid the chaos of revolution, suspicion, hate and conflicting allied purposes.

The "Liberated" group of thirteen nations with 98,000,000 people embraced Albania, Armenia, Azerbaijan, Belgium, Estonia, Latvia, Lithuania, Czechoslovakia, Finland, Georgia, Poland, Rumania and Jugoslavia.

The "Enemy" group comprised Austria, Hungary, Bulgaria, Germany and Turkey. The total population was about 102,-000,000.

During the acute period our organization brought from one quarter or another about 4,000,000 tons of food into the "Liberated" countries and about 3,000,000 tons into the "Enemy" countries which, added to domestic supplies, lifted the ration for adults to an endurable level.

FOOD AND REVOLUTION

Prior to the Armistice all the peoples under enemy domination, "liberated" as well as enemy, were being rigidly rationed. At the Armistice the people in the 13 "liberated" countries at once set up their own independent governments in democratic form. Most of their ministries were formed of revolutionaries who had been active against the old empires. In the shrunken enemy areas of Germany, Austria, Hungary and Turkey the old governments collapsed in revolutions and also emerged in democratic forms. They likewise were controlled by men of revolutionary type. Hungary in fact went through four revolutions while we were trying to feed her. Most of the former officials of all these nations were driven from office.

In these transformations and revolutions the disciplines, such as rationing food, either collapsed or near-collapsed. Control of distribution was weakened or non-existent. Everybody who could, grabbed food from the farmers, bootlegged it and hoarded it. There was at the start some rioting and pillaging of the countryside. The poorer people of the towns and cities were for a time much worse off than they were before the Armistice when there were rigid food controls.

Thus a considerable part of the 200,000,000 hungry people in the Liberated and Enemy groups were suddenly governed by men with little or no experience in administration and whose minds were more fixed upon political and ideological ideas than the hard toil of government housekeeping. Added to all the other growing pains of these new democracies was the fact that the Communists were stirring up more revolutions. And they found so receptive an audience in hungry people that Communist revolutions, one time or another, seized a dozen large cities and one whole country—Hungary.

SUSTAINING DEMOCRACY

Our major purpose was to save hundreds of millions of lives. But food and restored employment were the foundations upon which order could be preserved and the completion of the peace made possible. Moreover, we sought to sustain the feeble plants of democracy which had sprung up in all of these countries. We had hope that they would bring not only freedom to men but that they would make the firm foundations of lasting peace.

A weak government possessed of the weapon of food for

starving people can preserve and strengthen itself more effectively than by arms. Therefore, in our major operations we sought to work through these governments, even at the price of some lost efficiency.

In consequence, one of our first necessities was to stiffen or set up a Food Administration in each of these new governments. To secure the proper working of distribution we had to furnish to many of them experienced Americans as advisers. These new Food Administrations took control of agriculture and all domestic food stocks, plus the imports which we furnished, and to ration their populations anew. We set up machinery to check them constantly, to see that food reached the people equitably and sufficiently.

UNDERNOURISHED CHILDREN

I believed that the problem of restoring the acutely undernourished children was of such importance from a humane point of view and so vital to the future that we organized it as the "American Relief Administration" independently of all local governments, but in co-operation with them.

The love of children is universal in mankind. It seemed to me that this was a point where these peoples, torn with internal dissension, conflict and discouragement, could find a common cause and a common hope. We set up in each country a national committee, principally of women, who, with the assistance of our staff, extended their organization into every ward and village. We selected the initial staff from Americans who had already had experience in Belgium.

The plan was to give, under medical supervision, one meal a day to undernourished and undeveloped infants and children in addition to the national ration. This food and clothing for the children was a gift, partly American private charity and partly from our Government. We delivered the supplies to seaboard and these devoted women raised the money locally to transport it, to equip and conduct the canteens. School houses, public buildings, anything available were turned into kitchens and eating places.

Some 12 or 15 million of these children, enemy and friend alike, were thus fed until they were restored to normal.

We handled some 175,000 tons of second-hand gift clothing which was made over by work shops which we organized among the women in the different countries. Mostly for the waif and undernourished children we furnished millions of yards of new materials and new shoes to the value of several millions of dollars.

The total of our American charitable outlays amounted to about $325,000,000. The expenditure of the local committees for transportation and equipment amounted to at least this much again. We continued this work for over two years. The local organizations were strong enough to carry on thereafter.

PESTILENCE

Originally it had been intended that problems of pestilence should be met by the Red Cross organizations of the different countries, assisted by the American and Allied Red Cross organizations. But typhus developed on a fearful scale along the line of the old Russian front and began a march westward over Europe. The health authorities of the countries infected reported to the Supreme Council in Paris that there were one million cases and a mortality of 125,000 every week. It was not the province of my organization, but, the Red Cross societies finding themselves unable to cope with it, the job was assigned to us by the President and the Prime Ministers. As typhus is a louse disease our job was to quarantine a huge area and then delouse the population in those areas. We secured a staff from the Army Medical corps, some 8,000 carloads of delousing equipment of the British, American, French and German armies. The job required many months of steadily pushing back the invasion, but we completely succeeded.

PAST WAR ORGANIZATION TO FEED THE WORLD

In my previous article I discussed the inevitability of widespread food shortage and famine after this war and some of the experience developed after the first World War.

There are a multitude of problems to be met. Many of these will be different from our experience in 1918-21. But there is no more effective way to indicate what may be anticipated than by some account of what happened and what we did last time.

In some form most of the old questions will rise again. Preparedness includes an understanding of these questions and the measures to meet them.

FINANCE

All imported food to meet any famine must be financed from somewhere. The farmers, the processors, the transporters of the world must be paid. After the first World War, American Government "loans" were made to the "Allied" and "Liberated" countries covering the food furnished from America. Some comparatively minor loans were made by the allied and neutral governments to the amount of food furnished by them. That also included one enemy country—Austria.

We had no loan funds for Germany, Hungary, Bulgaria or Turkey. One result of the war blockade was that the enemy countries had not been able to spend their gold abroad to buy things during the war and they still had it. We supplied food against gold payments, against the service of their ships and against some goods which they exported.

Both the delays in removing the blockade and the delays in peace-making after the first World War contributed to increase the financial burden upon the United States.

THE EFFECT OF BLOCKADE AND DELAYS IN PEACE-MAKING

During the war, the Allies had maintained a food (and other) blockade against the whole of Europe, including neutrals as well as enemy-occupied countries. After the Armistice, the military authorities were fearful that they would not be able to enforce the Armistice terms on the enemy or to impose the peace terms if the blockade were relaxed before peace was signed. The neutrals and Belgium had been allowed a meager ration through the blockade during the war, but they were suffering a great deal of hardship. And the military authorities feared that if the blockade were taken off, even for the neutrals or liberated countries, there would be leaks into enemy areas.

After two months, we finally got the blockade removed from the neutral and liberated countries, except as to some special articles. But as to enemy countries, despite our strong urging, we were not able to secure even a partial relaxation of the blockade until four and a half months after the Armistice.

It was not until these countries were on the verge of collapse into Communism that relief from the blockade was given. Thereafter, a limited amount of food imports and the export of a few industrial articles were allowed until the peace was signed in July. Then all restrictions came down. That chapter is not an agreeable one upon which to expand.

Nine months were consumed in making the peace. This delay, together with the blockade, increased suffering, and stifled economic recuperation greatly in both the liberated and enemy areas. The unemployment was huge and dangerous. Had the blockade been promptly removed and peace quickly made, all Europe could have made more rapid recovery. We could have greatly lessened the social disturbances and the burden upon us to finance relief if exports could have been carried freely in our returning empty vessels.

The first lesson from this is that, in our own interest, the blockade should be taken down instantly when the enemy hands over his weapons.

The second lesson is the need for a quick—an immediate—provisional peace. We cannot afford to delay the revival of industry, exports and the re-establishment of private credit during the long months necessary to elaborate a final treaty of peace. The intelligent course would be for the United Nations to reach agreement in advance as to the terms of a provisional peace—recognizing *de facto* governments, drawing provisional frontiers and taking other steps to allow people to get to work. Such a peace could perfectly well be imposed by the military authorities simultaneously with the terms of surrender—and thus do away entirely with the armistice period. Then the process of reconstruction can begin at once. Arrangement of the final terms of peace can be completed later on.

The amount of loans or gifts by the victorious governments that will be required to fight the next famine, of course, cannot be estimated, but it is not likely to be less than after the first World War, save by the one possibility of the immediate removal of the blockade and a provisional peace.

COMMUNICATIONS AND PASSPORTS

For some time after the Armistice, the passage of mail, telegrams or persons over the frontiers of enemy and liberated countries was slow and uncertain. Fear, tension and hate were universal. The first need of our organization was communications and passport recognition. In order to secure communications, I requested each of the governments to lend us two telegraph circuits between principal centers.

All twenty-three governments involved willingly did so except the French. General Pershing solved this by giving me two wires from Cologne to Paris from the American military service lines. Within two weeks we had a complete telegraph system connecting every capital from Helsingfors to Constantinople with American Army and Navy operators at the clearing points.

Passage over the frontiers of the liberated and enemy nations was a great trial and filled with delays. I finally appealed to all the governments in the acute area to honor an informal passport signed by myself personally. They did so. Such arrangements as these should be agreed upon and established at once when firing ceases next time.

SHIPPING PROBLEMS

Shipping was scarce from war destruction and made more so by the frenzy of all the Allies, including our Americans, to get back to foreign trade.

The Germans and Austrians had some 3,000,000 tons of cargo and passenger ships held in their ports during the war. At once after the Armistice, we requested the allied military authorities to secure these cargo ships for use of our organization in carrying food. Furthermore, with the assurance of food, they could secure the passenger ships to repatriate the armies.

The ships were ultimately obtained, but some of our allies kept part of the cargo ships—aside from the enemy and neutral ships we still required allied ships. During the whole acute period we had daily to haggle, beseech and swear at our Allies and the American Shipping Board to get the millions of tons we needed to save the lives of this mass of humanity.

Our shipping division had not only the duty of directing a giant fleet but also of maintaining large warehouse facilities in some twenty ports. Obviously, one of the problems was to determine a program to meet the need of each of the countries.

Inexperienced, panicky officials, faced with heart-breaking situations and fearful that our organization might fail in deliveries, always wanted their food all at once. We were fortunate in having able and patient men in our organization to determine these programs. They successfully guided the flow of cargoes to meet the need.

Shipping problems will be with us again, but should be settled in advance by a fleet of approximately four or five million tons, definitely assigned to the relief organization.

CHAOS IN INTERNAL TRANSPORTATION

Another of the problems which will arise again will be to secure some unity of action among the liberated and enemy countries. These countries were dependent upon one another for inland transportation, coal, communications and many other things. Underlying and spread over them all were the violent hates resulting from centuries of oppression and outrage, conflict, jealousy and other mental disturbances that made it difficult to secure joint action.

There were just two points of unity—a realization that somehow there must be unified action if millions were not to die of starvation and disease; and a willingness of all (enemies and friends) to trust the Americans completely.

In the liberated and enemy areas the ports, railway and canals were demoralized by the war and more demoralized by the revolutions. Ten new states had been separated from the five old empires, and the boundaries in four other liberated states had been rearranged. Each government seized all the railway rolling stock and canal boats that it could lay hands upon and, out of greed or fear, refused to allow them to cross the twenty-odd frontiers.

The railways of Central Europe had been government-built and operated upon empire systems. When the empires cracked, the railways were disjoined so that, to move between places within a new country by rail, it was necessary to pass over the frontiers of neighboring countries.

On top of all this, some of the new government railway officials had never seen a railway before except to ride on one occasionally. The railway systems in several countries almost ceased to function. Therefore, part of our problem was to get the ports open and to arrange where necessary for shipment of food by rail or canal across one country to another. In order to persuade the different governments concerned to allow rolling stock to pass over frontiers, we undertook to check the locomotives and cars at frontier points and guarantee their return, and we did the same with canal boats. In some areas we had practically to take over operation of the railways under American and allied railway executives. We further furnished experienced American railway advisers to several of the governments and aided those who had secured little railway stock in the grab to obtain it from other countries. We required that each government pay all costs of internal European transportation and distribution.

COAL FAMINE

Beyond these troubles, the coal districts in the old empires came under new governments, some of which did not need all the coal but did not want to sell the surplus to hated neighbors. In any event, most of their neighbors did not have money or exchange to pay for it. Certain important coal districts were in the grip of bloody struggles by rival countries for their possession. In others, violent strikes were in progress. As a result, we had a famine in coal. In the grip of winter, the supplies were insufficient in certain countries to keep the people warm or to operate their railways and utilities.

We therefore placed American coal engineers in charge of certain coal districts; we established American coal advisers in the governments of others, and we had to negotiate the financial arrangements for coal purchases by those countries which were short. We had the same problems in moving oil from Rumania to the other countries. The abilities and tact of our Americans brought back the coal production in an astonishingly short time.

One day I received a telegram from the American colonel of engineers in charge of a certain coal district: "Sending $25,000. Send me that much tobacco." This was new in our experience in two directions, both the paying of cash and the use of tobacco for relief. I inquired for more details. It appeared that the colonel had found $25,000 in American gold certificates in the banks of the region, which they had held since before the war.

"These poor devils of coal miners haven't had a smoke in three years," he explained. "You know a miner must have a smoke. We could lift the production of this district by twenty per cent if we could give a tobacco premium."

We bought him the tobacco from the American Army.

BARTER SYSTEM FOR FOOD

Some limited districts had a surplus of food, and those which needed it had no acceptable money with which to pay for it. Currencies were breaking down and, during the stagnation of the Armistice, there was little movement of trade, even inside Europe. To aid generally, our organization furnished American financial and economic advisers to several governments. The handling of food and coal exchanges with neighbors mostly came down to barter under direction of these Americans as neutrals in the performance.

One day I had an appeal from one of our representatives to decide how many eggs from Galicia should be paid for a locomotive from Austria. Being stumped, I could only tell the man to decide it himself and to be guided by the age of each. We moved by this barter system some 600,000 tons of food internally in Europe, and millions of tons of coal.

PRICE AND ACCOUNTING PROBLEMS

In order to secure the great surpluses with which to carry the Allies in war over 1919 or to meet famine if peace came, we had guaranteed our American farmers $2.20 per bushel for wheat and $15.50 to $17.00 per 100 pounds for hogs. There were some other minor guarantees. The Armistice brought a temporary choke in the flow of our gigantic American supplies. It came perilously near breaking down our guarantees and bankrupting the American farmer and everybody who had loaned him money with which to produce. The situation came about because food prices for the dammed-back supplies from the Southern Hemisphere were much lower.

Some of the Allies naturally went at once to these quarters for this cheaper food. This, together with delays in removing the blockade, created a perilous situation for the American farmer, as we did not have storage capacity in the United States to hold such enormous quantities as he was marketing while we were settling these problems. We only solved it by transporting huge quantities of food to European ports and storing it there.

Ultimately the Allies had to come back to us for supplies. I have no doubt the farmers' prices would have crashed had it not been for the guarantees and the measures taken. We may experience this situation again.

All the huge sums of money, quantities of commodities, services of ships and men had to be accounted for. We worked out some simplifications in our accounting. We made the same prices for the various articles of food to every nation and made them at a level that would cover all our guarantees and outlays plus a "margin." We contracted that the receiving governments in the Liberated and Enemy areas would accept the final statements of a well-known firm of accountants without question. In turn we agreed that if we made any profits from our "margins" we would turn it over to "child feeding." We were able to turn over some $40,000,000 and lived a peaceful accounting life as well.

FOOD THROUGH MONEY EXCHANGE

As I said, the currencies of most of these countries had broken down or at least commanded little respect in the exchanges of the world. To accomplish a multiple job of relieving our government from making loans to pay for food and at the same time get the food into the hands of the needy, we set up some mechanism of exchange. We accepted remittances through banks in the Western Hemisphere to friends and relatives in the demoralized currency areas. We paid for food in the United States with these sums, and turned the food over to the governments concerned for local currency, which we then turned into their domestic banks for payment to the individual designated.

A little later we improved this greatly by selling through the banks in North and South America what we named a food draft. This draft called for a specific number of pounds of flour, lard, sugar, milk or bacon, and upon its presentation to any of our many warehouses, we delivered the goods. These transactions ran into many millions, saved that much in "loans" from the

American Government. We made a modest profit on the "drafts" and turned it over to the Child Feeding Division for charitable work—some $2,000,000.

The urgent question today is to lay some foundations in preparedness of supplies, especially in fats, to meet the inevitable need.

To understand the practical problem of food supplies requires a short digression to nutritional questions. Human beings cannot be kept alive or rebuilt in health by just any kind of food.

In nutrition terms, food should be a balanced ration of first, carbohydrates (principally bread, potatoes, sugar, rice, etc.); second, proteins (principally meats, fish, cheese, eggs, etc.); and third, fats (principally butter, lard, bacon, vegetable oil). There is some protein in the first and last two groups.

The high-protein foods are hard to come by under famine conditions. Any large supply of meats requires refrigerator ships, and there are not many to be had after a war. But we found, out of vast experience in the last war, that adults can be carried over emergencies on a bread and fat diet, supplementing their domestic supplies. The development of synthetic vitamins makes this easier to do, but a positive supply of fats is just as urgent as bread. Given time enough, people will die on bread alone.

Children must have a supplement of meat, dairy products and some other protective foods to a bread and other fat diet if they are to recover strength from their privations.

For reasons given later on we will most likely again go through the experience of a shortage of shipping which will require the utmost condensation and the exclusion of feed for animals at least in the initial stages.

In addition to our experience with the quantities required last time, we can get some idea of the forthcoming European need (supposing the war stopped tomorrow) by inspecting the rations now current in the diffierent countries as indicating their domestic supplies. On this basis, to bring the supply not to normal but to an endurable level for adults, would now require more than the last time. At this moment a rough estimate for the war would be, for the first year, a minimum of 24,000,000 tons of bread grains, rice, peas, beans and at least 7,000,000 tons mostly of animal and vegetable oil fats. This 7,000,000 tons would include a supplemental program for children. And Russia and China will also require help which are not included in this estimate.

A rough exploration of the food resources that will be available in the world discloses two pertinent facts—one good and the other terribly bad.

We have in the Western Hemisphere a surplus of wheat and other breadstuffs sufficient to meet any probable requirement. But at this moment, there is not in sight 20 per cent of the meat and especially fat supplies necessary.

SOURCES OF SUPPLIES

This volume of meats, fats and supplementary food for children cannot be mobilized unless there is definite advance food strategy. The situation at the Armistice in 1918 was much better than if we had to meet this problem tomorrow.

The shortage of shipping in the last war ultimately forced Britain, France, Italy and Belgium and neutrals to depend mostly upon the short route to North America. To help the then 180,000,000 people of our European Allies and their armies, together with neutrals whose ships we were pressing into use, the United States Food Administration undertook to produce for them for the harvest year of 1918-1919 a surplus from the United States of about 17,500,000 tons, of which 2,600,000 tons were to be largely animal and vegetable oil products. The balance was mostly bread grains, beans, rice and sugar. This huge program was far in excess of our normal pre-World War I annual export surplus of about 5,300,000 tons of bread-stuffs and 650,000 tons of animal and vegetable oil products.

Besides this Allied program we had to supply our own armies. Men in armies use up about twice as much food as when at home. We met all these requirements. We did it by elimination of waste and unnecessary consumption and by appealing to our farmers for their maximum effort.

I may emphasize again that the most difficult part of the future problem, just as it was last time, is the fat supplies. In the last war we decided that the shortest route to fats was the American hog. To insure the farmer against loss if the war suddenly ended, we, as I have said, guaranteed him from $15.50 to $17.00 per hundred for hogs. Under patriotic urge and our guarantees, the farmer certainly delivered the hogs. In the years 1918 and 1919 he sent an average of 66,000,000 of them to slaughter, compared with 57,000,000 in 1917. He increased the surplus of other animal products also. The Canadians had likewise built up their surpluses.

Altogether we had North America geared up in preparation to carry the brunt of the Allied situation until the summer of 1919 had war continued, or alternately we were prepared to aid in the inevitable famine if the war came to an end. With the Armistice in November we had a large part of these supplies in hand.

At the present moment the United States is geared up to supply less than one-half the meat and fat surplus of the last war, and the next famine will demand more. We are already feeling the pinch of shortages of this kind at home as the result of even these demands.

Moreover, after the last war we had large quantities of animal and vegetable oil reserves in South America, South Africa, Australasia, the Indies and Manchuria dammed back by the shortage of shipping. Japan will have exhausted these supplies from the East Indies and Asia. In fact, after the present war the only consequential sources of supply will be the Western Hemisphere and Africa with some supplement from Australasia.

The reason for our diminished American supplies of meats and fats is that, during the 24 years since the last European famine, the population of human beings in the United States has increased about 30 per cent while the animal population has not increased proportionally.

Animal statistics are difficult to compare because of several variants, but taking the Food Administration statistics as of January 1, 1918, and those of the Department of Agriculture for January 1, 1942, the figures are:

	January 1, 1918	January 1, 1942
Cattle	73,040,000	74,600,000
Hogs	70,880,000	60,530,000
Sheep	48,900,000	55,930,000

There is some compensation by increased productivity from improved breeding. No doubt, under the present admirable stimulation of production and reduced civilian consumption, our production will increase. But even these increases, after satisfying our domestic needs and those of our allies and our armies, have no present margin for the volume of fat that will be required for the next famine, without further preparedness.

If we look over the rest of the Western Hemisphere for afterwar supplies, and even if we include Australasia and Africa, we will find that their pre-World War II exports of animal and vegetable oil products amount to less than 200,000 tons a month. Of this, however, the largest part is fresh meat, which not only is in minor part fat, but requires refrigerator ships of which there will be but few.

The fat part of the problem will be unsoluble unless the strategy is determined now and unless Western Hemisphere agriculture is oriented to carry it out.

The only immediate source would seem to be to stimulate our hog production still further. And to do this the farmer may possibly need to be assured that his prices will not suddenly collapse when the war ends. Such assurances must be given to him a year before the hogs are ready for market. The product cannot be carried in storage for more than six or eight months. If the war did not end at that time, there would be another loss to chalk up against the cost of the war. Dairy products will be no less needed but they increase more slowly.

However, a stimulated American program would require much more agricultural labor than is now in prospect. With the heavy drafts upon farm labor and scarcer equipment, our production is more likely to decrease than to increase in a long war. If we are to solve our food problems, agriculture must be envisioned as a munitions industry and treated as such. If it is not done, we may be faced with gigantic failure after the war.

Certainly the whole question of fats needs urgent consideration. It would seem, outside our own possibilities, that stimulation of production could be undertaken in South America. They have the feed and labor. With Allied financial guarantees, they could do a great deal in preparedness.

IN CONCLUSION

All these are but a few of the possible problems that will arise again. In the last famine, the day-to-day purchase of food in eight countries from over seven seas, the fight for ships, their assignment to sources of supplies, their programming to keep the flow constant to a score of countries, the unloading, warehousing, distributing, accounting, disputing with dumbbells, listening to hourly advice from the well-intentioned but ill-informed and to the prayers of heads of needy governments, conciliating hurt feelings of our Allies, coordinating supplies with them and the neutrals and tempering the ideas of military authorities made a 112-hour work-week for a magnificent staff of Americans.

All this account may seem dry and statistical. But the high purpose was to meet the prayer of nations for a chance to live and the cry of mothers for their children. Beyond that, it was the hope that we were giving strength to the frail democracies which had been brought into being, that through them the world might find peace. We had won victory by arms, and we dreamed that this unparalleled generosity and service by a great nation would set new standards of human relationships in the world. And it expressed the Christianity that was within us. We will need to do it all over again as part of our effort to bring peace to a weary world.

Food Supplies for This War

NEW YORK CITY

[*January 21, 1943*]

I WISH first to express my own and your appreciation to
The National Broadcasting Company and their associated
stations for making the radio available for this occasion.
Their presentation of discussions of great public questions in
this time of crisis is a great national service. And on this occasion it has been done at great sacrifice to themselves.

I have been requested by your Board to say something on our
war food problem. I believe I can speak not alone from some
experience but in entire detachment from any group interest.
It is not a problem to be dealt with in emotional terms. Nevertheless its ultimates are victory and peace, the loss of millions
of human lives or the saving of them. And this is not a subject
for criticism, nor do I believe in the doctrine of—I told you so.
We need to face the hard facts and secure a remedy. And at
once.

Food supply has now become secondary only to military operations in determining the outcome of the war. And it will take
first place in saving the world from anarchy after the war.

When firing ceases we will be faced with three or four hundred million starving people. That such monstrous things should
be is but part of the crimes of Hitler, Tojo and Mussolini.

To save these millions of people after the war is not alone a
transcendent act of compassion. It is the only road to peace.
But we must be prepared.

In the meantime, we need more food for our own people and
to carry our Allies. The burden of furnishing food supplies to

the United Nations now and to a starving world after the war rests largely upon the American and Canadian farmer.

And at once let me say I have no sympathy with attacks being made by armchair consumers upon the American farmer. He is working a 70-hour week. He is working for a far less average income than any group in industry. No one is working harder to win the war.

We have at present ample stores of breadstuffs on the North American continent to supply our Allies and to contribute to the relief of the inevitable world postwar famine. The Biblical injunction was however that man cannot live by bread alone. The scientists have long since proved that the deficiency in that Biblical diet is meats and fats. And to maintain a cheerful and fighting spirit in the human animal, he needs frills and flavors like sugar, coffee and jam. He feels still better if he can have eggs and fruit.

There is today an acute shortage, especially in meats and fats, in the world. And fats include the whole gamut of lard, milk, butter, cheese and edible oil products.

All over Europe the flocks and herds are being consumed. There is already desperate shortage of meats and fats in every country ravaged by the Germans. And that shortage will grow steadily worse right up to the end of the war.

Britain and Russia are short of animal products and must be supplied by us if they are to carry on the war.

And every householder knows there is a shortage already in the United States. And we are confronted with the fact that our shortage of labor, of machinery and methods of price control are limiting the vitally essential expansion of this production and the flocks and herds upon which production depends. And unless we can quickly realize and quickly reverse these limiting forces there are dangers to the conduct of the war and winning the peace.

OUR PRESENT SITUATION

While we have Germany blockaded from overseas food, her submarines have done a fairly effective job of cutting off much of both British and our own meats and fats from the Southern Hemisphere. And the Japanese conquests have stopped much of our own and British vegetable oils from Asia and the Indies. Russia has lost a considerable part of her food areas and must have some support from us. China is at present cut off in every direction.

We in the United States are short of meats and fats because we must supply the deficiencies in our Allies, because our possible imports of meats and fats are curtailed, because our armed forces eat more of them than they do in civil life and because we are not increasing our production fast enough.

We had all these burdens and difficulties in the last war. Yet today, we are exporting less than half the meats and fats to our Allies that we did in the last war for we then had to support France, Belgium and Italy also, and with this lesser burden of exports we are threatened with greater shortages of meats and fats on our own home front than in World War I.

Our difficulties are increased because American livestock has decreased in proportion to the growth of human population since the last war.

At the end of that war we had 26% more beef cattle for each 1,000,000 of human population than we had twenty-three years later on January 1, 1942. We had 26% more hogs in proportion to the population. We had proportionately 5% more milch cows than now. But the improved cow gives more milk. We have in 1943 about the same sheep proportionately as in the last war. We have less chickens in proportion to our population, but the chickens work harder and produce more eggs.

IMPERATIVE TO BUILD UP OUR HERDS

The demands upon us today call imperatively and without delay to build up our flocks and herds and thus increase their production. And, further, we must increase our production of vegetable oils. We can of course, like the Germans, slaughter our breeding herds for immediate war purposes. But that would starve ourselves and the world afterwards.

Alternatively we can build up our flocks and herds and consequently their production. We did it during the last war. Over the whole period of that world war our hog population increased by 22%, our beef cattle by 27%, our milch cows 10%. It was this increase in production that enabled us to supply our Allies and prevented hardships on our own home front. And it was the salvation of Europe last time.

We can produce the feed with which to again greatly increase our food animals. For one thing the gas engine has retired 20,000,000 horses and mules from the national pastures and city feed bags.

WE ARE NOT MAKING THE PROGRESS WE SHOULD

That the progress we are making today is not satisfactory can be demonstrated. In January, a year ago, the Secretary of Agriculture gave to the country an admirable victory program of increased herds and increased production. The climatic conditions during the year were most favorable. Detailed statistics of actual farm results during the year are not yet available. But it is already obvious that this program was not fully met. This was due to various causes out of control of the Secretary. And now the Secretary warns us that production for 1943 may be less than that in 1942 in several directions.

THE CAUSES

The causes of this blockade on possible production are obvious:

First. Some 2,000,000 men have been drained from the farm labor supply into arms and munitions.

Second. The methods of food price control by which prices to the farmer in many instances are lower than costs of production.

Third. The manufacture of farm machinery has been reduced by 75%.

Fourth. We still go on subsidizing the farmer to restrict production in some commodities.

THE EFFECT

There is indeed ample evidence that without prompt remedy we shall not secure the increases that are vitally necessary.

A Congressional Committee reports that millions of dollars worth of crops in the Southwest were lost last year because they could not be harvested.

Word from farmers in many parts of the country indicate that unless their difficulties be remedied they will be compelled to reduce planting this spring.

And they are compelled to limit their herds below what they could otherwise do. The news comes daily from all parts of the country that the farmer is sending his dairy cows to slaughter for lack of labor. And this is amply verified by the arrivals at the slaughter houses. For the four months ending November 1, 1942, the inspected slaughter of female cattle increased 30% over the same period in 1941. In the same period the increase in the slaughter of steers was only 5%. The increased slaughter of female cattle in this four months' period was nearly 40% greater than the same period in the average of the three previous years. And there was still a further increase in the month of November. This does not increase our supply of dairy products. Also the cattle coming into the market during this four months ending November 1, 1942 were an average on different calculations from 30 to 40 lbs. per animal lighter than for the same period the year before. This beef loss would have supplied several million people during the period.

During this four months the number of sheep slaughtered has increased nearly 200% over the year before. Our national flock is less today than a year ago and will apparently be still less a year hence. There also seems to be some disturbance in the hog world, for sows have been coming to slaughter during the last four months faster than would seem desirable if we are to increase the herd with the rapidity needed.

This undue slaughter of cows, ewes and sows gives a temporary increase in meats, but it is an illusion as to supplies for the future. That is "eating the seed corn." The numbers slaughtered so far are not disastrous. We will not starve. Our Allies will not starve. But we can have far shorter supplies.

The evil is that these demoralizing forces are continuing. And if we keep traveling in this direction, we will see more hardships in our households unless we reduce our supplies to the Allies and armies. And with such a situation, it is nonsense to talk about furnishing meat and fat supplies to 300,000,000 additional famine-stricken people after this war is won.

Agriculture simply must be envisaged as a munitions industry. The farmer must be given men and tools if he is to perform his part.

REMEDIES FOR LABOR SHORTAGE

It is useless to talk about making up the farm labor shortage wholly from women or children. Much of farming is hard physical labor. Modern farming requires great skills in nursing the crops and livestock. Moreover farming has been mechanized. Now he is a mechanic. These skills cannot be learned quickly. But with organized preparatory training women can be of great service for lighter, simpler tasks.

There are other major remedies. The first is to cease the draft of labor from the farms into arms and munitions. The second is for industry to rigidly economize on labor and release the economies to the farmer. The third is for our munitions workers to contribute by removing all possible restrictions on effort, thereby increasing their production and freeing men to the farmers. The fourth is large and temporary import of Mexican farm labor. The fifth is to give consideration to the method of European armies. That is to furlough farm boys from the army for the few months of peak planting and harvest, they remaining under military direction, and in our case to draw both the army and farmers' pay.

THE RELATION OF PRICE CONTROLS TO PRODUCTION

Obviously price control of short commodities is necessary. Food cannot be allowed to go to the highest bidder. And prices and wages must be controlled to check inflation. But prices also dominate production. They can be the most powerful stimulant to production. They can stifle production. Prices can be made to produce the commodities we need and to minimize those which are the less necessary.

We give enormous wages and prices to stimulate planes and ships. Increased production of meats and fats are today just as important to win the war as planes and ships. And some bacon to the consumer at a few cents more is better than too little bacon.

At best price controls of food can be only a brake upon the pressures of shortage and inflation. We considered the method of retail price ceilings on food were a failure in the last war. And they have failed to keep the promises made for them in this war. Already prices on food have risen about 16% since they were partially applied a year ago and about 9% since they were fully applied. And that does not average in prices of the black market. There has been in fact a slightly larger rise in the past year than took place during the first year of food control in the last war under other and much simpler methods.

Systems of frozen retail price ceilings on food are not adapted to the problems of war production. They cannot single out and give premiums on production of the things we most need in parallel with the shifting demands of war.

The first reform needed is to abandon retail price ceilings on food and to substitute the alternative methods developed in the last war. That method is to fix prices as near the farm as possible. And they can then be fixed to stimulate production of the things we need. The consumer can be more effectively and more simply protected by regulating the turnover and profits of the food processor and the markups of the wholesaler and retailer.

The second reform is that all the functions of price control should be vested in the Secretary of Agriculture instead of several other places as at present. He alone can direct price so as to secure production and protect the consumer.

Above all, the best remedy to run away prices is increased production.

REDUCTION IN CONSUMPTION

Whatever we are able to do in increasing production of meats and fats, we will still need to reduce our domestic consumption, that is, if we are to feed the Allies and our armies. We have margins of consumption which can and must be reduced—and it means rationing. But with maximum production the hardships on the home front would be less.

I could talk at length on methods of rationing, having participated in that surgical operation one time or another on some five hundred million people. I do not on this occasion propose to discuss the alternative methods of reducing consumption. There are methods more simple and of less hardship on the housewife than those in use. But it is no use to criticize the mistakes that have been made during the last year or the hardships imposed. We should give Senator Brown, the new Administrator, a chance and our support in the revisions he will no doubt make. I will make only one observation. In rationing the American people with their widely different habits, products and problems, the system should be decentralized into the States and under State Administrators. We should also recognize the value of local government as opposed to centralized government. And we should rely to the maximum possible extent upon voluntary and cooperative measures rather than force. The American people are the most cooperative people in the world. And the hardest to drive.

Above all the greatest remedy to rationing is production and more production.

THE JOB BEFORE US

I realize that the calls for manpower and supplies pile in upon the Government from every direction. I realize that the Generals and Admirals, intent on their responsibilities, tend to accept the popular phrase that America has unlimited power and resources and that we can do anything. But there is a limit even to the resources of America. We have undertaken a job far greater than any other nation in history.

We can appreciate how great this job is if we look at Germany for a moment. It is true we have over a third more population than Germany, but we have undertaken a far larger task. The Germans have called about 9% of their people into their armed forces. We are calling about 8% or a little less. But the Germans are using 6,000,000 prisoners and imported labor, a large part working on her farms. Germany is impressing the mechanics, the machine shops and the food of 180,000,000 conquered people to her support. She does not have to build merchant ships to transport much of her armies overseas. She is not building much of a navy except submarines. She is not supplying her allies with food or munitions—she is taking from them. She is not financing her allies. She has much less mileage of railways to operate, for her whole population is in an area less than that of Texas. Yet Germany with all these differences in her favor is badly strained.

We, on the other hand, have undertaken to place almost as many men in arms. We must fight a war at 3,000 to 8,000 miles from our shores. We must build a host of merchant ships and a larger navy. We must furnish vast quantities of munitions and food to our Allies. We get little food from the outside. We must finance our Allies. We do not have 8,000,000 imported labor or prisoners, as would be proportionate to those in Germany. We exact no contributions of food or munitions from occupied countries.

But Germany is in the fourth year of total war. We are in the first year. She has passed the zenith of her strength. We are on the ascendant. Time runs in our favor. But we may run so fast that we get out of breath. Trying to do too much too fast may delay the inevitable Axis defeat.

CONCLUSION

We urgently need to determine what we can do within our strength of manpower, materials, shops, agriculture and the bottlenecks with which we must contend. We need to determine which of our tasks comes first.

And if we determine rightly, we will place agriculture in the first rank of the war effort alongside of planes and ships.

Our imperative necessity is the maximum food production. The American farmer will do it if he is given a chance. And the fate of the world may depend upon it.

In the Name of Humanity

The Christian Advocate
[February 11, 1943]

FIRST let us consider the history of the efforts to get relief to the starving women, children and unemployed men in German-invaded democracies.

During the four years of the First World War, relief was carried on under the direction of my colleagues and myself for the 10,000,000 people of German-invaded Belgium and Northern France. This was passed through the British blockade with the cooperation of the British Government. We secured guarantees of immunity of ships and food, both native and imported, from the Germans. And we supervised the distribution and saw to it that the guarantees were complied with. About $900,000,-000 value and 5,000,000 tons of food were delivered.

The major part of the funds came from the British, French and American Government. During the war the relief was repeatedly defended by the British and French Prime Ministers and Cabinet Ministers upon their own independent information from charges that the Germans received any military benefits from the operation. After that war these governments investigated the experience on the ground and not only reiterated their statements but fulsomely eulogized the whole management of it.

In September, 1939, Germany invaded Poland. In October, the exiled government of Poland requested my colleagues and myself to organize an operation for the Polish people similar to that in Belgium during the First World War. The exiled government offered and did find large sums of money from governments for its support, in addition to American charity. We at once established the Polish Relief Commission and began initial shipments of food to support about 300,000 of the most needy children. We secured the permission to pass the British blockade and we secured guarantees of non-interference from the Germans. This food went to Norwegian ports and was transshipped across the Baltic.

When Norway was invaded in April, 1940, we switched our shipping route to Genoa and from thence to Poland by rail. Soon, however, the British blockade was closed against us with Italy's entrance into the war. We then established buying agents in the Baltic and Balkan States and secured a meager supply of food sufficient to carry on for a few hundred thousand children until the German invasion of Russia, when we had to give up.

In November, 1939, upon the invasion of Finland, then invaded by Russia, that government appealed to my colleagues and myself for aid for their women and children. We organized the Finnish Relief Fund and provided special food to the extent of about $4,000,000. There were no governmental or blockade questions involved.

In May and June, 1940, the Germans invaded Holland, Belgium and France. During the following summer the Belgian exiled government requested my colleagues and myself again to organize the relief of their people on the lines of the First World War and they, having large funds, agreed to furnish the money. The agents of the Dutch and Norwegian exiled government asked that they be included in this relief. We received imploring petitions from the relief committees which were organized inside these different countries, especially to save their children. The United States was still a neutral nation and it was hoped we could set up a non-official, neutral agency to do the work. We initiated negotiations with the belligerent governments for some such arrangement as in the First World War.

In November, 1940, we organized the National Committee on Food for the Small Democracies to promote these negotiations and to mobilize American public support to this action. The committee comprised about 1,400 leading Americans among whom were over 500 religious leaders of every denomination, 400 leading educators, over 200 leading publishers, editors and writers, and some 300 leading citizens among whom were twelve former Ambassadors or Ministers, twenty former high government officials, together with General Pershing and Admiral Pratt. (I am glad to say that the minority of three or four clergymen who bitterly opposed us have now come to our point of view.)

In February, 1941, these negotiations proceeded to a point where the Germans agreed to give such guarantees but the British could not see their way to accept them, asserting that the Germans would not keep their promises and would get the food. We, therefore, changed our wider suggestions into a proposal of an experiment operation of limited scope to demonstrate the feasibility of relief under war conditions. The proposal was:

1. That we make an initial experiment in Belgium to test out whether these people can be saved without military advantage to either side.

2. That this test comprise the feeding only through soup-kitchens where the people come to get their food, and thus there can be no question of feeding Germans.

3. That at the beginning we provide for 1,000,000 adults and 2,000,000 children with bread and soup, the children to receive special food in addition.

4. That the German Government agree that there is to be no requisition of native food, and are themselves to contribute breadstuffs to the program.

5. Both governments to give relief ships immunity from attacks.

6. The whole to be under the supervision and checks by Americans or some neutral body.

7. If this experiment works, then it is to be extended as the need develops and to other democracies.

8. If at any moment the Germans take the food or the native

supplies, then the experiment is to be ended. As the stocks of imported food at any one time would not feed Germany for one day, even seizure of it would not affect the outcome of the war. And such an act would end the whole business in a demonstration to the suffering people that America had done its best. And it would demonstrate the utter brutality of the German concepts for all eternity.

This plan was accepted by the Germans but rejected in March, 1941, with the same reasons as had been given before.

About this time America became more involved, our neutrality became cloudy and obviously Americans would not be allowed to supervise relief in German-occupied territory. Therefore, we laid before the American Government (which now by virtue of the Lend-Lease had a right to a voice) a recommendation that the neutral governments (Sweden, Switzerland or the Argentine) be requested to negotiate this matter with Germany and, in case they were successful, to conduct and supervise the experiment. This proposal was rejected by the American Government in June, 1941.

Time drifted by; misery and death increased. Greece and Jugoslavia had been added to the invaded democracies and especially the former was suffering terribly.

In June, 1942, the Turkish Government intervened and insisted upon relief to Greece. The Turks sent in food. Soon after this, the British and American Governments regularized the matter by arranging that the Swedish and Swiss authorities, with the International Red Cross, conduct the operation and assure the protection of the food. That is now in operation, although upon an inadequate scale. Our State Department has now issued formal statements giving assurances that the imported food reached only the Greeks, that the native food was unmolested and supporting the efforts of the Greek committee in the United States to raise funds.

In effect, our proposed experiment was finally adopted. And here finally is proof that these suffering people can be fed without militarily benefiting the Germans. The success of the experiment in Greece is admission, even eighteen months late, that our contentions were right and practical.

Therefore, there can be no atom of reason why the Belgians, Dutch, Norwegians, Poles and Jugoslavs should not also have relief. The Swedish and Swiss authorities are ready to undertake it. The Swedes have ships that cannot be used by the Allies and therefore there is no deprival of the Allies in that matter. If there is no food to spare in the United States, it can be obtained in South America. Due to shortage in Allied shipping, food is dammed back and unused in South America. The exiled governments of Belgium, Holland and Norway have funds to pay for the food.

There is infinite need for it. Starvation is rampant. When the food supply falls to famine levels, people do not lie down and die from starvation. Long before they get to that point their physical resistance is so lowered by malnutrition that they die of disease. The children weaken first, the women and old men next.

In one Belgian industrial city, where a survey was made, thirty per cent of the children were found to be tubercular or to have rickets, forty per cent more were in the susceptible stage. The supply of meats and fats in these countries is now only ten per cent to twenty per cent of our normal American consumption. All these countries have local relief organizations conducting networks of soup kitchens in frantic endeavor to stretch out what little food there is in hopes of partly saving their children and thus their race. Their supplies are absolutely inadequate and these committees are imploring help.

Our governmental authorities have promised them food after the war.

These promises sound hollow to mothers watching their children starving across the empty table. As a Belgian publication puts it: "The whole question is whether the United Nations are fighting to liberate oppressed peoples or to liberate a vast cemetery."

There are long-view reasons why this experiment should at once be extended over these countries. Here are five or six nations whose whole philosophy of life and government has been and is yet opposed to totalitarianism. If the spirit of free men in the long years to come is to survive on the continent of Europe, it will be among these peoples devoted to freedom by their every instinct. Over centuries they have time and time again maintained their systems of free men from subjugation. They have done it not by military strength but by sheer moral and intellectual resistance. If the democracies of the West are to say to them now—as some of our citizens have in effect said to them—"We will make no effort to save your millions of women and children; they must die or grow up with stunted minds and bodies," then there is little encouragement to them to hold fast to our ideals. If confidence in the ideals of democracy is to be held, now is the time to hold it.

And there is also here an indeterminate obligation.

Most of these occupied nations live, partly even in times of peace, by importing overseas food for their people and feed for their animals. That is stopped by the British and American blockade. It is right—emphatically right—to say that the Germans have the primary responsibility in all this. They invaded these countries. The Germans can end the blockade any day by surrender. But these helpless peoples of the small democracies cannot end the blockade by surrender. They have to die. Does any American feel morally comfortable in maintaining this blockade if the food can be protected from the Germans?

Among those whose fates we are discussing are millions of children. Should Americans decide that these millions of children and women are to be a sacrifice that must be made to protect America in this war?

These little nations fought and sacrificed for the preservation of democratic institutions. That they are to be deserted without even a trial at their relief is not pleasant. And the more do these arguments become potent when experience in Greece shows that they can be saved without prolonging the war a day or giving important military advantage to either side.

And, overriding all this, there is the question of humanity. There are things in this world that are not silenced by ideological argument or declamation as to who is responsible. They are not to be settled in these ways because of the teachings of Christ which have resounded down these 2,000 years. The greatest Teacher of mankind did not argue and debate over the ideology and the sins of the two thieves. That teaching gave to mankind a new vision and part of that vision was mercy and compassion. And this question is today the test of our religious faith. For compassion is one of the major foundations of Christianity. And compassion is part of the warp and woof of democracy.

Without compassion there would be no legislation for the underdog. From this ethic have sprung our vast fabric of benevolent institutions, the relief of our unemployed, our hospitals, our solicitude for the weak and the unfortunate. Without compassion there is no progress for humanity.

We cannot as a Christian nation dismiss our concern. And the parable of the Samaritan has pungent implications other than the compassion of the Samaritan alone. Perhaps some will remember the condemnation, which has echoed over centuries, of the priest and the Levite who passed by on the other side.

I am aware that 3,000 miles away in the surroundings of our American homes it is difficult to envisage what all this means.

I am perhaps one of the few living Americans who have dealt with famine among millions of people. During the last war, my appointment was from the American people to represent their hearts and their religious faith in saving tens of millions from starvation and disease. I have moved continually among these hideous scenes. I have seen the agonies of famine. I have listened to the pleadings of children, the fierce demands of mothers for the right of their children to live. I have seen relief stations and hospitals filled with its consequences in distorted minds and bodies. I have witnessed it in twenty nations. I have seen generals of armies, to whom dead on the battlefields brought little emotion, melt into tears in the face of these spectacles. I have seen starvation's unending blight upon the world. I know starvation in the last war had a part in the causes of the world's agony today. I had hoped it would never again come to the world. But it has come, and I would be untrue to myself and to my country if I did not fight to the end to ameliorate it.

Feed the Starving Now

Jointly with Hugh Gibson

Collier's Magazine
[February 20, 1943]

FOOD is being sent through the blockade to the starving Greeks. We can rejoice that this heroic people is being saved from annihilation. Occupied by the Axis armies, Greece is being fed through the Allied blockade and under neutral supervision, and the operation is certified by our government not to benefit the Axis. It receives the approval and help of our government. As Americans, we can rejoice in the wisdom that has led to this total reversal of our governmental policy on relief.

It has proved workable in Greece—although on a scale our government describes as "still woefully inadequate"—so we are warranted in hoping for further and early action.

First: It is imperative that there be an immediate increase in the volume of aid to Greece if that gallant people is to be saved.

Second: The time has come to decide (before it is too late) what we are going to do for 50,000,000 starving people (including some 12,000,000 children) in Belgium, Holland, Norway and Poland.

Indeed, the march of events is accelerating at such a rate as to justify the hope of action before this article appears. But if there is no such action, a little straight-from-the-shoulder speaking may be of help in bringing a realization of some moral and political obligations. In any event, this article will serve its purpose: to advocate action if we are still lagging; to justify and support the government if it is moved to act quickly and decisively.

The slowly increasing trickle of help to Greece began in the summer of 1941. Its beginning is significant. One day in August the London Times printed a brief paragraph to the effect that the Foreign Office had consented to opening the blockade for certain quantities of food to go to the suffering population of Greece.

The second of the writers of this article was in London at the request of two of the occupied countries, trying to persuade the British to open the blockade so as to allow feeding of the other small democracies. He was at once deluged with questions from the exiled governments as to the foundation for this report. He was as puzzled as others, but was given an explanation that same afternoon. He received a visit from the Turkish Ambassador, an old friend, who came to talk about another problem.

On being asked if the report was true and if he knew how it had come about, the Ambassador replied that it was true and that he had brought it about himself. He said that, although the Turks and Greeks had been age-old enemies, they had settled their quarrels and were both determined to go on being friends.

When disaster overtook Greece, and wholesale starvation spread throughout the country, the Turkish Government considered it had a moral obligation to its neighbor; the Ambassador was instructed to approach the British Government and urge that relief operations be allowed for the Greeks. In due course, he received the customary reply, enumerating the usual arguments against any help for populations under Nazi occupation.

TURKEY MAKES FIRST MOVE

This unfavorable reply was forwarded to Ankara, and, a short time later, came a telegram instructing the Ambassador to inform the Foreign Office that on such and such a date, such and such ships loaded with food would sail from such and such ports in Turkey for such and such ports in Greece. This did the trick.

Most countries could not have carried it off in this way. But Turkey is a highly important neutral that could not be antagonized. Not only were the ships allowed to go through to their destination, but when experience proved that the operation involved no danger to the Allied armies, that it in no way benefited the Nazis, the volume of relief was increased, and financial facilities were provided by Britain and America. The whole operation was regularized by agreements set up by the Swedish and Swiss authorities and placed under the guardianship of the International Red Cross, exactly as the writers of this article had proposed eighteen months before.

Civilization may well be grateful to the Turks for opening the door to reason and compassion. The whole problem was bogged down in governmental refusal to examine the possibilities of relief. This was all the more baffling because the whole question of relief had been thoroughly tested during the last war by the feeding of ten millions of Belgians and Frenchmen living under the German armies of occupation.

Fortunately, the success of the Greek relief operation has served to confirm the experience of the last war and to demonstrate that it is possible to help our friends and allies without weakening the war effort. In the light of this, our government has come out categorically to defend Greek relief against criticism with the soundest of arguments. We have no hesitation in approving and applauding these arguments which are those we have been advancing for over two years.

With such a clear-cut governmental attitude having been adopted as regards the Greek problem, both compassion and loyalty dictate that we should try to do as much for other allies in desperate straits.

Time will prove how tragic was our failure to institute suitable measures of relief while we could still have saved millions from tuberculosis, rickets and physical and mental degeneration.

Recent reports give the following figures of combined meat and fat rations in some of the occupied countries:

Norway—3 pounds per person per month.

Belgium—2 pounds per person per month.

Poland—1½ pounds per person per month.

In the United States we consume an average of 20 pounds per person per month. The full horror of starvation in these Allied countries will not be brought home to us for years.

This situation is not "food shortage." It is *starvation*. Starved people degenerate in their resistance to disease, and such disease is rampant. There is typhus and tuberculosis in Polish cities. In one of the Belgian industrial districts recently surveyed, 30 per cent of the children are now tubercular—and an additional 40 per cent pretubercular. And there is an appalling increase in mortality of the children, the women, the aged and weak.

These are grim clinical figures and they represent more than cold figures. They represent children like yours and mine, with the same right to life and health and happiness, now slipping toward a miserable end for lack of food.

But a great ray of hope has come into their lives with the knowledge that at last food is being sent to the Greeks; that our authorities have recognized relief as desirable and workable. The hope of help, fast waning in the third winter of suffering, has revived in the belief that it will be their turn next. But the decision involves even more than dying children and starving millions.

If we take the right turning, we may save all that remains on the continent of Europe that stands for what we stand for— the forces on which we must count if liberty and decency are to prevail again—for these nations are the only areas of freedom in Europe.

We make a grievous mistake if we assume that the small democracies are willingly leaving this problem to our decision. This is not the case. They feel strongly and bitterly on the subject.

NORWEGIAN SAILORS PROTEST

One instance may be given: Since 1940, the Norwegian merchant fleet has been used to carry food and supplies to Britain and to fighting fronts. Only a few months ago the Norwegian seamen in New York, through their organizations and unions, made strong representations to their government in regard to the food problem in Norway. After consultation with the authorities, they took the stand that they would not "at present" take drastic action and strike. They were, however, emphatic in saying that they did not propose to go home at the end of the war and "have to go to the churchyards and find the crosses of their dead ones who have died of hunger"; that in that case, their present efforts in the common cause would have been in vain.

If we take the wrong turning, we shall come one day to find a strange Europe in which our defeated enemies alone have health and stamina, in which our friends are weakened in health and character—and perhaps embittered. To take the wrong turning is to adopt the course best calculated to thwart our own efforts at building a better world after the war.

We are fundamentally a just people and we want to have our country take the right course. It might be well to put ourselves in the place of people in occupied territory looking across the table at starving children and try to imagine how they feel.

They know that relief is feasible, for many of them owe their lives to its successful operation in the last war.

They know a great part of their food comes from overseas in peacetime and that they cannot hope to live unless it is allowed to come from overseas again.

They know the Greeks are being fed and that they, too, could be fed; and they have the bitter knowledge that the enemy in Germany always has the option of surrendering if they do not want to starve, but that the allies of Britain and the United States are deprived of even this miserable privilege, that they are helpless and must starve if the blockade continues.

They are not moved by broadcast promises that they will be fed when the war is over or when they have thrown off the Nazi yoke. They know they will be fed when the war is over, but that does not save their children from starvation now.

HELP MUST NOT BE DELAYED

We must be honest with ourselves to the extent of remembering that these wretched people are our allies and that they have a claim upon our loyalty and help; that it does not suffice to tell them they will be fed when the war is over and leave them to their fate in the meantime. If we proceed logically from the Greek experiment, we shall be following a course worthy of our high tradition in such matters.

There is no doubt in our minds that the American people desire that these people be helped. There are ample facts to support this statement. It is worth while to review some history of the efforts to save these people during the present war. The effort to secure our government's attention to this matter was supported by 2,000 committees of leading citizens of the United States under the leadership of the Committee on Food for the Small Democracies—itself a committee of 1,000 leading citizens.

Our Congress has long been on record. A joint resolution was introduced into both houses of Congress requesting the President to take up the problem to see what can be done about relief for the small democracies. This resolution was signed by a clear majority of the House and by a large minority of the Senate, equally Democrats and Republicans.

From the beginning, the major religious organizations have supported the idea of relief—Methodists, Baptists, Lutherans, Catholics, Jews and many others. There were some minor and vociferous church leaders, devoid of pity, who opposed it. They must have been surprised to see the non-Christian Turk take an effective stand for compassion.

Finally in December, 1942, the Federal Council of Churches of Christ in America added to the record by passing a resolution favoring action to save the peoples of the small democracies.

It may be added that in October, 1942, the Church of England, previously opposed, began to be moved. The High Chamber of the Synod of Canterbury, meeting in London, unanimously voted an order of the day which calls the attention of the British people to the tragic situation of the invaded countries. This resolution was proposed by the Right Reverend George K. A. Bell, Bishop of Chichester, who spoke of the misery of the Belgians and the Greeks. The Archbishop of Canterbury, who presided over the meeting, stressed the fact that competent authorities realize that vitamins or powdered milk, even if allowed through the blockade, would not suffice to save those who should be helped. He concluded by emphasizing the need for an effort to bring about some improvement in this dreadful situation.

For a long time, the refusal to allow relief—even of an experimental character—reposed upon a single statement made in the House of Commons by Mr. Churchill in August, 1940. In answer to a question, he stated in plain, blunt language that there would be no relief—and this was stated as a matter of British policy.

We can recognize that this statement was made at a time when Britain was herself in a desperate situation. Churchill was carrying on under great anxieties and pressures, when it was not easy to concentrate on any problem aside from the immediate problem of survival. However, there have been many developments since that time; and in view of these, particularly the success of the Greek experience, it may well be that Mr. Churchill himself would be ready to reconsider the whole problem from the broader aspect of saving our allies.

But in August, 1940, it did not appear in that light to the small democracies and their officials. They were frankly shocked that a problem involving the lives of millions of their citizens should be disposed of as a matter of British policy. There they were, recognized as Allied governments, contributing their armies, navies and air forces, their merchant marine, the resources of their colonies to the common effort. It seemed to them not unreasonable to look upon this as an inter-Allied problem which should not be settled out of hand without their being heard. But that is how it was settled and how it remains settled.

For a long time, our American government acquiesced—unwilling to say or do anything that might embarrass Britain in her epic ordeal. Even when we began participating in the struggle with Lend-Lease, we continued to treat this as a British problem and to refer the official and unofficial advocates of relief back to the original source of refusal. But with Pearl Harbor, our status definitely changed. We became allies not only of Britain but also of the small democracies.

Since that time we have had a more direct responsibility. We can no longer shrug it off with the assertion that this is a British problem, although anybody advocating relief is, even today, laying himself open to the charge of being anti-British. Curiously enough, this charge is not leveled against the many British subjects and British organizations professing the same views.

This is not a British problem. We Americans are also blockading these people. It is an Allied problem, and we are an ally. From the form of the recent announcements, it would appear that the relief problem had been transferred from London to Washington.

"TO SAVE A HEROIC PEOPLE"

As Americans, we can be glad that once the Greek experiment proved itself practical, our government came out with an unreserved statement of the facts. On August 3, 1942, Mr. Sumner Welles, Undersecretary of State, wrote a letter to the president of the Greek War Relief Association, expressing the satisfaction of the American government with what he described as "feasible attempts, with adequate safeguards, to save a heroic people from annihilation." On August 7, 1942, the State Department issued a statement to the press giving further details of this successful operation.

These documents will be worth remembering, for time may show that they mark an important turning point in the history of humane action in this war. The conditions indicated for passage of supplies through the blockade are obviously similar to those tested by experience in the last war. The reservation to the civil population of native crops and the condition that the work should stop in the event the Nazi authorities violated their agreements are the same we suggested in submitting the plan eighteen months ago. The statements of our government constitute an eloquent appeal for public support of Greek relief.

The declaration from our State Department goes far beyond the Greek problem. It disposes officially of the arguments previously advanced against relief operations in general and would seem to open the door for the other small democracies.

All the arguments in favor of relief having been proved up to the hilt in actual practice in Greece, on what conceivable ground can we refuse to do as much for our other allies? What answer can we make to the Belgians, for instance, when they ask why we left them to starve, after establishing all over again in this war that they could be helped without danger to the war effort?

This whole problem has been so distorted by propaganda that our national thinking needs to be straightened out before we can hope to make sensible decisions. We need a mental and moral housecleaning.

We owe it to ourselves to look at this problem from the humane point of view, to recognize that this is no cold question of figures but a problem affecting the lives of suffering women and children, depending on us if they are to be saved from lingering death. If there were no other reasons for feeding these people, compassion for their suffering should be enough. In the parable of the Samaritan, the greatest leader of mankind did not inquire into political consequences.

A letter just received gives a striking account of a visit to a Belgian village:

"I went on an independent mission to Belgium; I took an ambulance into Belgium, filled with food that had been given to me by Americans leaving Paris.

"Conditions as I found them in the few towns of Belgium I was able to visit were far worse than described. I had not expected to be greeted on my arrival like a savior angel or anything; on the other hand, I did not expect what I saw. In the first town I entered, Douache, a town of maybe 5,000 people,

I think, the inhabitants stood on the market square, completely quiet, completely immobile, until the ambulances stopped; then they threw themselves at us, tearing our clothes into shreds, several times almost upsetting the ambulances in their effort to reach the food.

"When, through the window of one of the cars, I screamed for them to be quiet, a woman in a momentary silence answered, 'Quiet? It is easy for you to say quiet; our children are starving—starving, do you hear?' And at that, the whole thing started all over again, only worse.

"Finally the five town elders managed to get them to line up and wait until their turn came. I visited many houses in this town; a woman told me that the death rate until then was something near 560; but I gather that in those, she included the children and old people who had been paralyzed and blinded. I remember her also pointing at a child with a water stomach, saying '*Il est mort*,' though the child was not actually dead."

THE CASE AGAINST RELIEF

For more than two years, there has been a systematic campaign carried on to defeat the relief movement. This campaign has been characterized by irresponsible and reckless talk, deliberate misrepresentation of fact and hysterical denunciation. One of the basic claims of the anti-relief people was that they were defending the British blockade against those who sought to break it down.

Another standby is the statement that the exiled governments of Belgium, Norway, Holland and Poland are opposed to relief for their people. This is nothing less than a clumsy lie —although by dint of repetition, it has gained considerable credence.

Another assertion is that the people in occupied territory are opposed to relief—that they would deplore the sending of food. Does it sound strange that starving people should take such a stand? But the zealous campaigners say they have thousands of letters from occupied territory protesting against relief.

Has anybody seen *one* of these letters—to say nothing about thousands of them? The writers of this article have not, although they have expressed their incredulity and their readiness to be convinced. On the other hand, they have seen multitudes of letters, cables and resolutions of all the relief agencies inside those countries—*all* of them praying for relief in terms the pathos of which would melt stone; *not one* clamoring to be allowed to starve to death or even expressing doubt as to the feasibility of relief.

American thinking has been confused by many leaflets and statements emanating from officials who are sadly uninformed on the subject.

AN UNFORTUNATE UTTERANCE

For instance, at the last Herald Tribune Forum, an official of the British embassy in Washington made the categorical statement that "the conquered allies have never asked for the blockade to be lifted."

It is unfortunate that an important official should be sent out to make speeches without being more adequately informed as to the facts. In this case, the authors of this article could have furnished the speaker with documentary proof that many of the conquered allies have not stopped asking that the blockade be lifted to let food through to their peoples.

Another so-called objection to relief is the statement that such matters should be left entirely to the military. Judging from the expressions of military leaders, that might be a good way of securing favorable action. Here are two of them:

General Pershing:

"I wish to send my greetings to those who are endeavoring to find a method by which food supplies can be furnished to the democracies in Europe occupied by the German armies. There is no doubt that millions are in jeopardy unless they are given aid from somewhere. From my own war experience and some knowledge of problems involved, I have every confidence that the salvation of these people can be worked out along the lines proposed by Mr. Hoover without military loss or benefit to either side."

Admiral Pratt:

"I have no hesitation in saying that this aid can be given under Mr. Hoover's proposals, without any damage to Great Britain. Taking the long view of the future of constructive forces in the world and America's relation to it, it is of vital importance to America that Mr. Hoover's plans be carried through."

With all these voices, with the actual successful experience in Greece, why wait longer to express the compassion of the American people and their solicitude for the future of civilization in Europe?

Our government has taken an admirable step in appointing ex-Governor Herbert Lehman of New York to organize American aid to reconstruction from the war. It would seem that the first step in this great task is to save the small democracies from future destruction. This would be a glorious inauguration of his mission. It would justify the religious faith for which we are fighting—for that faith lives only through action and compassion.

Food For Europe's Children

NEW YORK CITY

[*February 20, 1943*]

I N THIS tragic world there are a multitude of military fronts and home fronts. But if civilization is to be saved, there must be another front behind these fronts. That is, the front of human decency. That front is the front of ideals, of aspirations, of religious faith and humane purpose. It is the front of honor among nations and men, of sacrifice, of kindliness, of helpfulness, of fair play and sportsmanship. It is the front of justice and of compassion. It is the front of saving human life and suffering. The present leaders of Germany, Italy and Japan are stamping out such expression. It is to establish the front of decency in the world for which we are fighting.

The front of decency will survive only through deeds as well as words. Action on this front must often be expressed through governments, but it must arise from the people. Upon their thousands of organizations, religious and otherwise, rests the responsibility of making life better, happier and less bitter. From them must come the insistence upon amelioration of the hardships and spiritual destruction of war, and of upholding the front of decency. And we are here today to demand an action of that front.

To make the problem clear, I may give a little history of the efforts to get relief to the starving women, children and unemployed men in German-invaded democracies.

During the four years of the First World War, relief was

carried on under the direction of my colleagues and myself for the 10,000,000 people of German-invaded Belgium and Northern France. This was passed through the British blockade with the cooperation of the British Government. We secured guarantees of immunity of ships and food, both native and imported, from the Germans. And we supervised the distribution. About $900,000,000 value and 5,000,000 tons of food were delivered. The major part of the funds came from the British, French and American Governments. During the war the relief was repeatedly defended by the British and French Prime Ministers and Cabinet Ministers upon their own independent information from charges that the Germans received any military benefits from the operation. After that war these Governments investigated the experience on the ground and not only reiterated their statements but fulsomely eulogized the whole management of it.

In September, 1939, Germany invaded Poland. In October, the Exiled Polish Government requested my colleagues and myself to organize an operation for the Polish people similar to that in Belgium during the First World War. The Exiled Government offered and did find large sums of governmental money for its support, in addition to American charity. We at once established the Polish Relief Commission and began initial shipments of food to support about 300,000 of the most needy children.

This work was slowed down when sea lanes were closed by the German invasion of Norway and by the entry of Italy into the war. We struggled along with food from the Baltic and Balkan states, but this was closed out when Germany invaded Russia. The Germans invaded Holland, Belgium and France in May, 1940. During the following summer the Belgian Exiled Government requested my colleagues and myself to again organize the relief of their people on the lines of the First World War. The agents of the Dutch and Norwegian Exiled Governments asked that they be included in this relief. We received imploring petitions from the relief committees which were organized inside these different countries, especially to save their children.

In November, 1940, we organized the National Committee on Food for the Small Democracies to promote negotiation with the British and German Governments of some such arrangement as in the last war, and to mobilize public support to this action. The Committee comprised about 1,400 leading Americans among whom were over 500 religious leaders of every denomination, 400 leading educators, over 200 leading publishers, editors and writers, and some 300 leading citizens among whom were 12 former Ambassadors or Ministers, 20 former high government officials, together with General Pershing and Admiral Pratt.

The plan of systematic relief based on the experience of the last war failed of acceptance. Then in January, 1941, we proposed to the various governments that an experiment should be undertaken upon a limited scale to see if it would work. As the status of the United States changed in the meantime from neutrality eighteen months ago, we again modified the proposal.

I wish to make absolutely clear in the simplest terms exactly what we are proposing, why we propose it, both that it be understood and that it be not misrepresented.

First. Over eighteen months ago we urged that the neutral governments—mainly the Swedish and Swiss—be solicited to conduct an experiment in relief of the children, the women and the unemployed in the German-occupied democracies.

Second. We proposed that this experiment (a) be based upon permission to pass the Allied blockade with limited food supplies; (b) such agreements with the German Government that the enemy would obtain no direct or indirect advantage from this relief; (c) that the food be supplied directly to the people through the network of soup kitchens now operated by the devoted men and women of each of these countries; (d) that it be conducted under the supervision of the representatives of the Swedish and Swiss Governments; (e) that the stocks of imported food in those countries at no time amount to more than two days' supply for the German people—even if they seized it; (f) that the relief be withdrawn the instant there was any violation of the agreements.

Third. That experiment was refused at the time. But it was subsequently established in relief of the starving in Greece. Food has now been going through the blockade into Greece for over nine months. It is being distributed under the supervision of the representatives of these neutral governments. The amount is inadequate but it is saving thousands of Greek lives. Our government now certifies that the operation is successful and that the Germans receive no advantage from it.

Fourth. We now ask that these neutral governments be authorized to spread the same service to the other occupied democracies.

Fifth. The Swedes have idle ships that they will not risk in belligerent service. They are, however, ready to charter them for use in humanitarian service. Thus the question of depleting Allied shipping does not arise. There is ample food in South America which cannot be transported by the Allies and therefore there need be no deprival of food to the Allies, including the United States.

Sixth. Most of the occupied democracies have funds with which to pay for the food. It is not, therefore, a drain upon the American taxpayer.

Seventh. This service is long overdue. Every report is an appeal to not only the front of human decency, but it is an appeal to the self-interest of the United Nations. The rations these people receive are pitiful. Starvation is rife. With their vitality lowered, disease is claiming the children and the weak in thousands. The modern pestilence which first comes with famine is tuberculosis. Reports show whole districts in which 35% of the children react to tuberculosis tests and in some districts as high as 60%. If the child life of these democracies is to be saved it must be saved now.

Eighth. It is a hollow promise that these people will receive food after the war is over. It means little to a mother who sets her table only to watch her children wilt.

Ninth. These democracies have held the torch of free men for centuries. If we want the foundations of free men to survive in Europe, it must survive in these democracies. And it will not survive in bitter, frustrated, physically-distorted or dead children.

Tenth. I ask you if, in these dimming lights of civilization, it is not worth while that the lamp of compassion shall be kept alight? Can religious faith survive without it? Are we sustaining the front of human decency if we take no action?

The Food Situation

Press Statement, Chicago, Illinois

[March 1, 1943]

THE food situation cannot be blacked out by speeches. The acknowledged facts are:

1. We have been cut off by submarine and the Japs from our normal, large imports of food. Out of our larder thus depleted, we must supply Britain, Russia and the extra food required by our armed forces if we are to win the war.

2. I believe we can ration down our consumption to support this drain if we could maintain the 1942 farm production.

3. But we are faced with a serious decrease of farm products in 1943 due to taking manpower to the armed forces and munitions, to lack of farm machinery and fertilizers and to decrease in protein feeds. In some farm products the ceiling prices do not cover the farmer's costs. He is apparently expected to work a 72-hour week for less than nothing. The prospects of short planting, short harvesting, short animal products in 1943, as shown by the reports of the County Agriculture Agents, are most alarming. Already there are partial local famines in meat and dairy products in many parts of the country.

4. These forces of degeneration in agriculture are progressive and if they continue over a long war we can lose the war on the home front.

5. I have not proposed to reduce the ultimate size of the army, as Wallace and Green purport. I was the first to raise the whole question and proposed (a) that as there is a shipping bottleneck on the amount of men that can be sent abroad in

1943, further draft of farm boys can be deferred until after the planting and harvest of 1943; (b) that the army should furlough farm boys to help in the peak of planting and the peak of harvesting and to care for livestock; (c) that towns folk should be first trained and then used to help the farmers, although the problem cannot be solved by this means alone; (d) that as the bottleneck also limits the amount of munitions we can send, we might divert some manufacturing capacity to farm machinery.

6. The country is alive with black markets in many products, and thereby justice in distribution and this method of price control is breaking down.

7. Unless remedies are promptly applied, it is useless to talk of relief to the inevitable European famine after the war and even of a healthy supply to the American people.

Our Food Front

I CONSIDER it an honor to participate in this most important Conference of Mid-West Governors. You represent the great major food supply of the nation. And you have much to contribute to its solution. And that is our sole purpose here.

I have been deeply impressed by the single-minded attitude of every man at this Conference. You have sought solutions to this inevitable problem of total war. You have brought a wealth of knowledge and experience.

Every man at this Conference wants to help the government in its gigantic task of winning this war and the peace. The problem considered here is a problem of the home front.

We have a most difficult war to win. We must win. And to assure winning beyond any doubt we must organize our economic resources for a long war. Any other course would be national folly.

The strategy in total war is not solely a military question. The home front is as important as the military front.

The home front of the greatest physical staying power, of the greatest resources, of the greatest will to endure and work will give the greatest strength to the military front. A weakened home front will weaken the military front. Wars can be won or lost on the home front—in this war as in any war.

Our country is going strong on the military front. The magnificent ability, courage and devotion of our Army and Navy lift the spirit of every American. We have weaknesses on the home front. We at home must show the ability, courage and devotion to correct these weaknesses.

THE FOOD FRONT

One of these weaknesses is in the food sector. And indeed, of the different sectors of the home front, food is the greatest. It stands next to the military effort in importance.

Food serves on both the home and the foreign fronts. We have not only the job of feeding ourselves, but also our Allies. And if we would have peace after the war instead of the anarchy of starving Europe, we must be prepared to meet that also. Therefore our food production must be strengthened for a huge and a long sustained effort.

Moreover, while our civil population can be deeply deprived of most other consumers' goods, there is a sharp limit to what it can endure in food and still be physically effective for its part in the war. Failure on the food sector has lost wars before now.

We can well explore the experience of nations in the first World War in this particular.

RUSSIA

Prior to that war Russia was a surplus food country. She exported large quantities of food. Her warleaders devoted themselves solely to the military front. They neglected the food production front. Two years later the Russian cities were pinched for food. Mobs roamed the streets howling, "Give us bread!" "Down with the Czar!" The Czar went down, as he deserved. The Kerensky government came to power. It lasted nine months. It could not recover the food production and thus restore the home front of a great nation in the midst of war. The Communist slogan was: "The rich have hoarded the food; you will find it in their cellars." The cellars were empty. And Russia collapsed in the war.

GERMANY

Germany in 1914 produced about 85% of her food supplies despite the blockade. Her war leaders were sure they could ration the population down 15% and therefore had no anxiety about food. They neglected the food front. In three years Germany was dangerously short of food. In four years mobs were demanding bread and the Emperor's head. And Germany failed on the military front.

FRANCE

France was a self-sustaining food country before 1914. She had to concentrate her manpower wholly on the military effort to defend herself. Her food production decreased and she imported more and more from overseas. In 1917, she had exhausted her resources with which to pay for imports. We came into the war and saved her from collapse on the food front.

I do not contend that these collapses were wholly due to food, but it was the largest sector.

THE CAUSES OF DEGENERATION ON THE FOOD FRONT

And we can usefully explore the causes of this food degeneration in these European countries during the last total war. You will find some sinister parallels in America today.

Too much manpower was drained from the farms in all these nations. Their leaders said the women, children and inexperienced city people could serve the farms. They could not. The manufacture of farm machinery was turned to munitions and inadequate replacements were made. Fertilizers were diverted to explosives. The fisheries were restricted because of the dangers of the sea and the draft of seamen. The planting was less effective and harvesting less complete. More fields had to be turned to human food and thus feed supplies for the animals decreased. The import of feed from overseas was reduced or cut off. The loss of skilled manpower particularly affected the care of animals. The herds decreased and the animal products went down at an accelerated rate every year. As they decreased, more and more of the breeding herd had to be eaten for meat. The degeneration everywhere was first in meats and fats, which include dairy products, and then in breadstuffs.

Never has there been a greater demonstration of man's dependence on his food animals.

THE FOOD FRONT IN AMERICA IN THE FIRST WORLD WAR

Before the last war we in America were a great food-surplus producing country. We exported about 10 billion pounds of human food a year.

In that year our leaders fully accepted the fact that the food front was the next important thing to the military front. Early in the war, President Wilson announced:

"The importance of an adequate food supply . . . is superlative. Upon the farmers . . . rests the fate of the war and the fate of nations . . . The Government will do everything possible to assist the farmers in securing adequate seed . . . an adequate force of laborers . . . and farm machinery." And again he said, "The men and women who devote themselves to these things will be serving the country and conducting the fight for peace and freedom as truly as the men on the battlefield."

In that war we held enough of the boys on the farm. We increased our food production. We voluntarily reduced our consumption. From these two sources we were able to increase our exports from a rate of 10 billions to a rate of 30 billion pounds per year. We increased our total number of food animals over the war period. We were able to carry Britain, Italy, France and Belgium on our food back and we were able to save Europe from the after-war famine as well.

THE SITUATION TODAY IN OTHER NATIONS AT WAR

Now what is today's food situation abroad?

Britain, always a food-deficient country, is dependent upon

overseas imports. Now cut off from their normal sources of supplies from overseas, a large part of the burden must be carried by the United States.

Russia was self-sufficient in food before this war. But due to the drain of her manpower to the war effort and due to the German invasion she has become partly dependent upon the United States for food.

Germany sought to hold her food front by storing large stocks of food in advance. She has robbed her victims until they are starving. But implacably from the same causes as in the last war her food production is degenerating. In meats and fats particularly, she is steadily approaching a disastrous crisis. Italy is traveling the same road.

THE CONDITION OF OUR OWN NATIONAL LARDER

Now what is the state of our larder today? What will it be tomorrow?

For some months I have devoted myself to this problem in which I can claim some experience. I have traveled into twenty states in inquiry from the farmers, from the processors, from merchants, from housewives and from public officials. I have not depended solely upon statistics.

We have today five certain drains from our normal larder.

The First Deficit—We Are Part Blockaded. Surprising as it may be to some people, the United States had, before this European war, ceased to be a great food-surplus country. With the exception of the extraordinary harvest of 1942 we were on balance of all foods an importing country. The Japs and the submarine have cut off a large part of these imports. This shrinkage in our supplies of imported vegetable oils alone would be equivalent to the fat produced by 8 or 10 million hogs each year. And we imported large amounts of protein feed for animals. We imported vegetables and sugar.

We had a surplus of one major food line alone—that is cereals. But as the war goes on we can quickly expend that surplus in manufacture of industrial alcohol and necessary animal feeds. With this exception, the day after Pearl Harbor our national cupboard was potentially partly short of its normal food.

The Second Deficit—Our Obligations to Our Allies. We are compelled to open our larder, already depleted by blockade of our imports, to help Britain, Russia and others through lend-lease.

The Third Deficit—Extra Food for Our Fighting Men. Our armed men eat more than as civilians. They eat twice as much meats and fats. And they must have a priority on our larder.

The Fourth Deficit—Extra Food for Workers. Our increased numbers engaged in hard physical labor need more food.

I have no doubt we can tighten our belt and ration down our consumption to meet these four deficits in our normal larder. That is, the deficiency in imports, the drain from lend-lease, from extra supplies for our military forces and for our workers.

The Fifth Deficit—Decrease in Production. The most disturbing thing about our nation-wide larder is the prospective decrease in our food production. Secretary Wickard has repeatedly warned we will produce less in 1943 than in the last year. We lost some crops, many dairy cows and sheep last year for lack of labor. Yet we had more manpower and machines on the farm last year than we can hope for again during the war.

And we lived under two illusions last year. One was the spell of a record ground crop harvest far above normal.

The other was the abnormal killing of animals and thus a fictitious appearance of meat supply. A study of the increase in non-inspected slaughter of cattle based on the country hides which came into the market, the abnormal number of dairy cattle slaughtered, the abnormal number of sheep slaughtered all show that we had an abnormal meat supply. Yet we had a shortage in animal products during the latter part of the year despite this abnormal killing. And it is already much worse this year.

SIGNS OF DEGENERATION IN AGRICULTURE

But all that is not the greatest worry. There are symptoms of a dangerously degenerating agriculture that must be stopped.

Unlike our case in the war twenty-five years ago, we have today at work in America these uncanny parallels with the same degenerative forces that have been so disastrous in Europe. Like them we have drawn undue manpower from the farms. In the recent survey by the county agricultural service, seventy per cent of them report that due to decreased manpower there would be decreased acreage planted this year. Fifty-eight per cent of them reported prospective decreases from eleven per cent to twenty per cent in planting. And harvesting requires much more manpower than planting. The livestock situation is also acute.

Work as they will, it is impossible that women, children and city folks can wholly supply the lack in this skilled craft. That farming requires great skill needs no further indication than that we have replaced 16,000,000 horses with tractors. We have increased production by intense development of plant and animal technology. Like Europe in the last war, our farm machinery is wearing out faster than the replacement. Our imports of food are curtailed. Our fisheries are seriously restricted. Our protein feed for animals is very short. We are compelled to divert our nitrate fertilizers to explosives. All these are characteristic of European failures in the last war.

And we now have another degenerating force peculiar to ourselves. We have a price system in force that often strangles production and distribution. And prices are below the farmer's cost and just wage in many commodities.

All this sort of degeneration is progressive. Unless it is stopped in 1943, it will be worse in 1944 and still worse in 1945. And a prudent nation would plan for a long war. We must come in strong at the finish if we are to make the peace.

Unlike Britain and Russia, we have no great food country

standing behind us filling our larder from overseas in this emergency.

If we wanted any further evidence of this degeneration, we can find it in the despair that leads to auction sales, and in the abandonment of farms. We can find it in the undue killing of dairy cattle. We can find it in the shops without supplies for the housewife for days at a time. We can find it in local famines of meat or butter or potatoes or something else. We can find it in the epidemic of black markets all over the country.

REMEDIES

There is no cause for alarm, provided we set about remedy —and quickly.

Some of us, anxious over this problem, have had the temerity for the last five months to make suggestions to our authorities as to this strategy on our food front. We have supported the Secretary of Agriculture in his efforts.

We have from time to time made many constructive recommendations. They are familiar to you. I only mention them again because this vaccination has not sufficiently taken even yet. And time runs short—very short. No man can affect the timing of crops. That is inexorable.

We have recommended that agriculture must rank with munitions.

We have insisted that there must be more manpower and more machinery on the farms.

We recommended that the divided and competitive authorities over food in Washington should be consolidated under the Secretary of Agriculture.

We recommended that farm and food problems should be more largely decentralized to the States. That method contributed greatly to win the food battle in the last war.

We recommended that this ancient and inefficient method of price control now in use should be replaced by a simpler and more effective protection to both farmer and housewife.

We asked that prices to the farmer be increased to cover his costs and his labor.

We recommended definite organization for recruiting and distribution of agricultural labor, including training of women.

We asked that the former, large, seasonal immigration of Mexican farmers be organized and restored.

We recommended that the Army should consider deferring the draft of farm boys during 1943 and the furloughing of farm boys especially for the harvest and for some livestock purposes.

I have in mind a letter from President Wilson to Senator Capper in 1918 in which he assured the Senator that "men essential to the continued and undiminished operation of our farms shall be deferred" and that the Secretary of War had asked from Congress the authority to "furlough selected men during planting and harvest time."

We said an assurance of this co-operation in this war from the Army would help restore the confidence of the farmers that they can harvest this year and thus encourage them to plant.

We said: "There is a bottleneck in shipping which for the present limits your sending immediately all your men and equipment overseas." We suggested that this bottleneck should be examined in the light of the desperate agricultural need to see if some relief could be given in manpower and machinery in 1943 without weakening our military effort abroad. We have offered no opinion as to the ultimate number of the armed men required to win the war.

But we have a right to speak on what it will require to win it on the home front.

I would not repeat all these recommendations here if they had been heeded. However, an aroused public opinion is getting some results. I have no doubt the Governors of our States will be able to advance public understanding and to offer further constructive recommendations.

BETTER CO-ORDINATION

In traveling about I find there are from five to ten different federal agencies operating in each state, which in some degree affect the farmer. Many of them conflict with each other and with the efforts of the state and local organizations. It would seem to me that the time has come to recognize that the Governors of the States should be allowed to make a great contribution in coordination of these agencies. Especially, there should be set up in each state somewhere a single place that the farmer can go to and get attention to his particular problems.

BETTER DISTRIBUTION

There are questions of the control of food distribution and of the situation of housewives that I could comment on at great length. A price and distribution method which stifles production, produces great areas of scarcity and allows the constant spread of black markets that in consequence deprives the poorest consumers of their just share of food is amply subject to criticism. I am disposed, as I said three months ago, to give our authorities a chance to correct these things. But the patience of the country is running short.

FOOD AND PEACE

In all this I have discussed the question from our immediate point of view of winning the war. But food must also win the peace.

When firing ceases we will be faced with three or four hundred million starving people in Europe and China.

To save these millions of people after the war is not alone a transcendent act of compassion. It is the only road to peace. Unless we stop the degenerative forces on our own food front we will have no supplies for this purpose.

And unless we stop these degenerative forces we will weaken our military front.

OUR FARMERS

And I want again to say a word as to the people on the farms. There can be no doubt that the men and women remaining on the job are putting forth the absolutely maximum effort to produce everything they can. They are working a 72-hour week at wages less than any other group. They are showing the highest courage and fortitude. But there are things that cannot be remedied by them alone.

We must find solutions to these problems—we must not fail.

A Check-up of the Food Front

NEW YORK CITY

[*June 8, 1943*]

I PROPOSE tonight to make a check-up on where we have got to on the food front.

I propose to explore what happened during the 1942 food year.

I shall then examine the prospects before us for the 1943 food year.

I shall, from this experience and the world need, state our problem.

And I will make some recommendations for the future.

The strategy of the food front is second only to the military front in winning total war. It is of more importance than the military front in establishing peace. Total wars can be lost on the food front. Failure to recognize the importance of the food front has lost wars before now.

Through the glorious courage and ability of our Army and Navy we are making progress against a most cruel and mighty enemy. We grow stronger on the military front. We must now build up the food front. It should be reorganized again. Our job is not destructive criticism. It is to contribute constructive suggestions. The only thing that counts now is to win victory and secure the peace.

To those who are not familiar with food problems, let me say that our food year is approximately from July, when the harvest starts, to the next July, when it begins again.

THE FOOD YEAR 1942-43

We are still eating mostly on the 1942 production.

Newspaper headlines of official statements from Washington as to our present food year read:

"The most abundant harvest in 41 years."

"Harvest per acre 12% above all records."

"There are abundant food supplies."

"The ever-normal granary assures no shortages of food."

"Greatest food production in our history."

"We have more beef cattle, dairy cows and hogs than ever before."

"Food Administrator says food outlook is good."

This happiness and exultation in Washington did not seem to be reflected in the realistic land of house-wives. A few quotations from many thousands of city press headlines over the past four months carry less enthusiasm.

New York City: "City facing first famine in our history." "Less than 20% of normal meat supplies for 8 weeks." "Shops cannot supply the Government ration." "Prices above ceilings." "1055 black market convictions."

"Mayor comes to the rescue and imports 600,000 lbs. of potatoes."

Thus the Mayor was lighting up the dark scene with one potato for every third person among the seven million people in New York. The headlines blazed for days over the Mayor's having "secured one million pounds of meat." That nourished each person with a gorge of meat equal to the weight of two silver dollars for just one meal. The Mayor, however, was doing his best to keep up good cheers.

Boston: "A desperate food shortage." "Meat and vegetables non-existent to thousands of families." "Arrivals lowest in history." "Hundred indicted for black markets."

San Francisco: "Shortage meat and vegetables critical all along the coast." And even in the food belt we hear:

Chicago: "Shortage meat, vegetables; black markets all

about." "Housewives cannot find meat promised on ration cards."

In Philadelphia, Baltimore, Cleveland, Seattle, Omaha, St. Louis and a dozen other cities, are headlines of the same import. "Scarcity," "Famine," "Black Markets," "Shops Closing—Cannot Get the Ration in Meats, Fats, Vegetables."

Somehow all this leads me to the notion that the situation is bewildering.

The statistics are also perplexing. The Department of Agriculture states that the extraordinarily favorable weather at last harvest gave us a 12% greater yield per acre than ever before in our history. It shows a greater production of meats and fats than ever before in our history. Lend-Lease says we are shipping under 10% of our total meats and fats abroad. OPA says it has rationed down meat consumption by 30%. Seaboard city marketing officials say not half of the meat and fat ration is available in the markets. Perhaps some statisticians can tie these figures together. They might also try to tie up the potato figures. I am aware of all the explanations. But one thing is certain. If the statistics are correct, and I do not challenge them, then some bureaucracy is strangling the flow of food from the farmer to the housewife.

But underlying all this turmoil, there is a fundamental disorder. It may surprise some people to know that in the seven years between the harvests of 1932 and 1939, through Government restrictions, the acreage in 17 leading crops harvested was reduced by 47 million acres. These 17 crops are about 95% of our whole harvested area.

When Lend-Lease was passed in March, 1941, we undertook thereby a vast increased burden of food production. Yet payments to farmers to restrict production were not all removed for the two plantings of '41 and '42. By 1942 we had recovered only 9 million of these 47 million lost acres in the 17 leading crops.

During the past year we were saved, and our Allies were saved, from disaster by the super-bumper crop. It is not likely to be repeated soon.

1943 PROSPECTS

However, we have eaten our way to the end of that super-bumper crop. We may, therefore, explore the prospects for the next food year that is now just coming on the horizon.

Two years ago, one year ago, six months ago, you and I warned that failure to place food production on an equality with munitions would bring disaster. Last winter the Congress, your organization, all of us demanded drastic reforms in food control, increased manpower for the farms and more farm machinery. We wanted to recover more of the 47 million lost acres.

Following this, the Department of Agriculture issued a report on "farmers' intentions to plant," indicating an increase of 4% in the acreage the coming year over that of last summer. The implication of that figure to the public was a probable increase of 4% of food over the super-bumper harvest of last year. We vitally needed an increased production over last year. But, to assure this with normal yields, we should have had not a 4% increase but a 15% increase in planting. However, the use of this comforting 4% figure led the country into a statistical paradise. And such is the power of statistics that the demands for reform were flattened out. We were told we were alarmists and something worse.

We did secure part reforms. They were not accepted with the speed of light. But finally the War Department, after unkind remarks, gave concessions by deferring some farm boys from draft. The W.P.B. authorized a modest increase in farm machinery. One more agency was added to the eight separate and conflicting agencies dealing with food. It was all too little and too late.

Now let us examine what has become of this statistical paradise of increasing food supply. To present to you an independent view, I have canvassed the agricultural authorities in several leading farm states. These reports indicate that the 4% increase is likely to vanish. And the indication is that we shall have a normal, not an extraordinary, yield like that of last year. If so, we will have a decrease in the national grain crops of anything from 10% to 15% from that of last year. The outlook for wheat and rye is certainly a decrease of 260 million bushels less than 1942, or at least 26%.

We have increased our flocks and herds beyond our ability to feed them without the lost 47 million acres. The agricultural experts are estimating a shortage of 10% to 15% in full supply of feed for our animals during the next year. We can get some feed from Canada. But it appears that we will have about exhausted the surplus of feed of the whole North American continent during the next twelve months. Already we are feeding large amounts of wheat to our livestock and we are using it for industrial alcohol. By this time next year we will have little surplus of bread grains beyond our own needs.

Thus our supply of food is declining while, at the same time, the demand is dangerously rising. And these decreases cannot be blamed upon floods which have destroyed less than one-half of one per cent, nor upon the weather for that promises about normal crops. Nor can they be laid upon the farmer.

The American farm folks are the most skilled farmers in the world. They produce more per person than any agricultural people on earth. They have done a heroic job in planting this crop with but little help. In January last they were promised an agricultural army of 3,500,000 city folks. But it has not arrived at the food front yet. They must be there before the harvest.

The blunt conclusion from all this is: (a) our cities will have less food supply during the next winter and spring even than they had in the last few months; (b) we will not starve; (c) we can, by better organization and by tightening our belts, continue to feed our allies; (d) if the war in Europe should come to an end within the next 12 months, we should have no consequential food supplies with which to meet 3 or 4 hundred millions of starving people.

PREPAREDNESS FOR THE HARVEST OF 1944

Remedy for the 1943 harvest year is now too late, as the planting is mostly done. We must begin to build up the harvest of a year from now. That is, in 1944.

We still have time to redeem the situation. If it is to be redeemed, we must have far wider vision. We must have drastic changes in national policies.

We simply must take seriously certain elemental facts. We must realize that the major burden of the world's food front falls on the North American farmer and the American consumer. We must realize that in peacetimes on balance we are a food-importing country and today we are blockaded against many imports. We must furnish extra food to our military forces. We must ship large amounts of food to our allies to support them in the war. We must realize that there is a minimum level in food for our 130,000,000 civilians without impairing their physical and moral resistance.

And we have also pledged ourselves to hundreds of millions of people in the world that they will be rescued from the terrible famine, which has been brought upon them by a monstrous enemy. Without this action, there will be no peace.

We must realize that this food shortage will last for a minimum of four, and possibly six, years. These are stupendous burdens.

THE ANSWER TO HITLER

But we have an answer to Hitler.

We can ration down our own consumption further with good management. And we can make sure that we do not lose the war on the food front if we stop the degeneration in agriculture and bring in a far greater production in 1944. We must do it. Otherwise we are headed for world trouble. We have the resources to do it.

As a foundation for 1944 we must get all that lost 47,000,000 acres back into cultivation. To do that, our authorities must decide whether they will spare the manpower and farm machinery manufacture from other activities. And we must begin now or again it will be too late and too little.

REFORM IN FOOD CONTROL

Organizing the food front means far more than just increasing acreage, manpower and farm machinery. It also requires wise coordination of prices, of processors, of distributors and of rationing.

A month ago, the press reported a spokesman of the OPA as saying "food prices and food distribution are out of control." It was denied by another spokesman next day. But the second spokesman had not discussed it with the housewives nor with the farmers. However, when we are fighting a war, grief over spilled milk does not make more milk. Our question must be, Where do we go from here?

There is only one course which will clear up this muddle of uncontrolled food prices, local famines, profiteering, black markets and stifled farm production. That is to abandon the obsolete methods now in use which were proved a failure in other nations in the last war, or are copied from the British whose situation is wholly different from ours. We should start with the system which proved a success under the Americans in the last war and improve it.

And let me say this about food control while we were in the last war.

We steadily increased our food production. We shipped more food to our allies monthly than is being shipped today. We had no local famines in the United States as we are having now. We had no black markets. We had a people zealous in a moral crusade to help win the war with food, instead of lots of people trying to beat the game. Including the Department of Agriculture, we had only 23,000 paid Federal employees connected with food. Today we have over 120,000. Moreover, food prices rose only 17.9% in the 17 months after we declared war in 1917. Washington statisticians admit a rise of 24.3% in the

17 months since Pearl Harbor. The housewives will admit a rise of at least 35%.

I do not pretend that our methods were perfect in that war. We had to pioneer an unknown field. Results ought to be better in this war and not worse.

A PROGRAM

But what should we do now?

First. The first necessity is to consolidate all authority over food production and distribution under one single responsible administrator. There are too many cooks for too little food. Control of food is now divided nine ways over the Department of Agriculture, the O.P.A., the Lend-Lease, the Board of Economic Warfare, the Army, the Navy, the Manpower Commission and the W.P.B.

The recent addition of the 9th wheel, even through so able a man as Mr. Chester Davis as Food Administrator, does not make a Food Administration. The food functions of all these agencies must be moved into his office. He must have the right to hire and fire. The Food Administrator must today be Secretary of Agriculture. And the importance of food in the outcome of the war and peace should be recognized by his appointment to the new Office of Manpower Mobilization.

Second. Decentralize the work under state, municipal, and county administrators. In no other way can farmers' and consumers' needs be adjusted to our varied local conditions.

Third. Increase the manpower on the farms to a higher level than before the war and plant 40 or 50 million acres more in 1944 than in this year. On this question of manpower I offer a suggestion because we must have more skilled labor on the farms.

Public pressure upon our farm boys to join the forces is very great. They are not slackers and do not want to be called slackers. They do not want their gates painted yellow. They are doing a great and indispensable service. If we are to save this situation, I believe farm boys should be called to the army from the farms immediately after this harvest; that the farm boys should be called up from industry; that they should be given some military training. Then as many of them as are necessary should from time to time be ordered back to the farms with their uniforms. They should receive their pay from the farms, and not the army. They should be subject to call in national danger. That would give dignity to their service. They could constitute a great national reserve both for production of food and the direct military effort.

Fourth. Agricultural machinery on an average lasts about 12 years. Theoretically about one year's supply or one-twelfth of our machinery has been used up through suppression of manufacture. It will also require great additions to handle this extra 40 or 50 million acres in 1944.

Fifth. Abolish the system of retail and wholesale price ceilings. It begins at the wrong end. Price fixing in a great food-producing country must begin as near as possible to the farmer, and controls proceed from there on by regulation of the trades against profiteering. Prices rose less when this system was applied in the last war than they have under the present retail ceilings. We must regulate the flow of water at the nozzle instead of chasing the drops from the shower.

This present price system is stifling farm production. It is not stopping inflation.

Sixth. Ask the farmers to appoint their own war committee on prices and do a little collective bargaining with them in fixing prices. The so-called "parities" should be abandoned for the war. Prices to the farmer must include floors as well as ceilings. Prices should be fixed that will take into account labor and other costs and, above all, that will stimulate production.

Such a revolution in the price system would save a few tens of thousands of policemen. It is difficult to catch an economic force with a policeman anyway.

Seventh. Rations should be set to balance consumption to production. It only adds muddle to put the ration higher than the available supplies. And it brings great injustice, for some people get the ration and some don't. We should simplify the whole rationing business by over 50% or 60%. It can be done by decreasing the number and variety of articles rationed and by excluding all absolutely non-essential food from rationing. We might take caviar off of the rationed list. The many persons engaged in counting the caviar tickets could better be rolling bandages.

It would certainly give a mighty lift of spirit to the housewife and to the grocer. Also, it would save some of their time for other war duties. Also, a good way to check inflation is to let food luxuries go to the highest bidder. That would spigot off spare money and get it into channels where the 90% profit taxes can bite into it.

Eighth. We should recognize that processing and distributing foods are righteous and necessary callings. Thousands of small firms are being driven out of business. It would help win the war if left-wing reforms in our food economy were suspended for the duration. We should establish war committees in all the processing and distributing trades. They should be given major responsibilities in keeping the flow of food moving to the right spots. They could greatly assist state and local officials in policing the trades. They too have sons in the war. They are just as patriotic men as lawyers and economists. They are the only people who know how. Their interest is to stamp out black markets. And their profits can be absolutely controlled.

Enforce the condition of dealers' licenses so that they may deal only with another licensed dealer and then direct the railways and trucks to transport only for licensed dealers. This would stop most of the black markets.

Ninth. Such a system will avoid subsidies either to farmers or the trades or the consumers. Subsidies will not stop inflation. Subsidies are a delayed aggravation.

The *New York Times* properly says they "do not in the least deal with primary causes. They are like cleaning a room by sweeping the dirt under the bed."

And who is supposed to benefit by subsidies? It is supposed to be the worker, but the worker is also the taxpayer. So is the farmer. And taxes are, sooner or later, increased by just the same amount as the subsidy. Subsidies consist of taking money out of one pocket and putting it into another with an illusion attached that the cost of living has been reduced. It is both more painful and more costly to take money out of the tax pocket than it is to get it out of the price pocket. A wage based on subsidy foundations will break down sooner or later. Moreover, subsidy money increases government borrowing and debt to the banks and that adds to inflation pressure. Far more serious, however, is the result to the farmer and the consumer. Price fixing based on any such concept will strangle production. Its operation in the distribution trades will clog the flow of commodities and will in the end increase prices and black markets. Likewise, subsidies can become a weapon of favoritism or of punishment in the hands of the huge bureaucracy. They will sooner or later lead to scandal.

CONCLUSION

If these broad lines, policies and organization be adopted then food will flow naturally from farm to processor to wholesaler, to retailer and to the consumer. Prices will be better restrained. They will be lower, for the black markets can be blacked out. The housewives will have less trouble and worry. And above all, farm production will be stimulated, not stifled.

But over and beyond better methods of food control, we must absolutely assure the maximum production of America.

Let me say again that that is the only road that leads to the defeat of inflation, to decreased hardship in our homes, to assured support of our Allies and to peace for mankind.

If those in power and those not in power shall have wisdom, implacable resolve, a spirit of sacrifice, the fields of America will blossom with an abundant life that will save vast human life in a world given to human destruction.

Relief for Starving Peoples of Europe

WASHINGTON, D. C.

[*November 4, 1943*]

SUBCOMMITTEE OF THE COMMITTEE ON FOREIGN RELATIONS
UNITED STATES SENATE

S ENATOR THOMAS of Utah. President Hoover.

Mr. HOOVER. Senator, I do not believe there can be any doubt as to the general starvation amongst women and children in the occupied democracies. I do not believe there can be any doubt that relief could be given to those people, because of the experience in Greece and the fact that we are now delivering packages to prisoners in Germany under proper safeguards; and indeed, we are delivering packages to French, Belgian, Dutch and Norwegian military prisoners. At the moment, we are denying food to the children of those very prisoners. It seems to me they are as much in prison as are soldiers.

It does not seem to me that there can be any doubt that this question affects the whole future of Europe. It will be afflicted by a generation of stunted and diseased children and by the distorted minds that come up out of these miasmas.

Moreover, if we make no effort, it will affect our relations with those people for many years to come. For the last 2 years I have been steadily advocating that some effort should be made —that at least we should make a "try." I proposed a plan of procedure, and that plan was adopted as to Greece. The State Department has on numerous occasions certified that the Germans are receiving no benefits from the Greek relief and that it has saved the lives of millions of Greek women and children. The method now at least has had a demonstration.

In my original suggestions I proposed that the Swedes and the Swiss be asked to undertake this work, that they should be required to secure an agreement from the Germans that this food supply should be amply protected, that their ships should have immunity from attack and that they should have the right of complete supervision of distribution. That has been in progress in Greece now for nearly a year without any apparent failure.

It seems to me very urgent that we undertake it now, even at this last moment—perhaps the last winter and the most disastrous winter that will overtake these people; that the least we could do would be to ask the Swedes and the Swiss to see what arrangements they can make with the Germans; that, if they cannot make effective arrangements with them then, we will at least have discharged our responsibilities. If they succeed in making arrangements with the Germans such as they have made in respect of Greece and then the Germans should violate the agreements, we can withdraw it at any time and again have discharged our responsibilities.

There is no large military question involved in feeding the women and children of those areas. In the ordinary course of handling relief I do not presume we would have in excess of 75,000 tons of imported foods in stock in the whole group of western European democracies at any one time, and, if the Germans should violate their agreements and seize it all, it would not amount to 12 hours' food supply for Germany; so that the military question is a perfectly trivial one. I could go even further on that question, as a purely personal opinion, by saying that the defeat of Germany is not going to be the result of the food blockade—they are going to be fed anyway; they are going to be defeated by other measures entirely. At least in extending the food blockade to our own allies we are causing no damage to the Germans but solely to our allies; and we are causing an enormous damage on the whole future of Europe.

I am told, and I think the committee could confirm it at any time, that both the Swedish and Swiss Governments would be glad to undertake this. The Swedes have ample tonnage, which they cannot put into use. The food supplies are available from outside the United States if we did not believe we could furnish the quantities needed, and most of these governments concerned have funds with which they could even pay for it. Therefore, this is not a question of food, it is not a question of finance, it is not a question of ships, and it becomes solely a question of policy as to whether or not a relaxation in the blockade will be made sufficient to make an experiment.

At the present moment Swedish ships are running to Greece without interference. The Red Cross is sending ships to Marseilles at the present moment, carrying relief to the United Nations prisoners in Germany. One of the sort of cynicisms of the world is that those ships with those packages for our prisoners are being unloaded at French ports by underfed and starving men, and yet there is no loss. I have seen an account from one of the French newspapers of a French workman who had taken a part of a broken package of food and was given 5 years in the penitentiary for doing it.

We are sending this food through France with the aid of the French. We are sending it on into Germany without interference. I have a report from the service in charge of this relief to prisoners showing that they are sending food at the rate of perhaps $60,000,000 a year, and that the loss in shrinkage and damage and theft amounts to less than one-sixth of 1 per cent. In other words, foodstuffs can be delivered into German territory to its destination—that is proved.

I return again to the proposal that we should at least make an attempt to discharge our moral responsibilities. If we succeeded, we would have paved the way for a reception of our troops in those territories such as we cannot hope for when they have to move into starving populations.

I have no idea what the attitude of our military leaders is upon this question. I do know that General Pershing, who had to deal with this very same problem in the last war, was not only its staunch supporter during the war, but was its constant defender after the war; and he has himself made an extraordinarily strong pronouncement as to the necessity of doing it during this war. Likewise has Admiral Pratt, who was second in command of our naval operations in the last war.

In order to bring some public opinion into focus on this matter we created some time ago a committee called the Committee on Food for the Small Democracies. That committee comprises some 12 or 14 men who have been ambassadors and ministers; it comprises some 50 or 60 leading public men of all kinds from over the United States, including such men as General Pershing and General Dawes and Admiral Pratt. It includes over 600 leading ministers and prelates from every religious body in the United States. It includes some 200 university professors and educational leaders, and it includes several hundred writers and editors and publishers. That at least would indicate there is a great American public opinion in support of the proposal, that at least we should make an effort.

Food for the Liberated Countries

NEW YORK CITY

[*May 8, 1945*]

I PROPOSE in this 15 minutes to give you some evidence of the food situation in liberated countries, to recite a little history and make some constructive suggestions.

THE SITUATION

One of the most terrible and the most lasting of the hideous list of Hitler's brutalities is this starving and stunting of the bodies and minds of the children of the democracies.

Archbishop Spellman has recently returned from France, Belgium and Italy. You may have read his report in *Collier's*.

". . . The long denial of adequate food has so arrested brain-tissue development in children that mental growth has been stunted. . . .

". . . peace will not thrive among nations with a world half well-fed and half starved. To millions of children, democracy is still a word and a promise only. They have been exposed to hatred, hunger and a hopeless future, and if they are denied the right of taking their places in a world of personal security, they will form the underground army for the next war, and take by stealth and force what they cannot enjoy by right.

". . . Since the occupation, over a million children subsisting at famine level have died in France, and three-quarters of the children in Belgium are pre-tubercular from lack of food.

"Poland's tragedy has been the greatest, for more than half

of her eleven million children under fifteen years of age have been liquidated by starvation or enslavement. . . ."

To this statement of Archbishop Spellman I may add a few sentences from a multitude of recent official reports upon the situation of the children in the industrial areas.

The French Ministry of Public Health says: "In industrial areas three-quarters of children are underweight, nutritional diseases rampant. Children's growth diminished 70% to 80%. . . . 54% of children under 2 suffer from rickets. Death rate increased 37% due to debilitation during the war. . . ."

"Belgium: "33% of the children are tubercular. . . . 6 out of 10 children under normal weight. . . . Children's death rate increased 44%."

I could take your time for hours reading official reports on the condition of the children of the industrial areas when they came out from under the German yoke. And I could add heart-breaking accounts of children in Holland and Norway still un-liberated. The urgency of this situation has been confirmed in the last few days by Judge Rosenman's report.

A LITTLE HISTORY

Over five years ago, seeking to prevent this catastrophe, one thousand eminent Americans of every political and religious faith joined with me in urging that we be allowed to undertake the feeding of these children during German occupation. I need not remind you of the parable of the Good Samaritan. The greatest teacher of mankind did not refuse action because of the brutality of the two thieves.

We continued to urge the feeding of these children of democracy for over four years. The United States Congress, after exhaustive inquiry, passed a unanimous resolution urging that it be done. President Truman was among those humanitarian Senators. That it could have been done under the safeguards we proposed and the neutral ships we could have secured without prolonging the war one hour is now clear. While such relief was refused to the Western Democracies and Poland, it was permitted during two years for Greece. Both the British and American Governments have certified the Nazis had no benefit from it. And today responsible men who lived through the Nazi regimes in the other democracies are unanimous that it could have been done without helping the enemy.

Archbishop Spellman and hundreds of other observers now bring witness of the ghastly consequences of this refusal.

Equally heart-breaking are the scores of promises of United Nations leaders that immediately upon liberation abundant food would be furnished instantly. That promise has been poorly met.

THE PROBLEM

It gains us nothing to criticize, and my purpose in giving this background is only to show how immensely increased is our responsibility now. The dead are beyond our reach.

We have two separate problems before us today.

One of these problems is to save the working classes in the great industrial centers of France, Italy, Belgium, Holland, Norway and Poland from the starvation which marches upon them. None of these countries has produced enough food since the last harvest to carry them over until the harvest of next August. The farmers will keep enough food for themselves and their neighbors. The well-to-do in the cities will always get along. The real sufferers from this shortage will be the poor of the large cities.

We Americans should not be misled by the descriptions of American trippers to Europe of luxurious meals they are able to buy from $10 and up. Working people could not buy but one such meal with a week's wages.

In the twelve months after liberation during the last war, we organized the delivery of 23,000,000 tons of overseas food into Europe and Britain. Only a trickle of food has been supplied since the liberation of eight months ago. We dealt then with starvation not power politics.

The parallel problem is to rehabilitate the undernourished children. After the last war, we organized several thousand special canteens in which 16,000,000 undernourished children in fifteen nations were given one ample body-building meal a day. It was a gift from America. We furnished the special food they required. Tens of thousands of devoted women in these fifteen countries volunteered to furnish the canteens and they did all the work. They were inspired by the knowledge they were saving the future of their race. The children of that war were largely restored to life and hope. Could we not do that again?

SUPPLIES

You may well ask: Do we have the supplies for this great task?

We have 450,000,000 bushels of wheat in North America which we can export without reducing our own bread consumption one atom. Sixty per cent of the normal diet of the working classes in Europe is cereals. We have the resources to supply them with bread. If we could give all the bread they can eat, plus what margins they have of their own supplies, it would carry the adults in the industrial areas through. Release from restricted bread rationing would be a great step in liberation. It would be a great step toward political stability.

Our difficulty is animal products. We have a great shortage of meats, fats and dairy products in the United States. Yet this is the precise food these undernourished children must have. I believe we could squeeze out of our resources the amount these children need without harm to our own health even if we could not supply adults. I therefore have four recommendations to meet this situation:

FOUR RECOMMENDATIONS

My first recommendation is no reflection on Governor Lehman. He has been hampered by power politics. His organization has not had adequate transportation nor single-headed authority which these large-scale operations so urgently require. We could never have won the battle of the Western Front with committee control. But precious time has been lost. Unless UNRRA can start the flow of millions of tons of food monthly and begin within the next few days, there is only one sensible alternative. That is, for the United States War Department to take over the whole problem. They control the agencies of transportation in the United States, they control docks and wharves here, they control overseas transportation, they control docks and interior transportation in Europe and they have the personnel. If they start a great stream of food flowing within two weeks' time, they can do the job in time. It is now 11:59 on the clock of starvation.

Second, our Governmental agency, whatever it is, should at once follow the experience and the great success of the last war by joining with the women of the liberated countries to establish thousands of canteens in the industrial areas for rehabilitation of undernourished children. They should be furnished the special food, clothing and medical supplies they require.

Third, whatever the cost is, it could be paid out of the international contributions to UNRRA or the particular nations themselves.

Fourth, whatever agency undertakes this job should transport supplies for and make a place for such organizations as "Save the Children Fund," for you can give sympathetic help that official agencies cannot so fully accomplish.

CONCLUSION

We are today debating the structure of international trade; we are engaged in conferences on the structure of peace. But after all, peace, prosperity and freedom will not arise from stunted minds or stunted bodies. The preservation and rebuilding of these children is a far greater contribution to freedom, to prosperity, to peace than a hundred signed documents. Even if during the war the spiritual impulse of the American people to prevent this debacle was stifled, it must be released now to save what we can.

On United States Army Taking Over Food Relief to the Liberated Countries of Western Europe

NEW YORK CITY

[May 16, 1945]

A WEEK ago I stated that the time was rapidly approaching when the United States Army should take over the whole job of food relief to the liberated countries of Western Europe. That statement received such favorable response that I propose to amplify and clarify the subject further.

Now that fighting has ceased it is possible to look at the situation more clearly. Even above the need of repair of the physical wreck, the urgent problem now is food. There are two parts to the problem. I shall discuss the German problem and the liberated countries of Eastern Europe some other time. At this moment I refer only to the Western liberated countries to which we have full access. That is, Italy, France, Belgium, Holland, Luxemburg, Norway and Denmark—comprising about 100,000,000 people. None of these countries produced enough food in the harvest of last August to last them until the harvest of the coming August. In the meantime only a trickle of food has been sent to them and the inevitable shortage has been concentrating toward the period of the next three months.

Moreover, whatever amount of their own food they will have during the next 90 days, it cannot be evenly distributed. The farmer and the neighboring villages will hold onto enough food to carry them through. The European farmer, having been through famines before, takes no risks for his family and his neighbors. Thus the impact of the shortage will fall upon the cities. In the cities the well-to-do will live somehow. Therefore, the blow will fall upon the working people in the industrial areas.

The normal diet of adult European working people is about 60% wheat bread. If they could be given unlimited bread with such margins of vegetables and other things as they have, I believe the adult population could get through until next August. Unlimited bread, after five years of restriction, would be a powerful proof of liberation. We have in America and Canada a surplus of even more wheat than we need. But action has been delayed over eight months until now it is 11:59 on the starvation clock.

Apart from every humanitarian reason, food must be provided for the liberated countries if there is to be order and stable government. We cannot have our American armies of 3,500,000 men involved in starving populations on their communication lines.

A week ago I expressed the belief that the only agency in the world which can save this situation now is the American Army. They have the administrative ability, the personnel and the energy; they can control the transport of wheat to the American seaboard; they control the ships; they control transport in Europe; they know how to act quickly. They could do the job.

Of course Europe needs meats and fats, but we also have a shortage of those things. As I said, if the adults of Europe had unlimited bread they could get through. But their children must have some meats and fats. However, in this time of short supplies this should be organized so that it reaches the undernourished children only. We could tighten our belt a little and supply this comparatively small amount. But we cannot supply meats and fats to everybody in Europe.

And this is not a question of feeding Europe next winter. After they get their harvest three months from now there will be time to organize that.

I repeat, this is a problem of the next ninety days; it is urgent. It is urgent as a matter of humanity. It is urgent as a matter of preserving order. It is urgent in protection of our boys in Europe. It is a job so long delayed that only the American Army can solve it.

On the Organization and Administration of Animal Products

Letter to Congressman Thomas A. Jenkins

[June 20, 1945]

New York, N. Y.

Congressman Thomas A. Jenkins,
House of Representatives,
Washington, D. C.

My Dear Mr. Congressman:

I have your request for my views upon the situation and the method of organizing the administration of animal food products. I have expressed my views many times in the last four years, and particularly my recommendations of two years ago have been proved valid by all the experience since.

Let me say at once that this is not a partisan question either domestically or internationally. Not only does the well-being of our own people rest upon successful handling, but at least for the present we are unable to furnish the volume of meats and fats required for the restoration of undernourished children in the liberated countries of Europe. Therefore, we need full cooperation on all sides in finding solutions.

There can be no doubt that President Truman and the new Secretary of Agriculture, Mr. Anderson, have inherited a muddle in the production and distribution of animal products. We have an abundance of breadstuffs. Although we have not yet recovered the cultivated acreage of 1932, an unparalleled sequence of abundant yields have protected us and enabled us to supply these commodities for relief abroad. The meats and fats, however, are another story and chiefly due to bad organization.

I have read the debate in the Senate and the amendments proposed to the O.P.A. Act. I suggest, however, that what the Senate is endeavoring to secure in the conduct of that agency, so as to increase production and more equitable distribution, can be more workably brought about by an administrative revolution.

The Anderson Committee and the Senate Agricultural Committee have amply ventilated the faulty organization of the O.P.A., but for clearer understanding of my suggestions, I may summarize the consequences of these failures.

a. Altogether the meat and fat production will show a considerable decline in 1945—and this in the face of a starving world. While hogs are our greatest source of fats and fats rank equally with bread as a food necessity, yet, despite abundant feed, the hog population was decreased from about 81 million to about 61 million between January 1, 1944, and January 1, 1945, or about 35 per cent. In consequence, the production of pork products during 1945 seems destined to be over three billion pounds less than in 1944. The number of sheep as of January 1, 1945, shows a decrease of about 15 per cent in two years. Chickens have decreased about 12 per cent. The number of cattle has decreased about 1 per cent in 1944 and the number of calves being saved for dairy purposes has decreased about 7 per cent.

b. Certainly something is wrong with distribution. Even after deducting military and other governmental requirements there should still be over seventy per cent of pre-war meats and fats available to the civil population. Yet the people of New York and many other large cities are getting less than one-half of this proportion of available supplies.

The Department of Labor reports that, in April, 55% to 80% of the retail stores dealing in meats and fats in 56 large cities had no supplies.

c. The existence of black markets in meats and fats (except

milk) in every city of the country is sufficient evidence of a breakdown in control of both distribution and price. A large part of the civilian consumption is in fact being dealt with at prices up to 100% above the supposed ceiling prices. A survey within a week by the New York Board of Trade states that from 50 to 85 per cent of the meat and fat supplies in this city are in effect black market operations. An economic force like that cannot be caught by a policeman.

d. In frantic efforts to hold the supposed ceiling prices, subsidies are being given to processors and farmers amounting to millions of dollars. As these subsidies come out of the taxpayer's pocket, who is also the consumer, they do not alleviate anything. If they increase the debt, our veterans of this war will be required to pay part of our food bills after they have come home from war.

e. And in addition to all these considerations is our inability to provide meats and fats so necessary to the recuperation of minds and bodies of children abroad.

To sum up, our animal products are:

1. Diminishing in supply;
2. Affected by maldistribution which produces local famines in the cities;
3. Surrounded with black markets with all their fraud and corruption.
4. In reality selling at prices far above the so-called ceilings.

WHERE THE FAULT LIES

It is not the fault of the farmer for he has done an extraordinary job. Despite a drain of fully 35 per cent of the effective agricultural manpower into the military forces and the shops and a reduction of about 75 per cent in new farm machinery, he steadily lifted agricultural production up to 1943.

The fault does not lie in the Department of Agriculture (except perhaps in the hog program), for the controlling factors of production—that is prices, labor and machinery—have not been within the authority of that Department.

The causes of all this lie broadly in the method of organization where the control of food has been divided over six or seven agencies, where the whole price control machinery is based upon ill-advised concepts and where the organization has considered coercion more useful than cooperation with producers, distributors and consumers.

Price control is necessary in times of scarcity and of inflation pressure. The question is one of method. The original method in this war was to fix prices at the retail outlets and then work backward through the retailer, commission man and processor toward the farmer and to use subsidies and constantly changing prices to open the multitude of bottlenecks.

THE METHOD OF THE LAST WAR

The method in the last war was to fix prices as near the farmer as possible and to work forward to the consumer by additions of normal trade differentials and without subsidies. The method in this war leads logically to ridiculous actions such as the attempt of a year ago to standardize the hundreds of meat and fat items on the retailers shelves by the 40,000-word Presidential order as to how to cut up a cow.

Under the method of administration of animal products used in the last war we had:

  a. No black markets,

  b. No local famines,

  c. No card-rationing system.

  d. Prices advancing less rapidly than now, taking into account black market prices and subsidies.

  e. Less consumption per capita by the civilian population than that which was had in the year 1944;

  f. Constantly increasing production of all animal products;

  g. An enormous surplus which saved the children of Europe without privation to the American people.

Therefore, it would seem worth while now to reconstruct the whole method of organization and administration, taking advantage of the experience of the last war and the lessons from this war and adopting them to the present situation.

Without going into exhaustive economic discussion, I will simply suggest the form of reorganization that I believe should be done now.

1. The Secretary of Agriculture should be not only Food Administrator, as the President has already announced, but in my view the Secretary of Agriculture should also have physically transferred to him all of the price and other powers and staff of the OPA which are concerned in any way with animals and animal products, including feed, except the mechanical job of rationing. That the OPA should continue.

2. He should also have transferred to him the control of all allocation and buying of major animal products for the Armed forces, Lend-Lease and Relief.

3. The Secretary should appoint an Administrator of Animal Products.

4. In order to coordinate official buying, the Secretary should have an advisory Committee representing the Army, Navy, Lend-Lease and Relief allocation and buying, except for purely local purchases. The present methods not only result in competition among various agencies for supplies, but they also result in the piling up of unnecessary stocks by the separate agencies eventuating in dislocation, waste and spoilage. There should be in effect one national food pool under the direction of the Secretary of Agriculture and upon which the armed forces should have the first call.

5. There should be genuine organized cooperation with the farmers and the legitimate trades. They have the know how. The trades do not want black markets. Their sons are in this war. To bring this about they should be asked to create from their own organizations:

    a. A National War Committee of Livestock Growers;

    b. A National War Committee of Packers;

    c. A National War Committee of Commission Men;

    d. A National War Committee of Animal Products' Retailers.

These committees should not be fifth-wheel, occasional advisory boards, but should have definite responsibilities. There should be assurance given to these Committees that so long as they follow the directions of the Secretary of Agriculture they will be immune from prosecution under the anti-trust laws. For instance, by combined action they can secure distribution which will stop local famines.

6. If not already done, all of the legitimate packers, commission men and retailers should be licensed and be required under that license to deal only with other licensed dealers and to carry out certain other policies. The railroads and trucking concerns should be required to transport these products only for licensed processors and dealers.

7. The Secretary of Agriculture by agreement with the Livestock War Committee should set ceiling and floor prices, with some tolerances, upon various grades of cattle, hogs, poultry, eggs and dairy products to be paid to the farmers at the nearest point to production. That is, for instance, for hogs, cattle and sheep at the stockyards, the commission centers, etc. These prices must express the differentials between different qualities of animals or products and different markets, and must take into account a proper profit to the farmer, the cost of his labor, feed, etc., and must be so directed as to increase and not decrease production. If done properly, no subsidies will be required.

8. The Packers and Commission men should be directed to pay no more than these agreed ceilings and no less than the agreed floors. The Packers and Commission men can be protected against gluts by the Government purchasing.

9. The Packers should be given an over riding "mark-up" over their cost of animals to cover their costs and a proper profit. This "mark-up" should be averaged over a year's business as they must carry their stocks over long periods. If this average is exceeded, the difference should be paid into the Treasury. No subsidies need to be paid.

10. The Commission men and the Wholesale dealers should be given their usual trade commissions or a "mark-up" over prices paid by them. Where a "mark-up" is used it should

probably be averaged over a month's business or a fair period, depending on the trade.

11. The Retailers should be given their usual "mark-up" over cost of their commodities to cover rent, labor and profit, and this too should probably be averaged over one month's business.

Under this simplified method, the retailer can charge what he pleases for luxury meat, but he would be compelled to reduce the price correspondingly on necessity meat in order to keep within his average monthly mark-up covering all products in which he deals.

12. The Secretary of Agriculture should instruct these National War Committees that it is their responsibility to police their own trades. They can largely do this themselves although a countercheck by government agencies will be necessary.

The committees of the different stages of processing and distribution at once will know what the other stages are doing. A minor part of the present government inspectors will be necessary to assure compliance.

As a consequence under such a plan

a. The people will get their animal products for lower prices than they are paying today if black market and subsidies are taken into account;

b. Trade will flow in normal channels, for the dealers can vary the prices between products depending upon the demand for each so long as they do not exceed their average "mark-up."

c. The National War Committees can see to it that there are no local famines.

d. There will be no need for subsidies.

e. Production will increase.

f. It will require a minimum of policing by the Government.

That this plan of organization and administration works was shown by the experience of the last war. That the plan now in use has failed requires no demonstration.

Without reform our domestic difficulties will increase, and the hope of aid on meats and fats to women and children abroad becomes hopeless.

PART IV

EDUCATIONAL
SOCIAL AND SCIENTIFIC

Boys' Clubs in War

O UR problems at this Convention of leaders of the Boys' Clubs of America are largely problems of how we may serve in the war. We have a victory to win. That is the only road out of war for America. We will also have vast problems of making a lasting peace and of restoring national life. But these are problems which we will not introduce to these boys just yet.

Here are 350,000 boys daily gathered into our Clubs from the congested areas of our great cities. They are the sons of working people to whom less opportunity comes than to the great average. They constitute every race and color. But they are all Americans, and their Americanism is ardent with all the idealism of youth. And they want to do something about this war. Moreover, with that reserve of steam and that equipment of self-starters which are an anatomical part of every small boy, we need to find some useful outlet for their high desires to serve. And from it they will grow in the spirit of service to their country.

It is fortunate that the Nation has had the building of this great institution over the past 50 years. There are today probably a million men in America who have gone through these Clubs. At the most impressionable period of their lives they had a regime of health inspection and a physical training that only organized supervision could give. They were taught to do something useful with their hands. Their initiative and self-reliance were stimulated. They were introduced to gaiety and constructive joy which is the right of every boy. They were drilled in sportsmanship. And sportsmanship is the basis of morals second only to religious faith.

All this is the foundation not only for citizens but for the supreme duty of citizens—good soldiers. And we already find that of the thousands drafted from this multitude of Boys' Clubs' graduates most are passing into the Army with much higher physical standards than the average. This is a magnificent testimonial to these thousands of men and women, who over all these years have given their lives to make Boys' Clubs a place where boys turn into sound physical and moral men, infused with American ideals. Some day we will be able to tell you of the heroism and leadership of these graduates of the city pavements in this war. We know their backgrounds and we have no fear of what the record will show.

But our immediate concern is not with our graduates. Our job is with the 350,000 boys we have on hand and the further million or so who may have passed through our halls and into the war before this war is likely to be ended. For this stream of raw material we have also to provide training in health, training in hand, training in morals, training in the love of country and its institutions. And we have now to stretch the vision of these boys over the earth. Their imaginative equipment is equal to it. The explosive point of their enthusiasms and their idealisms light at once in the call to service.

In our regular work during the past year we have established many new clubs. We and they have expended upward to $800,-000 in additional buildings and equipment for old and new clubs and we have about $900,000 more in construction. For this we have to thank thousands of generous men and women who have given us their support. And that support not only involved this $1,700,000 for new buildings and equipment, but also many hundreds of thousands of dollars further to make up the deficit over the 25 cents a year that our boys pay as Club dues. We could have done more if we could have found still more money.

A part of our war program is the Boys' Clubs' Victory Volunteers, organized to aid the many senior emergency organizations in these congested areas of our cities. The Volunteers have a thousand duties already assigned to them in different cities. In some, air wardens have these boys organized to work the fire alarm boxes; others to inspect the roof sand; and others to spot lights in the black-out. In another place, the emergency nurses have them organized as orderlies. In our own shops the boys are making games for our soldiers and sailors. They are even putting on boxing matches between the champions of under 60 pounds to build up the morale of the Navy. And the boys are gathering up an unbelievable amount of scrap—iron, brass, tin, paper and what-not. They use the money from this scrap for their Club purposes and donations to the Nation's armed forces. I trust the junk dealers have become more liberal-minded than they were in my youth when I was dependent upon the sale of scrap iron in order to finance a proper celebration of the Fourth of July. Anyway, we want the country to know that when a boy wearing our badge asks you to do something, you ought to do it. And you can depend upon him.

And these multitudes of services are adapted to these youngsters. The world is new to every boy. To his adventures and discoveries and great undertakings he now takes war in his stride. His impelling passion for exercise on all occasions and his instinct to do battle and to hunt in the pack now have new outlets.

I must express our obligation and devotion to William E. Hall, the President, and David Armstrong, the Executive Director of this national association. For five months they have worked 14 hours a day, seven days a week in our service. Their physical home is in Pullman cars. Their immortal home is the affection and devotion of the greatest of human product—our boys.

United Church Canvass

SOMETHING has happened today that has never happened before in the United States. It means a great spiritual awakening that may transform America.

For the first time in history, sixteen great creeds and denominations, Christian and Jewish, are speaking with one voice to the people of America. Leaders of American life tonight begin a great work of spiritual unity. And this is what they say to you:

When our nation was founded, it drew its strength and being not only from great political and social truths, but from spiritual convictions . . . from a deep and abiding faith in Almighty God.

From our religious faiths came the great inspiration that men should be free. Free in worship, free in conscience, free in speech. From the churches of America came that revolutionary pronouncement of the dignity of individual men in the Declaration of Independence. That is, men "are endowed by the Creator with certain unalienable rights" upon which not even government may infringe.

These liberties cannot be sustained without religious faith. From that springs our spiritual guidance and our moral standards. These moral standards are sustained by faith alone. Without these supports Liberty degenerates into license, and is lost.

Just as our nation was founded by faith in God, so also can that faith sustain our nation in this time of dreadful trial. Our enemies have decried and sought to destroy our religious faiths.

378

Theirs is the boast that cunning and brutality can rule the world. We refuse to believe this. We know that if civilization is to live it must be based upon religious faith and upon compassion that is part of faith.

We know that America has become great, that civilization itself has marched forward because its people, its heroes and its martyrs were sustained by a courage that came from a Source above. Men who today face death and danger feel it sustaining them. On the seas and on the battlefields we know how much it means to them. Our spiritual life centers in the 200,-000 churches of America. As you worship there, you will feel it all about you. You will feel it as you fill the empty places of the men who have gone to serve their country in its time of need. You will feel it when you witness their great task of healing the hearts of those who mourn, of bringing strength to those who must be strong.

Beginning today, and until December 6th, the communions and faiths throughout America are joining hands to speak to you of their needs.

The churches call upon you to help rekindle the fires of our faith . . . to make that faith an active glowing part of your personal life . . . even taxing yourself for the spread of that faith.

The world hungers for spiritual strength.

Salvation Army Appeal

NEW YORK CITY
[January 14, 1943]

A S A sometime traveler over most lands and seas I can speak with personal knowledge of the work of the Salvation Army. I have seen it in every climate, in every nation. I have seen it always engaged in the same task and inspired by the same devotion. And I can speak with interest in its work since my early acquaintance of the Elder Booth.

The Salvation Army is the absolute expression of compassion which lies at the base of all religious faith. And it is not alone an expression of the compassion for poverty or misfortune. It also expresses itself in the redemption of man through the gospel of the dignity of the human soul. It builds the moral fibre and spiritual faith in the discouraged and suffering. By regeneration of faith and confidence in men and women, it lifts the hopeless into self-respect and faith.

The Salvation Army truly expresses its faith in works. It is one of our greatest organizations of social service and in a thousand fields. It has developed in its more than sixty years in the United States to an essential part of the machinery of our whole social structure. It has an almost limitless range of social work in the forty-eight states. And in the Eastern Territory alone— and we are here today in behalf of the Eastern Territory's needs —1,116,858 needy persons received lodging, and 1,320,052 were given good meals during 1942 alone, while 46 social service centers accommodated 13,709 men, and Day Nurseries, Maternity Homes and General Hospitals cared for 9,367 persons. It is a magnificent record.

The officers and members of the Army epitomize the spirit of devotion, self-abnegation and personal sacrifice which this nation needs to win this war. The men who once wore the Salvationist's blue are now in far quarters of the earth wearing the uniform of men fighting for freedom of the human spirit.

And this Army can present stories of physical and moral heroism of its officers and members which bring tears to our eyes but bring faith to our hearts.

On January 9, a member of the Salvation Army, Mrs. James Buckley, in uniform, christened at Hingham, Massachusetts, a naval escort vessel—a fighting ship—bearing the name of her son, John D. Buckley, who was killed while manning a machine-gun against the Japanese at Pearl Harbor. John Buckley had also been a member of the Salvation Army before he joined the Navy, to meet a hero's death.

In the last war and in this war, its canteens are those nearest the front line—and its moral support is welcomed in every branch of our armies.

After this war we will be confronted with the immense problems of rehabilitation of men. And it will be the Salvation Army which seeks out the desolate, the discouraged, the frustrated and puts them again upon the path of life. We will need them as never before. For they reach to groups in a way that can never be met by government. Governments can aid the material needs of men but their spiritual needs must come from our spiritual agencies such as this.

But the Army needs little of eulogy. The world knows its work. What it needs from us at this time is financial support. It knows how to do its job. It does it intelligently, efficiently and without waste. And it can make one dollar do the work of five. And its work is not to be measured in dollars. It is measured in men and women helped to a better life.

Thomas Jefferson and the Bill of Rights

Article for Bill of Rights
Sesqui-Centennial pamphlet
[April, 1943]

THOMAS JEFFERSON, of course, did not originate the Bill of Rights. He had much to do with its amplification and in securing that it be embedded in the Constitution. His flaming insistence in the Declaration that men "are endowed by their Creator with certain inalienable rights" had much to do with implanting them in the fibre of American life.

Jefferson knew well the centuries of struggle in which men had died fighting bitterly for these rights. Step by step they had been secured through the Magna Carta, the growth of common law, the "Petition of Rights" and the Declaration of Rights, until they reached full flower in the new republic.

During the first century and a half of our national life we saw no serious challenge to the Bill of Rights. We extended it and we accepted it as the air we breathed. But for the last quarter of a century it has been incessantly attacked both from without and within our country.

In the hurricane of revolutions which have swept the world since the Great War, men, struggling with the wreckage and poverty of that great catastrophe and the complications of the machine age, have in despair surrendered their freedom for false promises of security and glory. Whether it be Fascism,

Nazism, Communism or their lesser followers, the result is the same. Every day they repudiate every principle of the Bill of Rights. And where they have triumphed the first security of men has been lost.

Theirs is a form of servitude, of slavery—a slipping back toward the Middle Ages. Whatever these ideologies are, they have one common denominator—the citizen has no inalienable rights. He is submerged into the State. Here is the most fundamental clash known to mankind—that is, free men and women cooperating under orderly liberty, as contrasted with human beings made pawns of government; men who are slaves of despotism as against free men who are the masters of the State.

Even in America, where Liberty blazed brightest and by its glow shed light on all the others, Liberty is not only besieged from without but it is challenged from within. Many, in honest belief, hold that we cannot longer accommodate the growth of science, technology and mechanical power to the Bill of Rights. But men's inventions cannot be of more value than men themselves. But it would be better that we sacrifice something of economic efficiency than to surrender these primary liberties. In them lies a spiritual growth of men. Behind them is the conception which is the highest development of the Christian faith—the conception of individual freedom with brotherhood. From them is the fullest flowering of individual human personality.

Those who proclaim that the Machine Age created an irreconcilable conflict in which Liberty must be sacrificed should not forget the battles for these rights over the centuries; for let it be remembered that in the end these are undying principles which spring from the souls of men. We imagine conflict not because the principles of Liberty are unworkable in a machine age, but because we have not worked them conscientiously or have forgotten their true meaning.

Neither would sacrifice of these rights add to economic efficiency nor would it gain in economic security nor find a single job nor give a single assurance in old age. The dynamic forces which sustain economic security and progress in human comfort lie deep below the surface. They reach to those human impulses which are watered alone by freedom. The initiative of men, their enterprise, the inspiration of thought flower in full only in the security of these rights.

And by practical experience under the Bill of Rights we have tested this truth. Down through a century and a half this American concept of human freedom has enriched the whole world. From the release of the spirit, the initiative, the cooperation and the courage of men, which alone come from these freedoms, has been builded this very machine age with all its additions of comfort, its reductions of sweat. Wherever in the world the system of individual liberty has been sustained, mankind has been better clothed, better fed, better housed, has had more leisure. Above all, men and women have had more self-respect. They have been more generous and of finer spirit. Those who scoff that Liberty is of no consequence to the underprivileged and the unemployed are grossly ignorant of the primary fact that it is through the creative and the productive impulses of free men that the redemption of those sufferers and their economic security must come. Any system which curtails these freedoms and stimulants to men destroys the possibility of the full production from which economic security can alone come.

Nor is respect for the Bill of Rights a fetter upon progress. It has been no dead hand that has carried the living principles of Liberty over these centuries. Without violation of these principles and their safeguards we have amended the Constitution many times in the past century to meet the problems of growing civilization. We will no doubt do so many times again. New invention and new ideas require the constant remolding of our civilization. The functions of government must be readjusted from time to time to restrain the strong and protect the weak. That is the preservation of Liberty itself.

Jefferson was eternally right when he held that Liberty comes only and lives only where the hard-won rights of men are held inalienable, where governments themselves may not infringe, where governments are indeed but the mechanisms to protect and sustain these principles. It was this concept for which America's sons have died on a hundred battlefields.

The purification of Liberty from abuses, the restoration of confidence in the rights of men from which come the release of the dynamic forces of advancing spirit and enterprise are alone the methods through which the purpose of American life can be assured.

Aviation After This War

Press statement, New York City

[April 1, 1943]

THAT the airplane will assume a much larger part in the life of the world after this war needs no proof. As commercial transportation it will expand enormously, and the new inventions and improvements will make the planes bigger, faster, more comfortable and more economical to operate. We will have a host of trained personnel. It seems that the combat planes cannot be well transformed to commercial planes, and therefore there will be a large manufacturing demand to equip the world. And right here let me urge that our government give the manufacturers a chance to design the after-war commercial plane which will need embrace the many discoveries and inventions of the war. We should be ready.

From a commercial point of view, it is obvious that a larger part of passenger traffic overseas will move into the air from the slower and less comfortable crossings by ships. Passengers will increase overland. Those of us who live on the two coasts expect a ten-hour trip every hour on the hour. The use of planes for freight other than mail and express has great limitations. A recent estimate of 7 cents a ton mile as about the lowest cost possible by plane does not permit competition with a cost of a quarter of a cent by ships or one cent per ton mile by rail. Someone was enthusiastic in the press about shipping freight 7,000 miles to China by plane. There is little freight that will pay $490.00 per ton by air as compared with, say, $20.00 per ton by sea.

There will, however, be a big business in the air. And it will involve many international problems.

I doubt if the larger area victorious nations will give up their sovereignty of the air. That is, will give a free right for foreign planes to fly indiscriminately over their territory. They are not likely to want foreign planes constantly looking down upon their domestic, military or other affairs. All the victorious nations want to build up commercial aviation in their own countries. They will want to maintain their airplane-manufacturing industries for military reasons. To protect their commerce from foreign monopoly, they will no doubt give some privilege to their own national planes in their own boundaries.

But there must be some organized international relations as to air services. It would seem that there is an analogy with ships insofar as passage over the seas is concerned. In peace times, ships of foreign countries can go to and from the ports of any nation, except inter-coastal services. It is possible that this may be the key to international rights. But this degree of freedom in the air implies open airports at coastal points everywhere for foreign landings and it implies international weather and radio service. We have another analogy in seas transport that might be considered. We have in some countries so-called "free ports," being small areas of the ports set aside where sea ships can land goods without red tape or tariffs, where the passengers and crews can change planes without inspections or bother except as to health and carrying of infections. If they want to go outside this walled area into the country, they are subject to any current requirements. If we had such free airports established along the coasts of the world or on national frontiers, then there could be full freedom over the seas for all nations' airplanes. It might well be that this right of free navigation should be extended over certain land areas of backward nations which are in reality governed in trust for the whole world, such as Central Africa.

Flying over the land of other nations or landing at their interior airports of course could be done by consent of the nations concerned. Many countries do not have the means to maintain their own services or are on through-routes which they themselves would like to see maintained, such as South America, etc.

If we wish for real advance and improvement in air transport, we must retain private enterprise and competition. That made the airplane as we know it today. But in the very practical world that will evolve after this war, we will have to meet foreign, government-owned services, and there will be, and in some cases need be, government subsidies by mail or otherwise. We will need some sort of international agreement on rates if competition is not to be smothered by government action. We ought to be thinking of all these questions of rights which should be established in the peace treaties.

It is probable that the enemy countries would, as a part of disarmament, at least be deprived of the right to manufacture airplanes until the world was satisfied that their faces are firmly directed toward peace. While the war plane is now about as differentiated from the commercial plane as the warship is from the commercial ship, still they can be made in the same factory. In enemy cases, if they are allowed to have their own air services—which is not certain, they will probably have to buy planes from the victors so as to make sure that they are not building up for war under a disguise.

The airplane looms large as a potent instrument for keeping peace in the world. If combat planes were reserved to the victorious powers after this war, they could, by a comparatively small combined force, keep the world free of aggression with planes alone. It opens a great vista of land and sea disarmament if the world acts intelligently about it.

Neither a Hitler nor a Tojo would be so ambitious if there were a prospect of a continuous air attack until such persons came to reason.

Boys' Clubs Boys in the Army

NEW YORK CITY

[May 6, 1943]

Mr. Hall, men and women who direct the Boys' Clubs of America:

FOR our radio audience I may say a word about this annual meeting of the Boys' Clubs of America. These are 240 real clubs of 350,000 boys from the congested areas of our cities. These clubs belong to the boys, and the property value is over $20,000,000. They each pay their dues of a few cents a month like any gentleman. These are actual clubhouses in which there are swimming pools, gymnasiums and directed sports that build them physically and teach sportsmanship. There are workshops where their vocational bent is developed. And above all, there is solid character building. In this war the Boys' Clubs have undertaken a nation-wide program as their contribution to victory.

This war makes it possible to reappraise somewhat the American Boy in general. Judging from the literature of a few years ago, we might conclude that he was not so good as his dad. More idle time, more candy, less chores, less family discipline, all were supposed to have softened him up physically. Movies, funnies, automobiles, radio and the bright lights were supposed to have undermined his moral stature. He no longer had the initiative, the pep, the fibre we had "when we were boys."

What does this war disclose to us? The millions in the draft have on the average higher physical levels than those in the

war of 25 years ago. The main drink is milk. The educational
rating is much higher; the individual initiative is better. The
boys may sing less but they are more serious and more determined. They are thinking more deeply. And these American
boys today are showing extraordinary endurance in hardship
and a magnificent courage in battle. They are the best the race
has produced.

And how do our boys compare with the boys of other nations?
We have already some great tests in the Pacific and in the air
war over Europe. And how about our Marines at Guadalcanal?
Here our boys have already demonstrated their ascendency,
man for man, over the boys of every enemy country. They have
demonstrated a far greater initiative and character. And this is
a war of individual initiative as never before. Our boys are the
product of democracy. They have never been regimented. They
are individualists. The war will be won by the much-defamed
rugged individualism.

And what part have these Boys' Clubs had in this? Truly,
we are but a small segment. But we do have thousands of our
alumni in draft groups and we have 350,000 pavement boys in
our charge of whom thousands are emerging into draft age
every day. They come from near the ground in the economic
scale and most of them from recent immigrant parents. We
have no complete statistics, but I can give you some indications
of what the Boys' Clubs have done physically for these boys.
Remember that the average rejections as physically unfit in the
draft of this war are somewhere over 30 per cent. The reports
we have from 2,700 of our boys drafted show that only 16 have
been rejected, or less than one-half of one per cent.

Does that not mean that the Boys' Clubs have done something for these boys and their country? If we had the resources
to organize all the 1,500,000 pavement boys into these clubs,
we would have made an even greater contribution toward saving our country in this danger.

And what are the Boys' Clubs doing now? They are doing a
multitude of daily chores in aid of the war effort. But beyond
this, our 240 Clubs with their gymnasiums and swimming pools,

their mechanical shops, their physical inspection are giving a pre-draft training unequalled in the country. Our alumni have already furnished the equal of four whole divisions to our armies. These 350,000 boys we now serve may yet contribute five more divisions to our army of fit, know-how, patriotic boys with self-starters within them, before this war is done.

I have the privilege of introducing to you a great American soldier who today has one of the greatest responsibilities of our times. And is equal to it. That is, the Commandant of the United States Marines, Lt. General Thomas Holcombe.

Enchanted World

This Week Magazine
[August 1, 1943]

THERE are two jobs for American boys today. One is being a boy. The other is growing up to be a man. Both jobs are important. Both are packed with excitement, great undertakings, high adventure.

Sometimes a boy's elders seriously interfere with his sheer joy in being a boy. They fill the department of growing up to be a man with grief and trouble. They create daily problems about everything: about health, about being made to eat food that is "good for you," washing around neck and ears, keeping neat, with special unreasonableness about rusty jack-knives and prized collections of snakes and toads.

There is a constant check-up to make sure that a boy's every waking activity is a constructive joy, not destructive glee. There is moral and spiritual instruction. And there is going to school. There are many disciplines, directions, urgings and pleadings from elders that no boy understands until he has become a man himself.

But then he looks backward to the enchanted boy's world in which he once lived so splendidly. And he finds its memory one of his most precious personal possessions.

I was a boy in the days before our civilization became so perfect, before it was paved with cement and made of bricks. Boys were not so largely separated from Mother Earth and all her works. And that was before the machine age denied them their natural right as primitive, combative animals to match their wits with bird and animal and insect.

In the course of my life, I have eaten presumably the best food in the world, served with the customary ceremony and ritual. But no royal gourmet or no Ritz has ever provided me with game of such wondrous flavor as birds cooked over a small boy's campfire; pigeons from Iowa's woods and prairie chickens from her hedges, hunted down by our gang with homemade bows and arrows, and sling-shots.

We cooked and ate fish of our own catching. Not with tackle assembled from the steel of Damascus, bamboos of Siam, tin of Penang, silver of Colorado or artificial flies of many colors. We got more fish with a self-made willow pole, a butcher-string line, and ten-for-a-dime hooks than I have ever got since. Our decoy was a section of angle worm, dug by us, and our good-luck incantation was to spit on the bait. We lived in a time when a fish used to bite instead of strike, and we knew it bit when the cork bobbed. We were masters of the art of trapping rabbits in cracker boxes half-opened by a figure 4.

On crisp winter nights we whizzed down gigantic, snow-clad hills at death-defying speeds—on sleds made by us. And on hot summer days we went swimming in a hole under willows by the railroad bridge. There was nice healthy mud in that hole, and it always attached itself to us. No spa has a more satisfactory mud-bath to offer its clientele.

But my boyhood was not all adventure and high living. There was also school. There were also farm chores. There was also strict discipline, for mine was a Quaker family with strong views regarding the corruption of youth. It was a condition of the other freedoms that I read and be questioned on one chapter of the Bible each day. At times I felt injustice was done by the extra-long chapters. They were kindly folks. They believed in a boy's being a boy, but they were resolute on a boy's growing up to be an honest, self-respecting member of human society.

Since one of the saddest things in the world is that boys must grow up into the land of realities, I think there should be a special Bill of Rights for boys, as boys:

Like everyone else, a boy has a right to the pursuit of happiness. He has the right to the kind of play that will stretch his imagination, tax his ingenuity, sharpen his wits, challenge his prowess and keep his self-starter going.

He has the right to the satisfaction of that thirst to explore the world around him, every bit of which is new to him, and to explore the land of make-believe at will.

He has the right to affection and friendship. He has the right to the sense of security in belonging to some group. He is by nature gregarious, and the cultivation of that instinct will bring him many joys and helps in life.

He has the right to health protections that will make him an inch taller than his dad. He has the right to education and training that will fit him into a job he likes when he becomes a man.

These are the rights of boys and it's up to us, as adults, to see that they have them. The glory of the nation rests in the character of her men. And character comes from boyhood. Thus every boy is a challenge to his elders. It is for them that we must win the war—it is for them that we must make a just and lasting peace. For the world of tomorrow, about which all of us are dreaming and planning, will be carried forward by the boys of today.

The Front of Human Decency

Woman's Home Companion

[April, 1944]

IN WRITING this article for the Woman's Home Companion it is my purpose to put a challenge to the women of this country. For the moral life of America is in danger. Many years of personal experience have taught me that our women can always be counted upon to meet a national emergency with energy and intelligence. That is why I venture to challenge you to assume an even graver responsibility than that you now bear so splendidly. You are already fighting on many fronts, the military, home, farm and industrial fronts. But if civilization is to be saved, you—and all of us—must fight hardest of all on the front of human decency, on the front to maintain standards of human rights, behavior and morals.

It is the front where we must fight for that dignity of men and women which rests in the spirit as well as in the letter of the Bill of Rights, of liberty under law.

It is the front of truth, intellectual honesty and moral courage in statesmanship.

It is the front of financial honesty and an honest day's work.

It is the front of compassion and tolerance and kindliness.

It is the front of sportsmanship, of my brother's keeper and of good neighbors.

It is the front of private as well as public justice, of private as well as public morals.

It is the front of religious faith, for that is the greatest safeguard of all decency.

In sum, we must fight to preserve decency both abroad and at home. And this will be a fight in realism as well as in idealism.

This war is not being waged to punish military aggression only. The leaders of the Axis seek to implant a system which would destroy personal liberty and the dignity of the individual man. We are fighting to prevent that.

We are fighting against a system that regiments man's very soul, raises boys and girls to be cheats, liars and worse; against intolerance that murders Jews; against atheism that destroys religious faith, brutality that kills and starves women and children and innocent civilians; against military aggression that would enslave whole nations.

These are real things we are fighting abroad. What we have to fight on the front of human decency at home is no less real. At home we have to fight not only the degeneration of standards and agencies that make for human decency now, during the war, but we must fight to recover after the war the ground we lose now. For some loss, I know, is inevitable. High moral and ethical standards in private life are more important to the nation than a particular economic system. But the economic system can affect morals.

We must accept the fact that total war relaxes moral standards on the home front and that this imperils the whole front of human decency. The inevitable brutalities of war accustom us to brutality. Righteous indignation against our enemies teaches the pattern for intolerance. Untruth and half truths, necessary to deceive our enemies and to keep discouragement from our own people, become familiar and thus seem no longer so monstrous as they seem in a peaceful world.

Again, men, women and whole families must be shifted to new localities. Old restraints and disciplines are often lost. The facilities for education and care of children are overstrained. Mothers must be drawn into war work, and thousands of children are deprived of watchful care. The hot emotions of war break down many moral restraints.

These are some of the problems on the home front of human

decency. They must be faced and solved if we would preserve what is finest in American life.

If you, the women of America, enlist in this fight, what armies will be fighting with you?

Your allies are the churches, the colleges, the schools, the press and the government. They are the character-building organizations for our youth, the organizations for relief of suffering at home and abroad. They are the responsible men and women of every community in this nation who demand that decency be supported and violation denounced.

Most of the action on the front of human decency must be expressed through government. But the driving power behind government must come from us, the people, and more particularly from the women. From you must come the insistence that government reflect our best instincts, our finest ethics. Our public leaders are guardians of our birthright, trustees and protectors of our honor as free men. You must insist that America practice what she preaches.

Even during the war we must ask ourselves some searching questions about our conduct.

Are we upholding the front of human decency when we permit untruth and dishonesty in government officials to go unchallenged, whether in our home town, our home state or in Washington?

Are we holding the front of human decency when we refuse possible relief to millions of starving women and children in occupied democracies?

Have we the courage to criticize when criticism is due?

Can we sustain the principles of law, justice and liberty abroad if we sit by without protest and see these principles violated at home?

Are we not violating the whole spiritual basis of tolerance?

Are we not breaking down respect for law when we fail to boycott the black markets?

Are we not ignoring juvenile delinquency? Are we not allowing the morals and disciplines of our homes to drift? Are we upholding our agencies of religious faith?

These are the specific weaknesses we must combat if we wish to demand restoration of essential values after the war.

Space does not permit the discussion of all these questions. I may, however, emphasize one of them—the rising tide of juvenile delinquency. Here is a black spot that the women of America could rub out at once.

Do I need to recite the scenes around many of our camps, our war work communities, our city streets? Do I need to recite the heart-breaking statistics of children going wild and of the havoc among our teen-age boys and girls? You are all too familiar with these conditions. Nor do I have to emphasize the fact that loosened morals and disciplines in the home are allowing this spread of delinquency, especially among teen-age girls. And as we all know, this delinquency is not confined to families of the less fortunate or to café society.

I recognize the earnest work being done by the churches, the Boys' Clubs, Boy Scouts, Girl Scouts and other character-building institutions. I know of brave and devoted work being done by volunteer women in the munition centers through the provision of crèches for babies and recreation and rest centers for young children of mothers engaged in war work. I know of the great service of women trying to minimize the evils of juvenile delinquency in our cities. These efforts must be more generously supported in our giving. But these agencies and individuals cannot do all that must be done.

Here is a problem in which an organized crusade of our women is required—a crusade to furnish facilities for proper recreation but also to force preventive and remedial action by police and military authorities. The stench of juvenile delinquency must be cleared up or the whole front of decency in our race will be impaired physically, morally and spiritually.

Could not the women leaders in centers where juvenile delinquency is strong start now to survey the problem, start to formulate plans whereby the community would assume responsibility?

The fight against juvenile delinquency, important as it is, nevertheless is only one battle on the front of human decency. We must battle all along the line if we are not to see the individual rights, the spiritual and moral standards of our people, their honesty, their obedience to law, their tolerance, all sadly impaired by the war. It is vital to winning the war that we uphold these strengths in the nation now. The spiritual forces and virtues of our nation need to be harnessed into action. The women can do it.

Let's Go Fishin'

Collier's

[April 22, 1944]

RECENTLY I made some suggestions for an economic and social tidying-up of our country in preparation for the return of our boys from overseas. As I wrote, I was depressed by the thousand mournful voices chanting daily of "post-war problems" in such powerful terms as recovery, reconstruction and regeneration.

But in their research efforts in speech and their labors in type, they all concern themselves solely with what we are to do while we are on their promised jobs. Civilization, however, is not going to depend so much on what we do when we are on the job, as what we do in our time off. The moral and spiritual forces do not lose ground while we are pushing "the instrumentalities of production and distribution." Their battle is in our leisure time.

When the guns cease firing, and the gas comes on again, some of us are going fishing. We American men and boys (and some women) are born fishermen—twelve million of us. We have proved it in bygone days by the annual licenses we took out from thrifty state governments.

We have had mostly to postpone the fishing beatitudes for the duration. Many of us are busy at the military front. Some of us on the home front could possibly get a day or a week off, but the fishing holes can only be approached by automobile or motorboats, and a stern government refuses to recognize that fish do not flourish near railway depots.

In the meantime, I suspect that Mother Nature is making the fish bigger and more plentiful by way of preparing to celebrate peace, and our paternal government is doing its duty to solve our postwar problems by running the hatcheries full blast, turning out billions of infant fish and trying to decrease infant mortality.

I have discussed this important subject in years past, but some review and extension of those remarks are not out of place in these days when we are groping for post-war regeneration. Nothing can stop these regenerative forces.

Even the Four Horsemen cannot stop them. War, murrain, famine, pestilence, dictators, the rise and fall of empires or republics may defeat the game fisherman temporarily, but he rises again to invade the streams and the sea. More people have gone fishing over more centuries than for any other human recreation.

Sometimes the uninstructed and the people who have bad "isms" scoff at the game fishermen and demand to know how they get that way. It is very, very simple. These regenerative impulses are physical, spiritual and economic—and they are strong.

The human animal originally came from out-of-doors. When spring begins to move in his bones, he just must get out again. One time, in the spring, our grandmothers used to give us nasty brews from herbs to purify our blood of the winter's corruptions. They knew something was the matter with the boys. They could have saved trouble by giving them a pole, a string and a hook. Some wise ones (among them my own) did just that.

THE CALL OF THE OPEN SPACES

Moreover, as civilization, cement pavements, office buildings, radios have overwhelmed us, the need for regeneration has increased, and the impulses are even stronger. When all the routines and details and the human bores get on our nerves, we just yearn to go away from here to somewhere else. To go fishing is a sound, a valid and an accepted reason for such an escape.

It is the chance to wash one's soul with pure air, with the rush of the brook or with the shimmer of the sun on blue water. It brings meekness and inspiration from the decency of nature, charity toward tackle-makers, patience toward fish, a mockery of profits and egos, a quieting of hate, a rejoicing that you do not have to decide a darned thing until next week. And it is discipline in the equality of men—for all men are equal before fish.

Necessarily, fishermen are gregarious. Otherwise, the mighty deeds of the day or of a year ago or of ten years ago would go unsung. No one else will listen to them. Also, they are an optimistic class or they would not be fishermen. Therefore, as two or three are gathered together, the spiritual vitamins of faith, hope and charity have constant regeneration. And we need all that in these years of creaking civilization, especially in the coming years of post-war tribulation.

Nor does this source of spiritual vitamins require any governmental bureau to administer it. All that is required of Congress is to restore our freedom from the fellows who restrict the use of gasoline, and the rugged individualism of the fisherman will do the rest.

His joys are not all confined to the hours near the water. I asserted years ago that one of the elements in the advance of civilization was the progress in the equipment to overcome the mysteries of fish. We have moved upward and onward from the primitive willow pole with a butcher-string line and hooks (ten for a dime) whose compelling lure was one segment of a worm and whose incantation was spitting on the bait. We have arrived at labor-saving devices and increased efficiency in tackle assembled from the bamboo of Burma, the steel of Sweden, the lacquer of China, the tin of Bangkok, the nickel of Madagascar, the silver of Nevada and the feathers of Brazil—all compounded into mass production at Akron, Ohio.

For magic and incantations, we have moved forward to cosmetics for artificial flies and wonders in special clothes and bags with pigeonholes for everything, including mosquito repellents. We no longer call it a "pole," for it is a "rod"; and we no longer say that a fish "bites," he now "strikes."

Out of all this progress, a good fisherman can secure many regenerative hours of winter, polishing up the rods and reels, greasing the lines and discussing the relative merits of gay-colored flies and dead-sure lures—thereby recalling that Big One from the pool just below the rapids and the fly he rose to.

Nor is fishing a rich man's regeneration. That boy with the worm and a grin is always a reminder that men are equal before fish. However, that boy misses out in one particular that I hope to see attended to in our next era of national reform. There is regenerative joy in contemplating and fondling adequate tackle, which he cannot get out of a collection of angelworms. And his joys are more seasonal because he cannot put in the winter nights polishing up that tackle with its reminder of that Big One from that pool and thereby the renewed smell of battles to come.

NEW DEAL FOR YOUNG ANGLERS

I acknowledged to a prominent official an idea to reform this. All boys should be guaranteed from birth to manhood a quart of polish and a collection of tackle with an assortment of special flies. There has been sad neglect in this question of assuring artificial flies to the youth of our land, for flies proved their inspiring worth perhaps four hundred years ago—long before Izaak Walton.

When I was a boy and lived at the social level of worms, a true fisherman gave me three flies—a coachman, a gray hackle and a professor. I treasured them greatly and used them successfully for two or three years—until the wings were all worn off. But there were more fish in proportion to the water in those times.

There are some class distinctions among fishermen. The dry-fly devotees hold themselves a bit superior to the wet-fly fishermen; the wet-fly fishermen, superior to the spinner fishermen; and the spinners, superior to the bait fishermen. I have noticed, however, that toward the end of the day when there were no strikes each social level sometimes descends down the scale until it gets some fish for supper.

This class distinction may perhaps be ignored in the general reformation, for it is not based on the economic levels. The best dry fisherman I have known is a lady cook at a lumber camp in Montana. She scorned the wet-fly fisherman and rose to indignation at bait.

The swordfish and tarpon fishermen likewise have some social distinctions on the basis of the size of line and reel. The lower-thread line operators are the dukes and earls in that aristocracy. Also, the swordfish and marlin devotees are naturally superior to those who take mere mackerel, amber jacks or flounders. The bonefish fishermen claim a little superiority to the tarpon seekers. But again it is not economic status that counts in such good society so much as knowing what the fish bite.

Someone propounded the question to me: "Why have all Presidents in modern times been fishermen?" It seemed to me a worthy investigation, for the habits of Presidents are likely to influence the nation's youth. Some of us had been fishermen from boyhood and required no explanation. But others only became fishermen after entering the White House. In examining this national phenomenon, I concluded that the pneumatic hammering of demands on the President's mind had increased in frequency with the rising tide of economic and international complexity, and he just had to get away somehow, somewhere and be alone for a few hours once in a while. But there are only two occasions when Americans respect privacy, especially in Presidents. Those are prayer and fishing. So that some have taken to fishing.

President Cleveland was both a stream and a sea fisherman from youth. His stiff trout rod is still preserved by a devoted fisherman, and it is recorded that his sea-fishing boatman was chosen for silence. Whether President Coolidge fished in his youth is uncertain. He was a good deal of a fundamentalist in economics, government and fishing, so he naturally preferred angleworms. But when the fly fishermen of the nation raised their eyebrows in surprise, he took to artificial flies. However, his backcast was so much a common danger that even the Secret Service men kept at a distance until they were summoned to climb trees to retrieve flies.

But I should return to expanding on post-war regeneration and its moral and spiritual values in a gloomy world. Statistics tell us that the gainfully employed have steadily decreased in hours of work during the whole of thirty years. And in shorter hours and long week ends and holidays, we have devoted more time to making merry and stirring the caldron of evil. Crime has increased. Yet nobody ever was in jail or plotted a crime when fishing. The increase of crime is among those deprived of those regenerations that impregnate the mind and character of fishermen.

Our standards of material progress include the notion and the hope that we shall still further lessen the daily hours of labor. We also dream of longer annual holidays as scientific discovery and mass production do our production job faster and faster. But when they do the job, they dull the souls of men unless their leisure hours become the period of life's real objective—regeneration by fishing.

THE PROBLEMS OF LEISURE

Moreover, while we are steadily organizing increased production of leisure time, the production of what to do with it still lags greatly. We do have some great machinery of joy, some of it destructive, some of it synthetic, much of it mass production. We go to chain theaters and movies. We watch somebody else knock a ball over the fence or kick it over the goal post.

I do that and I believe in it. But these forms of organized joy are sadly lacking in the values which surround the fish. We gain none of the lift of soul coming from a return to the solemnity, the calm and inspiration of primitive nature.

Nor is it the fish that we get that counts, for they can be had in the market for mere silver. It is the break of the waves in the sun, the joyous rush of the brook, the contemplation of the eternal flow of the stream, the stretch of forest and mountain in their manifestation of the Maker that soothes our troubles, shames our wickedness and inspires us to esteem our fellow men —especially other fishermen.

The Need of Boys

THE Annual Meeting of the Directors of the Boys' Clubs of America is convening at this moment in an adjoining room. I have been requested to give to you some account of this important movement. It is indeed a ray of sunlight in this sombre world. For it is from the success in building of character in our youth that must come the hopes of the future. And this institution is one of the aids in this work.

For those not familiar with the movement I may state that the Boys' Clubs comprise some 240 active clubs in 177 cities and represent an investment in buildings and endowment of fully $25,000,000. A quarter of a million boys between 7 and 17 are active members of these clubs. And there is nothing inactive about their membership. The clubs are located in the congested districts of our cities. The boys are mostly the sons of workmen, and their parents are proud of their sons' membership and glad they have these facilities instead of being driven onto the pavements for the adventure that every boy must have. They come from every racial stock, many of them only second generation Americans. Our purpose is first to provide constructive joy with training in the second great moral code, which is sportmanship—all of which prevents delinquencies. Second, to provide careful supervision of health. And third, to discover and to guide the natural bents of these boys toward some definite occupation in after life.

This 38th annual meeting is one of particular rejoicing, because we now have proof of tangible results from all the effort of many years in building up a great institution. This meeting will be addressed by J. Edgar Hoover, who, as the head of the Federal Bureau of Investigation, is particularly concerned with the appalling increase in delinquency in our teen-age boys and girls due to the loosening of restraints by the war. Yet among the 250,000 boys in these clubs there have been very rare cases of delinquency. And, mind you, this is the human material of our cities about which our social students moan with such despair.

Over a quarter of a million men in our armed forces have been members of these clubs when they were boys. Of these we have records of about 90,000. And here is an astonishing fact. Those 90,000 were in such health that less than half as many of them were rejected as 4-F's for physical defects as the average of the country. But even more gloriously, we have word of several hundred who have been decorated for bravery. We have fear that more than a thousand have died for their country.

General Hershey has recently shown that about 30 per cent of the men of draft age are rejected for physical defects. That is about the same as in the last war. In other words, while our advances in medicine and public health have decreased sickness and prolonged life, there is something lacking in physical fitness of the individual American. I believe, if General Hershey would canvass all the men in the Army who have gone through our Boys' Clubs and all the rejects from among these former Boys' Clubs members, he would find that we have one answer to his question. That is, to give opportunity for youngsters beginning at 7 for regular medical inspection and physical training until they are 17.

It is our hope to extend this movement to cover another 1,000,000 less-privileged boys in our cities. But the times are against expansion. We know from long experience that these clubs cannot succeed unless they have buildings of dignity; equipment for physical training; equipment to develop their occupational bents; and above all, they must be guided by men of sympathetic and experienced understanding. We have many cities which want to build new clubs, but for the moment we must bow to the national necessity not to use building materials. Today we have also lost much of our skilled staff to the military forces, yet the remaining staffs have cheerfully doubled their tasks, and we carry on. And we are carrying on in even larger fields than in peace time. For every one of these boys in our clubs is now mobilized into national service—they are recovering waste materials; they are serving other organizations in a hundred capacities. They are part of the national effort.

There is no greater refreshment of the soul that you, my listeners, could have than from a visit to these clubs. Here are tens of thousands of cheerful, chattering youngsters, proud of their buildings, of their organization, of managing their own affairs with firm discipline, of sitting in solemn judgment upon their problems and of governing themselves. Here is that training in cooperation and sportsmanship which must be the basis of successful national life. And you could be helpful in encouraging them to carry on.

I have said we would like to expand. There are these further hundreds of thousands of boys who should be served. It would, more than any other method, reduce delinquency in our cities. There should be a similar service for the girls in these same areas. But we must acknowledge the fact that we, with other character-building organizations, have competition of the war agencies, and funds are hard to come by. But I have faith that the demonstration of the value of our past work under the supreme test of war will bring the needed support to us some day.

This war has brought home to us the full effect of the organized Nazi and Fascist training of boys and girls. They are trained for cogs in the gigantic military machine built to conquer the world. Theirs is not training for peace. We have now met them in battle. Our American way is to build individual character, to develop free will. When the nation needs them in battle, they are better soldiers. And also they are fitted to aid in reconstructing a world of peace. When these and all our other American boys come home, we shall find in them the fibre and moral resources from which America will emerge to a happier land.

Chicago Boys' Club

CHICAGO, ILLINOIS
[*June 6, 1945*]

Ladies and Gentlemen, Friends of Boys:

THIS meeting has been called to promote the interests of boys in the congested districts of Chicago. They are the pavement boys. I am proud to speak to you in my capacity as the Chairman of the National Boys' Clubs, because Chicago has been a greater leader in this movement.

The Chicago Boys' Club, Incorporated, was organized forty-five years ago, starting initially with one room and three boys. Today it operates seven clubs and five camps with assets of over $1,100,000 and a membership of over 10,000 boys. You, Mr. Regnery, and the Directors are to be congratulated on this magnificent achievement. It is a record of great vision on the needs of boys who, through no fault of their own, are condemned to live in the blighted areas of Chicago. I must not fail to mention, in addition to the efforts of this group, that there are eight other finely conducted Boys' Clubs in Chicago, two of which are conducted by the devotion of the Union League Club. Altogether these Clubs serve over 16,000 boys. But there are still 30,000 to 40,000 more in Chicago who need this leadership. I wish I had time to mention all the men and women to whose devotion the people of Chicago are indebted for the conduct of this service—and not the least of whom is Mr. Rudolph.

Together with his sister, the boy is our most precious national possession. We do not exclude their sisters—if anything, our sentiment for them is even more tender. But tonight we are here engaged in the business of this special group of boys and what we are going to do about them. In it are problems of morals, of delinquency, of health, of citizenship and of manhood. And although I devote myself particularly to the boy question, I am no less enthusiastic over the efforts of the Chicago Clubs to also provide for girls.

To arrive at an understanding, we ought to proceed like scientists and examine the behavior characteristics of the animal. We must determine the anatomy of a boy's mind. And also what civilization has done to him.

BEHAVIOR CHARACTERISTICS

This sort of boy, and all boys, are endowed with a dynamic energy and an impelling desire to take exercise on all occasions. He has tremendous potentiality even when he sits still.

His every movement is a crisis. He lives in more emergencies than the New Deal. Indeed, every boy must discover the world all over again. To his eyes it is a world filled with great adventures, discoveries and vast undertakings. And he doesn't come into the world with much information on pains and penalties—he must also pick up these items. Like all pups, he is born with a bounding instinct to play. Also his primary instinct is to hunt in a gang and that multiplies his devices. He is a complete self-starter, and therefore wisdom in dealing with him consists mostly in what to do with him next.

And truly, if he is to be a successful adventurer in life he must grow in mind and imagination, and for that he must live at least part-time in the land of make-believe. One of the sad things for him is that he must grow up into a land of realities.

From all this you will see that he presents not only joys and hopes, but also paradoxes. He strains our nerves, yet he is a complex of cells teeming with affection. He is a periodic nuisance, yet he is a joy forever. He is a part-time incarnation of destruction, yet he radiates sunlight to all the world. He gives evidence of being the child of iniquity, yet he makes a great nation. He is filled with curiosity as to every mortal thing. Every one of his body cells contains an interrogation point. Yet he is the most entertaining animal there is.

WHAT CIVILIZATION HAS DONE TO HIM

Now all that is mostly happy and encouraging, but modern civilization has bumped into this special group of boys. It has gone and built up great cities. It has stupendously increased the number of boys per acre. It has covered all the ground with bricks, cement and cobblestones and surrounded it with brick walls. All the natural outlets for the energies of these boys have been upset.

The normal boy, being a primitive animal, takes to competition and battle. In the days before our civilization became so perfect, he matched his wits with the birds and bees and the fish. He is today separated from Mother Earth and all her works, except the weather. The outlet of curiosity in exploring the streams and the fields is closed to him. The mysteries of the birds and bees and fish are denied to him. He cannot even see all of the sky at one time.

This pavement boy in fact has a life of stairs, light switches, alleys, fire escapes, bells and cobblestones, and a chance to get run over by a truck. Inasmuch as he cannot contend with nature, he is likely to take on contention with a policeman.

There are some three million of these confined dynamos in the congested districts of American cities and probably 60 to 80 thousand of them in Chicago.

The Constitution provides these boys as well as grown-ups, or at least at one time it did, with the inalienable right of liberty and the pursuit of happiness. His chief use of the Bill of Rights, however, is free assembly and free speech. But we are not so much concerned at the moment with his liberties as we are with his method of pursuing happiness. He will find the tragedies of liberty when he becomes a taxpayer. He and his gang can go on this hunt for happiness either constructively or destructively.

Therefore, our proposal is to channel him into constructive joy instead of destructive glee.

I dislike to refer to these boys as "under-privileged." That is only a half-truth. Our country provides the pavement boy with better schools and better health protection than any other in the world. He has more chance of becoming a policeman or a mayor or even an editor or a banker than they have anywhere else on earth. He suffers far less than his grandfather from mumps and measles and more quickly do we heal his broken bones. The electric light has banished that curse of all boys which was cleaning lamps and everlastingly carrying them about. And the light switch has driven away the goblins that lived in dark corners and under the bed. It clothes drab streets with gaiety and cheer by night. And it is these very bright lights that increase our problem.

But we are more concerned at the moment with the privileges which this civilization has taken away; and the particular ones which concern us are those that influence or make his character and his physical stature. Now this brick and cement foundation of life is a poor soil for physical, moral and spiritual growth.

WHAT OUR JOB IS

Somebody will say morals are the job of parents. But the best of parents cannot keep him indoors all the time. And his world in the streets is a distorted and dangerous world, which the parents cannot make or unmake. So it becomes a job of public responsibility.

That job hinges around what these boys can do every day between school hours and bedtime, on holidays and on Sundays after church. The most estimable organizations, such as the Boy Scouts, do not constantly serve these hours.

Ours is a problem of creating a place where these pavement boys can stretch their imaginations, where their inborn bent to play and where their unlimited desire for exercise can be channelled and led into the realms of sportsmanship. For sportsmanship is the second greatest code of morals.

Ours is a problem of diverting his fine loyalties to the gang from fighting it out with fists to the winning of points. We must let off his explosive violence without letting him get into the police court.

It is a problem of creating a place in which his curiosity as to what makes the wheels of the world go around may be turned into learning how to make some of the wheels himself.

All this will make the boy a citizen and not a gangster. Even the taxpayer can understand that the cure of a gangster is a thousand times more expensive than the diversion of a boy away from the gang. We can do the latter for $10.00 a piece, while the former costs $10,000 and often doesn't succeed at that.

As I sat here this evening I could not avoid a contrast. Fifteen years ago I was, as President, called upon to bring all the powers of the Federal Government to rid this city of Al Capone and his gang. They were one sort of product of the congested areas of this city. We eliminated them, but it cost the taxpayer a million dollars to do it. On the other hand, you have seen here the product of the Boys' Clubs from these same surroundings. Here we have seen the stream of enthusiasm, music and talents which are being poured into the life of Chicago. It thrills one with confidence in America.

But there is more to this than even exercise, morals and physical health. There is the job of stretching his vision of life. The priceless treasure of boyhood is his endless enthusiasm, his high store of idealism, his affections and his hopes. When we preserve these, we have made men. We have made Americans. But the hard pavements do not reek with these things.

THE FUNCTION OF THE BOYS' CLUBS

Many years ago, devoted souls, apprehending this problem, established Boys' Clubs in some of the most crowded areas of our cities, including Chicago. They sought to stop the gap that idle hands can fill with evil. Today there are about 280 clubs spread in 153 cities. They have an operating budget of nearly

$4,000,000 a year and about $30,000,000 worth of equipment. They are a great, new form of university in American life.

In these places boys find outlets for that explosive energy in play and the land of make-believe. Their activities stretch all the way from checkers to sandlot baseball, from orchestras to bands. There are boxing matches, libraries, gymnasiums and swimming pools. They are led into shops of the arts and the trades to discover their occupational bents. And above all, they are taught the spirit of sportsmanship and cooperative living. They are not only taught the rules of health. But they are examined for physical weaknesses and repaired. And here also are given glimpses of the opportunities of a greater America.

The juvenile delinquencies in the areas where these clubs work invariably show a striking decrease. They have produced men of leadership in their communities. There are great editors, sculptors and actors who came from this boys' mill. And they have produced five players in major league baseball. The feet of thousands have been set on the road of American opportunity.

Lately there has been a magnificent test of these Boys' Club boys. The national average of 4-F discards in the draft is nearly 32 per cent. Yet in some 200,000 draftees who came from these Clubs whom we have been able to trace, there were less than 5 per cent in 4-F. And this from the least promising material in America.

And from another direction these Clubs are proving of superlative importance. The totalitarian countries also adopted these benevolent ideas of handling boys. They grouped them, they systematically cured their physical defects, gave them recreation and found their occupational bents. But they pounded in Communist and Fascist modes of thought. They built their minds into mental and moral submission and to a brutal mold. Their concept was that each of them is simply a molecule in a mass-directed state. That is exactly the opposite to what our Boys' Clubs do. We build into our boys personalities, personal responsibility, dignity, character and moral discipline, not regimented minds. And now these concepts have clashed on the field of battle. And ours proved the better men, man for man, and we won.

If you believe I am over-stating the case for the Boys' Clubs, inquire of your police, of your magistrates. Look into what has become of their alumni in the world.

THIS BLACK SPOT

These drab congested areas with their battalions of boys and girls are one of the black spots of American life. In the advancement of national life, the powerful initiative of our people creates many bright spots of progress. But in the wake of that progress, we leave some very black spots.

And I do not believe in looking at black spots only. It is the white spots in our civilization that keep up our courage and faith and that keep us fighting the black spots.

And we can well take a moment to look at a bright spot. In all history, there was never such care of youth and such opportunity for youth as 75 per cent of the children of America now enjoy. Our job is to give the same chance to the rest.

In a civilization 6,000 years old, it was only a hundred years ago that not one-third of our children had elementary schooling. Today that black spot is pretty well cleaned up. It is not fifty years ago that 85 per cent of our children had no secondary or vocational schooling. That spot has been reduced to 35 per cent. Fifty years ago we had only 150,000 of our youth in institutions of higher learning; today in peace there are 1,200,-000 of them. I do not know whether those left out are a black spot or not. It depends on what they would do with this higher learning.

Therefore, despite a few black spots, this mass of American youth is a magnificent army for carrying forward civilization. And by their valor in this war they have proved it.

However, the incessant job of democracy is to clean up black spots. Or their infections will destroy it. And that includes a lot more than just improving the boys' and girls' resident in these spots. We ought to wipe them out altogether.

GOVERNMENT RELATIONS

Government, with its ever-expanding activities, will no doubt concern itself to a greater and greater extent with the affairs of our young people. But it will be a sign of degeneration when we, as private citizens, shall surrender character building to the state. That is not the place where morals, personality and character can ever be built. The methods of a dictator are simple and easy. Ours is more difficult, but it is the only kind of society that self-respecting men and women can cherish. It is one which holds every boy and girl to be worthy of its confidence, which sees in the poorest born and the least privileged the material of greatness and which aims to preserve and develop their talents, their personality, their honor and their virtue wherever they may be found. From the sum of the individual achievements of such personalities alone comes the real achievement of the nation.

Chicago does not do things in a small way. And here is a problem where Chicago's great vision can give leadership to the country. It can make good and great citizens from its least fortunate boys and girls.

CONCLUSION

And what do I say in conclusion? But little. You picture that pavement boy entering the door of that house of constructive joy. The light of his face—the gleam of honest devilment in his eye—the feeling of trust and security in his heart.

And there is a sense of safety and gratitude which warms his mother's heart also when she knows where her boy is tonight.

Japanese Surrender Day

Press Statement, Los Angeles
[August 14, 1945]

WE GIVE thankfulness to God that this greatest and most hideous war of history is ended. We rejoice that our loved ones are now to return. We rejoice that this slaughter of men, women and children is ended. We rejoice that we have overcome monstrous evil forces that have been directed against us. But our rejoicing must be sobered by our solicitude for the hundreds of thousands of America's sons who have been disabled. And our rejoicing is still more sobered by our grief for those who have given their lives for our country. We owe unending gratitude to their memory. We owe gratitude to the sons of America whose skill, whose magnificent courage have brought victory. We thrill that the virility and sacrifice of our race for an ideal is undiminished. Perhaps thankfulness and rejoicing are sufficient for this day.

But solemn thoughts arise within our rejoicing. This year 1945 marks the end of a hideous era. And tomorrow we must take up the responsibilities of the new era which confronts us. It can be a glorious era if we have high statesmanship in the world and are willing to sweat for a few years during a transition period from war to peace. And that statesmanship cannot succeed unless it establishes in the country that climate of personal freedom which stirs the initiative and labor of men.

In the long-view of the new era, the bright hope is enduring peace. With peace, we can have recovery; with peace, we can hope for a regeneration of civilization. With peace, the ever-lasting stir in the hearts of men and nations to be free will return to the world. The new era opens with hope. We can make it the golden era of all history if we have the will and the wisdom in our statesmanship.

Index

Acquisitiveness, 239

Administrative law, reform of, 233

Administrative organization of war agencies, Hoover on, *see* specific agency, Home front organization (U.S.), War agencies

Adults, effects of malnutrition on, 269, 271, 309; nutritional requirements, 290; *see also* Foodstuffs, Rations

Afghanistan, 103; alliances, 99, 101

Africa, 180, 184, 193; food supply, 292, 293; independent nations of, 52

Aggrandizement, 114, 131

Aggression, 36, 67, 81, 113, 136, 396; armament a threat of, 121; attempt at stopping by Congress of Vienna, 98; control by force, 49-50, 122, 126; definition, 116, 128, 132-133, 135, 138; freedom from, 131; non-aggression pacts, 99, 100-101; policing against, 58, 76, 138; sanctions against, 50, 122, 126

Aggressor nations, determination of, 116; disarmament of, 114; sanctions against, 49-50, 126; and veto power in Security Council, 127, 138

Agnosticism, 239

Agricultural Commodities Control, 156

Agricultural labor, depletion of, 293-294, 298, 300, 329, 337, 367; Hoover proposals, 197, 200, 338, 339; importation of Mexican, 191, 300, 339; increase of, 266, 345, 349-350; military furloughs and deferment for, 191, 300, 329-330, 339, 345; women, 300, 339, 341

Agricultural machinery, 196, 267, 296, 298, 329, 337, 347, 350, 367

Agriculture, acreage, 344, 345, 347-348; administrative organization of control agencies, 265-268, 302, 338, 340; crop harvest, 333, 335, 336, 344, 345-346, *see also* Agriculture wartime production; decentralized control agencies, 302, 338, 349; Department of, 266, 267, 268, 293, 344, 345, 348, 349; Hoover's proposals for, 196-199, 295-304, 338-339; in

occupied countries, 186; in warring Europe, 270-271; livestock, 265, 266-267, 292-293, 297-300, 336, 345, 366; Lutz report on Hoover proposals, 202; postwar problems, 234; Secretary of, 265-268; 298, 302, 338, 349, 369 ff.; wartime degeneration of, 337-338; wartime production, 196-197, 269, 293, 296, 297 ff., 329, 334, 335 ff., 345 ff., 367; wartime regulation of, 265-268, 338, 350; *see also* Price control; *see also* Food production (U.S.)

Air, freedom of, 37, 387

Air force (U.S.), 257

Air power, in hands of Trustees of Peace, 41; Japanese, 185; limitation of, 112, 121, 128; in total war, 180, 183, 189, 191

Air transportation, postwar, 235-236, 386-388

Alaska, 195

Albania, 278

Alliances, *see* Military alliances

Allies, World War I, Allied Blockade Council, 277; Allied Food Council, 277; Allied group, food relief administrative category, 272, 277; Allied Shipping Council, 277; disarmament, *see* Disarmament; punishment of war criminals, 65

Allies, World War II, and food relief, 269-270, *see also* Food relief; as only military force, 9, 388

Allocations of materials and supplies, 149, 177, 190, 369

Altruism, 239, 396

America, *see* United States

America at War, Baker, quoted, 215

America in the World War, Harbord, quoted 208-209

American Archivist, The, 205

American Army in France, Harbord, quoted, 210

American Expeditionary Force, Its Organization and Accomplishments, Harbord, quoted, 209-210

American Expeditionary Force, World War I, development of, 208-216

421

Date Due